PENGUIN BOOKS

THE HUDSON RIVER AND ITS PAINTERS

John K. Howat is Chairman of the American Wing at the Metropolitan Museum of Art in New York City. He is coauthor of *Nineteenth-Century American Paintings and Sculpture*, published by the Metropolitan Museum of Art, and author of the exhibition catalog *John F. Kensett*, published by the American Federation of Art. He has also contributed to *Antiques* and *The Metropolitan Museum of Art Bulletin*. Mr. Howat was educated at Harvard College and Harvard Graduate School of Arts and Sciences, where he received his master's degree in art history. He did further graduate work at the New York University Institute of Fine Arts. Subsequently he was a Ford Fellow and a Chester Dale Fellow at the Metropolitan Museum of Art. In 1970 he traveled to Tokyo to set up the exhibition of American paintings in the United States Pavilion at Expo, selected from the collection of the Metropolitan Museum. Mr. Howat lives with his wife and two daughters in New York City.

James Biddle is the former president of the National Trust for Historic Preservation.

Carl Carmer, author of *The Hudson, Listen for a Lonesome Drum*, and many other books, is Honorary Chairman of the Scenic Hudson Preservation Conference.

BY JOHN K. HOWAT · PREFACE BY JAMES BIDDLE · FOREWORD BY CARL CARMER

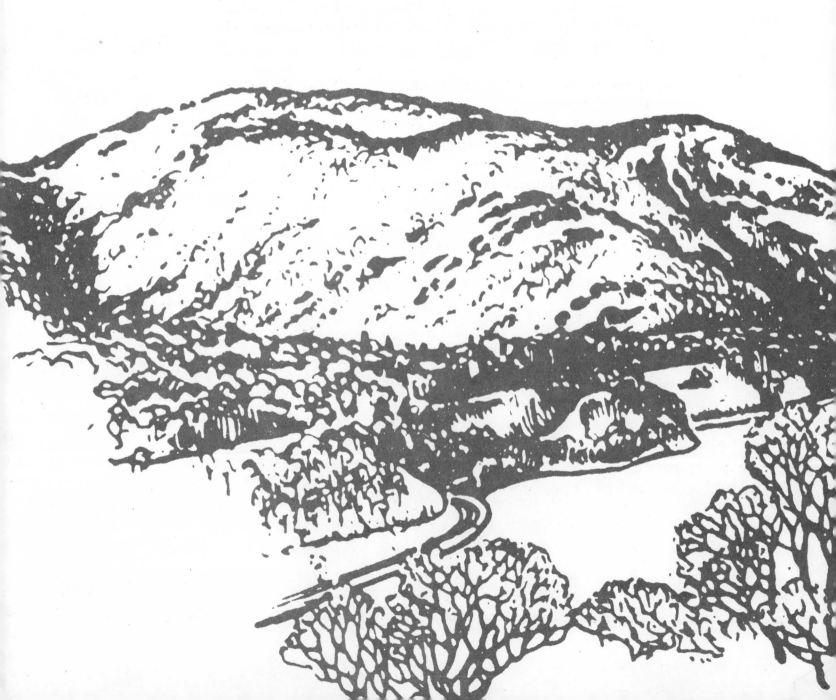

THE
HUDSON
RIVER
AND ITS PAINTERS

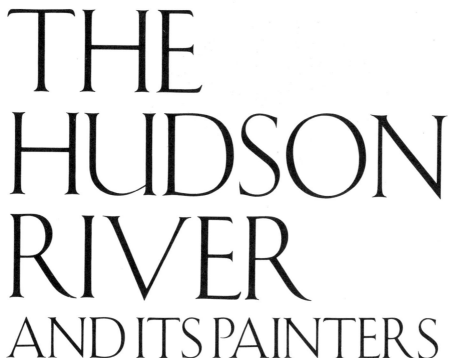

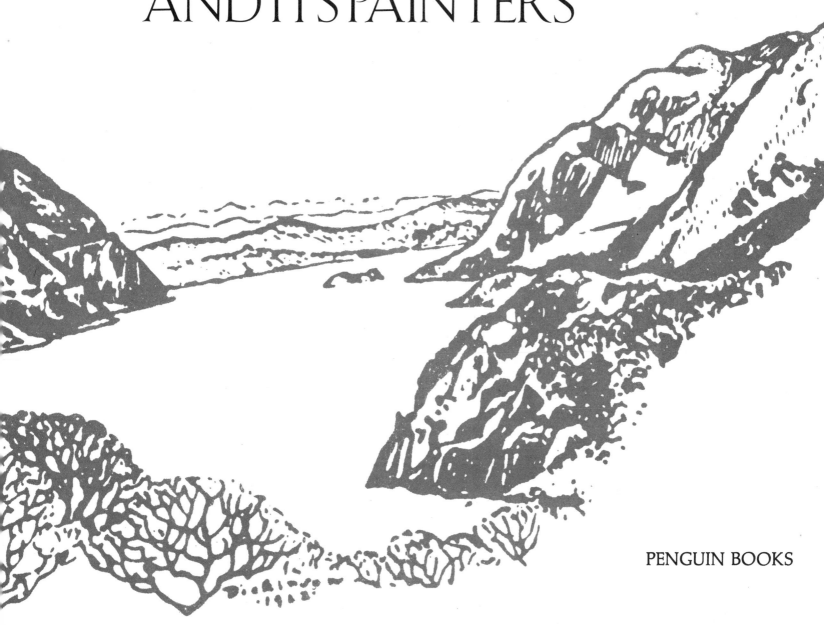

PENGUIN BOOKS

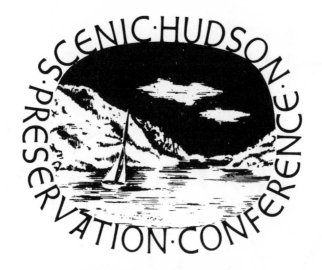

Penguin Books Ltd, Harmondsworth,
Middlesex, England
Penguin Books, 625 Madison Avenue,
New York, New York 10022, U.S.A.
Penguin Books Australia Ltd, Ringwood,
Victoria, Australia
Penguin Books Canada Limited, 2801 John Street,
Markham, Ontario, Canada L3R 1B4
Penguin Books (N.Z.) Ltd, 182–190 Wairau Road,
Auckland 10, New Zealand

First published in the United States of America by
The Viking Press 1972
First published in Canada by
The Macmillan Company of Canada Limited 1972
Published in Penguin Books 1978

LIBRARY OF CONGRESS CATALOGING IN PUBLICATION DATA
Howat, John K.
The Hudson River and its painters.
Bibliography: p. 193.
Includes index.
1. Hudson River School.   2. Landscape painting,
American.   2. Landscape painting—19th century—
United States.   4. Hudson Valley—Description and
travel—Views.   I. Title.
ND1351.5.H6   1978   758'.1'097473   78-12734
ISBN 0 14 00.5080 9

Manufactured in Hong Kong

"The Heritage of the Hudson" by Carl Carmer originally appeared,
in slightly different form, in *Art in America* as "Of Art and the River,"
copyright © Carl Carmer, 1964, and subsequently in *Saturday Review* as
"Irving and the Misty Valley," copyright © Saturday Review, Inc., 1971.

To Storm King Mountain and

the Hudson Highland Gorge

ACKNOWLEDGMENTS

This book is the result of the ideas and enthusiastic efforts of many people who have worked together in an admirably smooth and thoughtful manner. Particular thanks are due to Frances Stevens Reese of the Scenic Hudson Preservation Conference, whose brain child the book is, and to Nicolas Ducrot of the Viking Press, who first encouraged the idea of the book. Other members of the Scenic Hudson Preservation Conference joined in freely and unselfishly to create a book that for the first time fully illustrates views of the length of the Hudson Valley painted by artists of the Hudson River School, in combination with discussions of the school's history and the general history of the valley. Charles P. Noyes III provided many of the fine color photographs of the paintings illustrated, as well as the striking photographs of the present-day Hudson Valley. Mr. Noyes was especially helpful in locating many of the paintings considered for publication. James Hamilton was an early adviser and morale booster to the project. Sandra Feldman was an indefatigable researcher, writer, and endlessly helpful assistant in the preparation of captions for the illustrations. Natalie Spassky has been extremely helpful with suggestions, as has Sally Muir, who served both as typist and kindly critic of the text.

James Biddle, President of the National Trust for Historic Preservation, and Carl Carmer, a Scenic Hudson Preservation Conference founder and Hudson historian par excellence, have written the preface and foreword, for which deep thanks are due. Benjamin W. Frazier III gave generously of his time to supply historical and legendary background and identify many of the locations depicted in the paintings. Alan Gussow and Donald Halley helped with their cooperation and made very constructive contributions in the early stages of the book.

Greatest thanks are due to those individuals (among them several who prefer to remain anonymous) and institutions who have consented to the use of pictures they own and who have provided pertinent information:

Mrs. Henry Allen. Mr. Lee B. Anderson. Miss Martha Andrews of the Corcoran Gallery of Art, Washington, D.C. Mr. Tom Armstrong and Miss Barbara Luck of the Abby Aldrich Rockefeller Folk Art Collection, Williamsburg, Virginia. Mr. Charles Buckley and Mrs. Carl Fox of the City Art Museum of Saint Louis. Mr. Clarence K. Chatterton. Mr. and Mrs. Howland Davis. Mr. and Mrs. Olin Dows. Miss Pat Eargle of Chapellier Galleries, New York. Miss Sarah Faunce of the Brooklyn Museum. Mr. St. Julian Fishburne. Mr. and Mrs. George Corning Fraser. Mr. Thomas T. Fraser. Mr. and Mrs. Maitland Lee Griggs. Mrs. Lytle Hull. The late Mr. Rutger Ives Hurry. Dr. Louis C. Jones of the New York State Historical Association, Cooperstown, New York. Mrs. John Kean. Mrs. Linda Kershaw of the Boston Museum of Fine Arts. Miss Cecily Langdale of Hirschl and Adler Galleries, New York. Mrs. Beatrice Larned, Mrs. Maria Naylor, and Mrs. Rudolph Wunderlich of Kennedy Galleries, New York. Mr. Martin Leifer of the New-York Historical Society, New York. Rev. James T. Lindsley. Mr. and Mrs. Henry Livingston. Mrs. Elizabeth McAndrew and Mrs. Hilda Cameron of the Crandall Library, Glens Falls, New York. Mrs. Peter McBean. Miss Elsa McCormick of the Wadsworth Atheneum, Hartford, Connecticut. Mrs. John C. Newington. Mr. Kenneth M. Newman. Mr. and Mrs. I. David Orr. Mrs. Wilhemenia Powers of the Adriance Library, Poughkeepsie, New York. Mr. Robert Preato of *Art News* magazine, New York. Mr. Norman Rice of the Albany Institute of History and Art. Mr. Christian Rohlfing and Mrs. Elaine Dee of the Cooper-Hewitt Museum, New York. Miss Caroline Rollins of the Yale Art Gallery. Miss Elizabeth Roth, Print Room of the New York Public Library. Miss Jean Saunders of the Putnam County Historical Society, Cold Spring, New York. Mrs. Betty Saxon of the Art Institute of Chicago. Mr. M. R. Schweitzer and Miss Karen Plaks of the Schweitzer Gallery, New York. Mr. George Shriever. Mr. Richard E. Slavin of the Olana Historic Site (New York State Historic Trust). Mr. Robert S. Sloan, Mr. Herbert Roman, and Mr. Harold T. Schatzberg of Sloan and Roman Galleries, New York. Miss Eleanor Snider and Miss Robin Bolton-Smith of the National Collection of Fine Arts, Washington, D.C. Mr. Frederick Stanyer of Boscobel Restoration, Inc., Garrison-on-Hudson, New York. Mrs. Norman R. Sturgis, Jr. Mr. H. J. Swinney, Mr. George Bowdwitch, Mr. Warder Cadbury, and Mr. William Verner of the Adirondack Museum, Blue Mountain Lake, New York. Miss Van Arsdale and Mrs. Marie Laurent, Rare Books Room of the Buffalo Public Library, Buffalo, New York. Dr. Roland Van Zandt. Mr. Robert R. Very of The Old Print Shop, New York. Dr. Elliot S. Vesell. Mr. Hudson Walker. Miss Katherine Warwick of the National Gallery of Art, Washington, D.C. Mr. Robert

Paul Weimann, Jr. Mr. Ian White of the M. H. de Young Memorial Museum, San Francisco, California.

Abby Aldrich Rockefeller Folk Art Collection, Williamsburg, Virginia. Albany Institute of History and Art, Albany, New York. Art Institute of Chicago, Chicago, Illinois, The Baltimore Museum of Art, Baltimore, Maryland. Boscobel Restoration, Inc., Garrison-on-Hudson, New York. Brooklyn Museum, Brooklyn, New York. Butterfield Memorial Library, Cold Spring, New York. Century Association, New York. Chapellier Galleries, New York. Cincinnati Art Museum, Cincinnati, Ohio. Cooper-Hewitt Museum of Decorative Arts and Design, Smithsonian Institution, New York. Corcoran Gallery of Art, Washington, D.C. Crandall Library, Glens Falls, New York. Hudson River Museum, Yonkers, New York. Kennedy Galleries, Inc., New York. Library of Congress, Washington, D.C. Lyman Allyn Museum, New London, Connecticut. The Metropolitan Museum of Art, New York. Munson-Williams-Proctor Institute, Utica, New York. Museum of Fine Arts, Boston, Massachusetts. National Collection of Fine Arts, Smithsonian Institution, Washington, D.C. National Gallery of Art, Washington, D.C. Newark Museum, Newark, New Jersey. The New-York Historical Society, New York. New York State Historical Association, Cooperstown, New York. Olana, Hudson, New York. Schweitzer Gallery, New York. Sleepy Hollow Restorations, Irvington, New York. Sloan & Roman, Inc., Gallery, New York. Union Club, New York. Vassar College Art Gallery, Poughkeepsie, New York. The Vermont Council on the Arts. The Wadsworth Atheneum, Hartford, Connecticut. Yale University Art Gallery, New Haven, Connecticut.

The proceeds from the publication of this book will go to the Scenic Hudson Preservation Conference in support of their important work.

—JOHN K. HOWAT

CONTENTS

PREFACE

Throughout history the natural landscape has inspired the artistic expression of man. Thus it is not surprising that a region so richly endowed with great natural beauty as the Hudson River Valley should have produced countless individual works of art, poetry, and music. One of the most important contributions to the development of American artistic tradition is the work of a group of landscape painters of the last century known as the Hudson River School.

Regarding natural landscape as a direct manifestation of God, these men attempted to record what they saw as accurately as possible. Unlike European painters who brought to their canvases the styles and techniques of centuries, the Hudson River painters sought neither to embellish nor to idealize their scenes. They approached nature with reverence and portrayed it with the detailed care of a naturalist. Yet the results were more than photographically accurate. "The artist as a poet," explained one of their leaders, Asher Durand, "will have seen more than the mere matter of fact, but no more than is there and that another may see if it is pointed out to him."

The respect for nature shown by these painters was characteristic of the nineteenth century. Life had for the first time become comfortable enough for men to regard the wild landscape of the American continent as beautiful rather than threatening. James Fenimore Cooper and Washington Irving extolled the virtues of rural and frontier life in their novels; Emerson and Thoreau wrote of an elemental human need for wilderness; the common man believed in the greater purity of the natural environment.

The artists of the Hudson River School were part of this tradition—pantheists who thought that nature was shaped only by God and therefore "fraught with high and holy meaning." In search of that meaning, they left their studios to wander in the Catskills and along the Hudson; they often ranged as far as the White Mountains in New Hampshire, the Maine seacoast, or the great mountains of the West.

Today man has lost the reverence for wilderness that pervaded so much of nineteenth-century thought. Seeking to subdue nature rather than conserve her, man has succeeded in putting his mark on even the most inaccessible reaches of the continent. The wild river valley which gave its name to the first truly native American school of painting has itself fallen victim to his onslaught. Its vistas marred, its mountainsides raped, its very waters clogged with filth, the majestic Hudson limps along to the sea.

More and more private citizens are demanding that the Hudson Valley, its gorges, and its highlands be rescued and have joined in making determined efforts to fight for their survival. In 1965 valiant and eventually successful efforts were made to save Olana, the home of the Hudson River School painter Frederic E. Church. With the subsequent formation of the Scenic Hudson Preservation Conference and the appointment of the Hudson Valley Commission, the battle has become continually more heated. National leadership in the area has been given by the Sierra Club, which is helping to lead the fight to save Storm King Mountain from being developed for the site of a pumped-storage generating plant.

The presence and the influence of the National Trust for Historic Preservation is also felt, not only through assistance with preservation causes but through the ownership and management of one of the region's national landmarks. The Trust protects for all Americans the great architectural monument Lyndhurst, near Tarrytown, overlooking the Hudson River. The Gothic Revival mansion, former home of railroad tycoon Jay Gould, was left by Gould's daughter Anna to the Trust, which administers it as a historic house museum. Built in 1838 for William Paulding and enlarged in 1864 for George Merritt from designs by Alexander Jackson Davis, the great American architect, Lyndhurst is surrounded by acres of open and wooded landscape which extend to the river. Lyndhurst is a national treasure—a nineteenth-century architectural document situated in the type of nineteenth-century picturesque setting espoused by horticulturalist Andrew Jackson Downing.

How appropriate it is in our preservation efforts to re-evaluate the great school of painting inspired by the Hudson River and its valley in their wild state only a hundred years ago. Today the paintings of the Hudson River School can uplift us in the same way that the wilderness uplifted the souls of the artists. We must reaffirm the contention of Hudson River painter Thomas Cole that "the great works necessary for the progress of commerce" can be achieved without sacrificing the quality of our environment, "if man were not insensible to the beauties of nature." At the same time we must join with Cole in denouncing the "copper-hearted barbarians" who have brought their ugliness to despoil the great American wilderness.

—James Biddle
President, The National Trust
for Historic Preservation

Washington, D.C.
February 1971

FOREWORD

The Heritage of the Hudson

Writing about the romantic Hudson River is a welcome task since it can begin at home. From the eight-sided, many-windowed cupola which surmounts my eight-sided house, I can behold not only the wide stream moving massively toward the sea but many a century-old dwelling which was planned long ago by people who thought it would be a credit to its neighborhood and a reminder of their period's dedication to beauty.

A little to the east I can see without the aid of binoculars the turrets of the Beltzhoover Castle (now known as the Halsey Castle) and I know that a rippling lake lies beside it—a lake that bears upon its surface the slow white swans that every visitor feels are essential to so beautiful a dwelling.

If I look south, I see the old home of Colonel James Hamilton, son of Alexander, and I must again wonder what motives led to the wild and untrue legend that the Colonel built the house in which I stand as a convenient dwelling for his son's mistress.

As I look to the Hudson, I see projecting into its waters from the far side the long railroad pier which gave the little town of Piermont its name. History tells me that Daniel Webster once sat in a rocking chair on the floor of an open flatcar and was borne away by the first train of the just-completed New York and Erie Railroad toward a magnificent dinner in Fredonia, New York, on the banks of Lake Erie. The new railroad was not allowed to come farther than the middle of the river; hence the pier that would allow the new line to transfer all New York City–bound cargo to river boats for the rest of the journey.

As for my northern view I can only say that, as soon as the War for Independence ended, building a house on the banks of the Hudson became an indication of status and many an ambitious and well-to-do citizen of New York City took advantage of the opportunity for becoming highly respected by his contemporaries.

If a good friend visited me on the east bank of the Hudson, I would take him first to look at the big yellow house called Nuit and tell him that its very name suggests the hours of evening when shadow supplants a western glory. I would make him aware that the cobbles which he treads toward the entrance had been shipped across an ocean from the streets of Marseilles and had a history of their own long before they had left the shores of France to glint under a stretch of American sunset.

From this home onward my guest and I would travel north to pass other homes or sites of vanished houses romantically named. Netherwood, Locust Grove, Windcliff, Ellerslie, Leacote, Tivoli, Rose Hill are only a few of the names that give evidence of the poetic fancies of their owners.

Broadway is the river road on the east side of the Hudson—the same Broadway that all America knows, it runs all the way from New York City to Albany. It passes the top of Main Street in Irvington and, as it does, the summer traveler may look down through a long, leafy tunnel to a splatter of shining Hudson water. Running parallel to that green-lined tube lies another, named Sunnyside Lane, which leads down to the charming and whimsical cottage that housed Washington Irving in his latter days. Restored to the exact image it presented when America's first world-famous author was its occupant, the house still looks as if it were wearing a cocked hat, as Irving said it did.

No restoration in the nation makes its guests feel more at home, perhaps because it continues to exist in the more august company of castles and mansions that grace the countryside. As it sits in delightful modesty beside the great river, I believe that it conveys more successfully than any other restored dwelling in America the character, the sly humor, the imaginative fancy of the man who chose to live in it. Somehow it creates a *neighborhood* in which at dusk the Hamiltons await, as they often did, the arrival at their home (now next door to my own) of the town's quite unpretentious author living a half mile away. Sometimes Irving would bring with him one of his own houseguests, such as the renowned Swedish spinster-writer Fredrika Bremer, who was so elated when her host did not fall asleep before the dessert, as he usually did, that she must record the fact in her diary.

The staff of the Sunnyside Restoration has been so successful in its researches that many of the homely day-by-day practices, routines, and habits which assume significance only when attributed to a great man are revealed. The sensitive visitor of today grieves with the long-dead Irving when he comes upon the gravestones of his dogs, or rejoices with him when he finds that shaving after midnight provides a temporary relief from the torture of sleeplessness. It is no wonder then that the writer's warm humanity seems to lie concentrated within the old Dutch house and the simple pattern of his living out his remaining years.

When Irving died in 1859, just after completing his biography of Columbus, ours was not the only nation that was in tears. England and Spain—particularly Spain—have mourned him until today. And many an American ignores the current revolt of the uncompromisingly literary against oversentimentality when he stands before the simple grave at Sleepy Hollow Cemetery and reads the first lines of Longfellow's tribute:

> Here lies the gentle humorist, who died
>   In the bright Indian Summer of his fame.
> A simple stone with but a date and name
>   Marks his secluded resting place beside
> The river that he loved and glorified.

Irving, one of the most famous men of letters, was also interested in art, for the river stirs every facet of the creative instinct. Were he alive today, he would be rejoicing over the current interest in the paintings of his contemporaries. When he was young, he had considered becoming an artist as a life-work, and his enthusiasm for art never left him. The fact that he sometimes chose the pen name of Geoffrey Crayon indicated his feeling for and knowledge of the products which he was given every opportunity to praise.

A new and spontaneous spirit rose among hills and groves through which the Hudson passed. The landscapes offered by the river were superior in their beauty to any that might be admired in Europe, said the sensitive Thomas Cole, and he set out to prove his statement. A believer in the close relationships of the arts, he took his flute with him and sought rocky ravines, the channels whitened by splashing waters which inevitably ran through steep tributaries to invade the level surface of the three-mile-wide Tappan Zee. Having found a scene that moved him, the young painter let his flute speak for him and, once it had spoken, began to imitate with his brushes and colors that part of the divine creator's universe he had chosen for a painting.

The immeasurable expanses of an untamed land challenged Thomas Cole and his artist colleagues, and they all were accepting the challenge. On enormous canvases for the most part, they set about impressing potential patrons and purchasers. They believed that their products were meticulously accurate as to subject matter. They also were encouraged by the fact that they *and* the possible purchaser were convinced that a good picture cannot fail of having a praiseworthy "moral effect." On a highly artistic plane they were evangelists.

A high respect for art and artists had permeated the Hudson Valley, and no man who had an inclination toward graphic excellence was wasting time. Cole became successful. So did Durand and Kensett and Bierstadt. A recent catalog entitled *Hudson River School*, produced by an earnest and enthusiastic researcher, Agnes Halsey Jones, lists about fifty painters who have usually been considered as belonging to what has been designated the only "school" that American artists have produced. The majority of these men lived happy and prosperous lives. They created a feeling of pride in our national culture which satisfied a yearning long shared by the fellowship of successful merchants and professional men of the area. The curious visitors who came from Europe to observe the life of the new republic could no longer return to their homes abroad with sneers at "American money-grubbers" whose lives were impoverished by a lack of indigenous and worthy cultural achievement.

The approval won by the Hudson River School began to disappear, however, at the turn of the century. For more than two generations it had met with little criticism. Now a virile, realistic, more individualistic attitude began to develop in the history of American art. Yet when I came to Irvington about a quarter of a century ago, old residences near mine were still called by the names of distinguished artists who had once lived beside the river—"the Cropsey house," "the Bierstadt house," and the like.

It has long been my contention that landscape has an especial influence on those who inhabit it—not merely in economic ways, as the wheat or cotton spring from the earth, not in geographic ways, as rivers and mountains become boundaries to be crossed, but in spiritual and psychic ways. The look and feel of a land communicate not easily described messages to those who are sensitive enough to receive them. Perhaps because rivers in their courses offer poetic parallels to human life, people are inclined to attribute to them influences that strongly affect their lives.

In 1609 the Great River of the Mountains (as the Elizabethan explorer Captain Henry Hudson called it) had long awaited the inevitable dramas for which it would serve as a setting. Upon entering the wide stream, Hudson's crew were aware of the backdrop. Its banks, they said, "were so pleasant with grass and flowers—and goodly trees—as ever we had seen." They were more deeply concerned, however, as are most explorers, with their own roles on the great stage which encompassed them. The fortnight of sunlit September days during which the dusky natives sang choruses of welcome, and their ship drew near the blue mountains to the north, held no omen of the climactic day years later when the treacherous keeper of their log—old Robert Juet—would set their captain adrift in the arctic sea.

No change of backdrop would be necessary for ensuing acts. As might have been expected, then, characters and plot would supersede place. Early depictions of life along the river would therefore be more concerned with those stalwarts who lived it than with the river valley itself.

The Dutchmen who came from the Netherlands to the river were audacious adventurers, eager for profits in beaver and wildcat pelts obtainable in the valley woods. Their prosperity was immediate and the patterns of their living had little time to change from those they already knew. Portraits, showing the distinction of their wives and their own qualities as successful merchants and landholders, were symbols of high status. Painters were soon competing for commissions. Called "limners" by our frontier society, not many of the newly developed artists indulged in the subtleties of their professional European prototypes. They emphasized, rather, the obvious. The result was a group of boldly realistic portraits. The stamp of major characteristics was realized in them more directly than it would have been by more sophisticated painters. The carrying of this method further might have resulted (as it did in Washington Irving's amusing word portraits of Dutch dignitaries) in caricature. Hence the work of the "patroon painters" (so-called because their work was commissioned by the privileged Dutch patroons, or landowners, of the period) was not so important a contribution to American art as it was to American history. It might be noted in this connection that consciousness of place had already begun to grow, for Hudson River scenic backgrounds became both symbols and decorations in some of the limners' portraits.

Though, as always in time of war, the portraits of heroes assume authority, the fact that the Hudson River was of the greatest strategic importance and the realization that its beauty was overwhelming drew the attention of all who looked upon it. Even the British officer sent under a flag of truce by General John Burgoyne to offer surrender of his army at Saratoga discoursed for the first ten minutes of his visit on the colors of mid-October foliage in the Hudson Valley.

So compelling was the Hudson's beauty that it was regarded as a special gift of God. Painters, awed by the "divine architecture" they beheld in the mountains, hollows, and waters of its valley, chose to convey what God had said to them through these media of the "sublime subject" in terms of canvas and paint. They paid tribute to the blue stream and its bluer mountains with a conscientious and disciplined artistry which resulted in skills never before obtained by American artists. Not long after the mid-nineteenth century they were designated as the "Hudson River School." Proud that they had won for themselves this unique distinction, they sought to express wild natural glories with ever larger canvases. On these they exulted in meticulous representations of foreground plants, of middle-ground waters, of distant peaks rising beyond both into mist-strewn heavens. Having nearly exhausted Hudson River scenes, they used their techniques on other subjects—the less dramatic, elm-punctuated slopes of the Genesee, the greater challenge of Niagara's plunging waters.

As art directions changed in the last quarter of the century, American landscape gave way to canvases depicting Americana—genre paintings, representations of life in the almost measureless gray city at the big stream's wide mouth. The river retired into its mists. Artists, stimulated by metropolitan vigor and excitement, began, to the stunned surprise of the public, to paint ashcans, dreary tenements, and drearier saloons.

As if fleeing from the cruel realism of these sights, other painters sought release in a dream world where juxtaposition of unrelated objects was a commonplace; but even there their surrealism produced little hope or joy. River water continued, however, to flow by their doors, and the incredible river itself offered so varied and glittering a pile of incongruous and challenging materials that an age of empirical and highly individualistic experiment began.

It still continues. Always, as in our past, the tidal waters of the river-that-flows-two-ways fill the brain with images so intimate that on occasion the artist must become interpreter as well as creator, and the viewer is often entranced by the strange language the paintbrushes speak. The lively minds that exist among the eight million inhabitants of the river-girt City of Greater New York leave few avenues of artistic endeavor untraveled.

I believe that conservation is imperative today. I believe that nowhere is it more important than in the Hudson Valley.

Progress is a relative term, and no more silly aphorism has been invented than that which declares that it cannot be stopped. True progress involves preservation of the people's inheritance of their scenic, historic, and recreational values.

I believe that ugliness begets ugliness, and I know that nature's beauty, once destroyed, may never be restored. I would offer to our children the same beauty our fathers offered us a century ago—the matchless loveliness of our stream, our valley, and our mountains.

I would offer, too, the peace and healing our river gives to those who seek its waters for respite from the tensions of their lives. I believe that the time for opposing those forces that would defile the Hudson is now.

—CARL CARMER

THE HUDSON RIVER SCHOOL

THE FIRST NEW YORK SCHOOL

THE HUDSON RIVER SCHOOL

The First New York School

The Hudson River School, America's first homegrown, coherent, and sizable group of landscape artists, began in the 1820s, building on previous example. It grew rapidly, developed its own theories, and occupied the center of the national art stage until it faded in the 1870s and 1880s, thrust aside as an unfashionable, provincial, and tedious occurrence in our art history. The term "Hudson River School," according to Worthington Whittredge, one of its members, was invented by a hostile critic writing for the *New York Herald*, but as Whittredge commented, "This critic probably never reflected that the Hudson River School, if it were a school, must have something distinctive about it and instead of the term being, as he intended, a term of ridicule, it might become a term of approbation." The term is accepted today, not for its accuracy, since its members traveled widely and painted an almost endless variety of locations, but for the similarity of thought and style of its members. The growth and development of the school, which was centered primarily in New York City around its patrons and promoters, paralleled but outstripped contemporary American movements in portrait, still-life, genre, and history painting in much the same way and at the same time that landscape under the impact of naturalism outgrew in importance other types of painting in

Europe. The youthful American nation and its rapidly growing commercial capital, New York, were ambitious culturally as well as commercially, scientifically, and politically. Both had discovered themselves, following independence and the renewed unity after the War of 1812, to be behindhand in providing the humane delights of art, literature, and music that made Europe such a discovery for Americans to visit and made most European travelers to these shores so condescending about the "New Man" and his apparently rather crude and lusterless way of life. Self-consciousness and proud reaction to criticism were not the least reasons why thoughtful leaders like Washington Allston, Samuel F. B. Morse, Thomas Cole, and Asher B. Durand among the artists, and Washington Irving and James Fenimore Cooper among the writers set out to establish the arts on a firm footing in this country. Few art or literary movements are begun by an interested group setting out specially to be a "movement" or a "school," but the development and wide success of the Hudson River School came as close as any American art movement to being willed into existence as a concrete gesture and contribution to national life. The successful development of the school depended upon a number of factors and situations, such as the new importance of New York following the opening of the Erie Canal and Hudson River as the primary water route between the East Coast and the Middle West, the urge of an expanding nation to record and celebrate its primitive and untapped natural wonders, the resumption of cultural and commercial ties with Europe and particularly with England, the increasing number of painters and engravers who relied upon the growing patronage of business and businessmen-collectors, the development of art schools and galleries where artists could learn their craft and display their works, and a felt need to promote and develop a sense of our own history. There was nothing new about artists receiving patronage in this country in the 1820s, but to have that patronage greatly expanded in the hands of numerous "new men" of business centered in New York or other large cities, men who wanted greater artistic variety than mere portraiture provided, was a new and portentous development.

Landscape painting occupied a relatively minor place in the roster of the arts during the eighteenth century in Europe and England. Indeed, Sir Joshua Reynolds, the leading tastemaker for late-eighteenth-century English society, advised that Claude Lorrain and Willem van de Velde II, among the most admired seventeenth-century landscape masters, had, "in general, the same right, in different degrees, to the name of a painter, which a satirist, an epigrammatist, a sonneteer, a writer of pastorals, or descriptive poetry, has to that of a poet." In the end of the eighteenth century dilute versions of such opinions were important determinants in this country among the cognoscenti of what "should" be painted. Allston and Morse went to Europe to learn the "Great Style," based almost entirely upon Italian High Renaissance figure and history painting, which Reynolds believed to be the pinnacle of art. Dealers in America, such as New York's Michael Paff ("Old Paff"), during the 1820s fooled themselves and rooked their clients as they dealt in supposed "Old Master" canvases in preference to dealing in contemporary local work. In the 1880s the elderly Daniel Huntington recalled Paff, "a noted dealer and restorer ... in whose dimly lighted and musty den the connoisseurs of early New York congregated to wonder at the 'Raphaels, Correggios, and stuff' which the lean and keen-eyed 'Paff' had raked up, begrimed and daubed over, in some obscure pawn-broker's shop, and cleaned and brought out in gemmy brilliance and over whose beauties he would expatiate enthusiastically for hours." More important, however, as a restraint on landscape painting in America had been the simple economics of the situation: poor men could not buy art, and rich men without too much imagination preferred to cover their walls with impressive wallpapers, looking glasses, sconces, richly inlaid cabinets and chests, and portraits of themselves and their families. The sources of the Hudson River School depended upon a new milieu, a major change of taste, as well as an increase in the number of men with extra money to spend.

The traditional and by now almost hallowed date for the beginning of the Hudson River School is 1825, when Thomas Cole was discovered by three of New York's leading artists, John Trumbull, William Dunlap, and Asher Durand. Two of the three Hudson River views which Trumbull spied in a framemaker's shop window rapidly found their way into the collection of Philip Hone, then in his one and only term as mayor of New York. Such recognition by the wealthy and most important collector of the city went far to establish Cole and the type of art he represented. Eight years later Hone himself wrote that Cole's "pictures are admirable representations of that description of scenery which he has studied so well in his native forests. His landscapes are too solid, massy, and umbrageous to please the eye of the amateur accustomed to Italian skies and English park-scenery, but I think every American is bound to prove his love of country by admiring Cole." A critical non sequitur perhaps, but such thoughts were a vital basis for the school, especially since they were not held solely by Philip Hone.

Before this important artistic event, relatively few landscape painters could be found in New York, or any other American city, but vital groundwork was done by a variety of not very well known draftsmen and painters who produced views primarily for reproduction as mezzotints, engravings, etchings, and woodcuts, most often illustrations in travel books. In great contrast to today's military recon-naissance through electronic and photographic means, military officers of that era relied on their skills as surveyors, draftsmen, and diarists in gathering information. Among early examples of their works were *Scenographia Americana or A Collection of Views in N. America and the West Indies ... From drawings taken on the spot by several officers of the British Navy and Army* (London, 1768), in which appeared "A Southeast

View of the City of New York," and "A South West View of the City of New York," both after drawings by the American Captain Thomas Howdell of the 7th Company of the Royal Artillery; and *The Atlantic Neptune*, in which numerous maps and views of the coastal region between the Saint Lawrence and the Gulf of Mexico were produced for the Admiralty between 1763 and 1784. In addition to the military artists who recorded our landscape were a number of trained and not so well trained English watercolorists and oil painters who came to this country in the 1790s and afterward in quest of subject matter and an open field for their activity. England in the late eighteenth and early nineteenth centuries produced innumerable view-painters, among the best known of whom were Richard Wilson, Alexander and John Robert Cozens, Thomas Girtin, and Joseph M. W. Turner. The Anglo-artistic outpouring to this country included a number of lesser figures who worked in the shadow of these men and who imported their diluted style to this country. Archibald Robertson and his brother Alexander both came to New York in the early 1790s and were colleagues operating the Columbian Academy of Painting, attended primarily by young ladies and probably New York's first art school. Archibald specialized in miniatures and watercolor landscapes. His somewhat laborious views of New York and vicinity were usually done in ink with colored washes added. Alexander was subsequently Secretary and Keeper of New York's American Academy of the Fine Arts, successor to the Columbian Academy, which was founded in 1801 by the gentry of the city for their own amusement and the occasional instruction of local artists. William Winstanley, another English landscapist and portraitist, came to New York in 1790 and is primarily remembered for keeping the original of a George Washington portrait by Stuart and sending on his copy when he had been asked to pack and ship the original. "This swindling genius," as Dunlap called him, painted "portraits, landscapes—anything." His surviving landscapes are rather attractive, but in a smooth and conventional manner strongly reminiscent of Richard Wilson's. William Russell Birch and his son Thomas, both English-born, settled in Philadelphia in 1794 to work as engravers, miniaturists, and landscapists. Thomas's fruitful career covered the next sixty years, in which he devoted himself to painting very simply arranged land- and seascapes of considerable beauty, filled with light and air. Nonetheless, his pictures, like those of other English painters who followed him to America—William Groombridge, who arrived in Philadelphia about 1794; Francis Guy, who came to Baltimore about 1800; Joshua Shaw to Philadelphia about 1817; William Guy Wall to New York in 1818; John Hill, the engraver, to Philadelphia in 1816; William J. Bennett to New York in 1826; Robert Salmon to Boston in 1828; and others—were essentially topographical or reportorial works characterized by conventional spaciousness, airiness, and pastel tonalities which prefigure the atmosphere painting of the full-fledged Hudson River artists but lack the darker, more highly detailed, and moody quality of the later work of Cole or Durand, who, not surprisingly, considered themselves the true pioneers of American landscape painting.

Such a feeling on the part of Cole and Durand is understandable in view of the chauvinistic mood of the era but does not consider the previous contribution of certain native Americans who tried their hands at landscape painting in the earliest years of the nineteenth century. Leaving aside the usually perfunctory landscape backdrops to eighteenth-century portraits by such painters as Smibert, Feke, Stuart, and Earl, among the first pure landscapes done by native Americans are those by Trumbull, Vanderlyn, and Allston.

Colonel John Trumbull, the crusty old autocrat of the New York art world, made numerous landscape sketches in Europe and in this country before he painted several views of Niagara Falls between 1806 and 1808. Three views, preliminary to a large panorama now owned by the New-York Historical Society, are dark, naïvely constructed, generalized observations, but they are dramatic in conception.

John Vanderlyn anticipated Trumbull's Niagara views by several years. His patron Aaron Burr wrote him a letter of introduction to a friend in September 1801: "Mr. Van Der Lyn, the young painter from Esopus, who went about six years ago to Paris, has recently returned, having improved his time and talents in a manner that does very great honor to himself, his friends, and his country; proposing to return to France in the spring, he wishes to take with him some American views, and for this purpose he is now on his way through your county to Niagara. I beg your advice and protection. He is a perfect stranger to the roads, the country, and the customs of the people, and in short knows nothing but what immediately concerns painting. From some samples which he has left here, he is pronounced to be the first painter that now is or ever has been in America." Vanderlyn's ambition was to be a great painter of history, in the tradition of Jacques Louis David, and landscapes such as those were little more to him than reportorial bread-and-butter.

The most beautiful, but at the same time the most imaginative and least naturalistic, American seascapes and landscapes done in the first two decades of the century were those by Washington Allston, of Cambridgeport, Massachusetts. Allston spent most of those years in London, Paris, and Rome, painting figure compositions and landscapes remarkable for their glowing color and forceful arrangement. His landscapes are imaginary scenes, not topographical, which presumably accounts for the minor impact they had on the more sharp-eyed romantic naturalists of the Hudson River School. Allston, a friend of Coleridge, was regarded as the grand old man among American painters until his death in 1843, especially by his Bostonian friends, who apparently preferred hearing his poetry and philosophical discourses to looking at his wonderful pictures.

Of all the predecessors to Cole and his followers, the single artist who could most reasonably claim Cole's mantle as founder of the school is the appealing figure Thomas Doughty, who at one juncture was hailed as "the all-American Claude Lorrain." Doughty was born in Philadelphia and began his career there as a leather currier, but he gave up this work in 1820, in his words, "contrary to the wishes of my friends and family, to pursue painting as a profession." He subsequently was the leading landscape painter in Boston, traveled in England and France, and lived in New York City, Newburgh, and western New York before his death in 1856. Doughty traveled extensively throughout the northeastern United States, painting rivers, mountains, and woods interiors that are memorable for their mood, tonality, and quality of light, especially the pink and gold sunset tones, rather than for their local specificity.

An emotive but perceptive critic wrote, "Doughty's paintings are subdued, quiet, and almost uniformly sad. . . . In all his pictures, however, we see the manner of the artist, or we should say, perhaps, the mind of the poet, softening the tints, the grouping, and the incidents of the scene to the same love and spirit of sadness." Despite Tuckerman's friendly comment, written a decade after Doughty's death, on his woodland landscapes, that "there was often a cool, vivid tone, a true execution, and especially a genuine American character about them, which, in the early part of his professional life, rendered the studies, sketches, and finished landscapes of Doughty more characteristic, suggestive, and interesting to lovers of nature and of art among us than other works of the kind," Doughty encountered throughout his painting career criticism and neglect because the art public felt he painted by formula rather than by observation. Although Nathaniel P. Willis, the poet and author of numerous travel books and musings on scenery, thought Doughty was "one of the first painters in the world," the art critic for the *New-York Mirror: A Weekly Journal of Literature and the Fine Arts* wrote in 1840 about "Doughty, as clever and good hearted fellow as ever lived," who, however, has "glaring faults": "He does not give character to his trees, and has not variety enough. His water is seldom transparent. All his pictures purport to be from nature; but we think he is particular in taking the outline from the spot, and then finishing from recollection or according to fancy." The critic did grant that "in his skies Doughty excells." Later collectors and critics, perhaps tougher-minded and more demanding than their predecessors had been, rejected Doughty's "tea-tray" style. Tuckerman in his *Book of the Artists, American Artist Life,* published in 1867, listed three public and ten private New York collections of American painting in which works by Cole, Durand, Kensett, Church, Cropsey, and others abounded. All told, only five landscapes by Doughty were listed in the collections of imposing Knickerbockers like A. M. Cozzens, John Taylor Johnston, and Robert L. Stuart, while their famous competitors W. T. Blodgett, Cyrus Butler, Robert Hoe, James Lenox, Robert M. Olyphant, Marshall O. Roberts, and Jonathan Sturges had nothing by the artist.

The Crayon, the New York journal and notice board of the mid-century landscape painters, had the melancholy note in 1856 that "a movement is on foot in favor of Doughty, the landscape painter, who is said to be in absolute want. Why not get up an exhibition of his works? Doughty is one of the pioneers of our landscape Art, and has painted many noble pictures in his better days. . . . If any will contribute to the fund, they may remit to W. C. Bryant, Esq. . . . " Doughty died shortly thereafter, having made an original and useful contribution to American art, but one that was admired more for its impulse than for itself.

Thomas Cole early in his progress as landscape painter looked in 1823 at landscapes by Thomas Birch and Thomas Doughty on display at the Pennsylvania Academy of the Fine Arts in Philadelphia. Impressed by what he saw, he determined to go beyond their example. Cole, writing in 1826 to his Baltimore patron Robert Gilmore, who had been critical of Doughty's "mannered" pictures, replied, "You say Mr. Doughty had failed in his compositions: perhaps the reason may be easily found—that he has painted from himself, instead of recurring to those scenes in Nature which formerly he imitated with such great success. It follows that the less he studies from Nature, the further he departs from it, and loses the beautiful impress of Nature which you speak of with such justice and feeling. . . . I believe with you that it is of the greatest importance for a painter always to have his mind upon Nature, as the star by which he is to steer to excellence in his art. He who would paint compositions, and not be false, must sit down amidst his sketches, make selections, and combine them, and so have nature for every object that he paints. This is what I should endeavor to do: and I think you will agree with me that such a course embraces all the advantages obtaining in painting actual views, without the objections. I think that a young painter ought not to indulge himself too much in painting scenes, yet the cultivation of his mind ought not to be neglected, it is the faculty that has given that superiority of the fine over mechanical arts." Thus privately Cole articulated the operative basis for his work and the whole flourishing of the Hudson River School that followed his example in the production of both pure landscapes and imaginary compositions.

Cole, like the great majority of his colleagues, came from a simple background. Born in Lancashire, England, in 1801, he worked as a calico designer and engraver's assistant before coming to America with his parents and siblings in 1818. He worked in Philadelphia as a wood engraver, after which he was an art teacher, itinerant portraitist, wallpaper designer, writer, and general artist-handyman. His assets in 1825 were his dissatisfaction with his so-far spotty career, his love of the countryside, and his new-found dedication to landscape painting. There is no question that Cole's individual performance, success, and public recognition were the model for what ensued, as numbers of painters and draftsmen took up landscape painting.

The year—1825—of Cole's debut in New York and the opening of the Erie

Canal was also the occasion for "An Address Delivered Before The American Academy of the Fine Arts, November 17, 1825, By Richard Ray, A Member of the Academy," to cite the title page of the subsequent publication. The address speaks the prevailing optimistic mind as it extols the arts and their important role "when society has become in some degree established—when the division of property gives to a favored class the choice of amusement and relaxations of leisure." The Academy believed firmly in the subservience of the artist to the aristocratic patron. Such an attitude had led to the founding by artists at just that moment of the New York Drawing Association, immediate forerunner of the National Academy of Design, and Thomas Cole was a founding member of the protesting organization. Ray's speech was an attempt to placate the aroused artists of New York and bring them back into the Academy fold. He praised the arts as "not merely ornamental— though as such it is too common to consider it—they may be thought to exercise an immense influence on public virtue. As the softener and refiner of the manners of the people—as the means of uniting in one common feeling of pride every class—as the recorder and the witness of honorable actions and eminent men, they claim no humble regard from the politician and the moralist. But [in order that] these results may be produced, the Fine Arts must be brought out among the people: they must not be secluded in private houses, nor appropriated to individual or- naments, but they must be consecrated to public and national works. They have been found ever connected with the highest advances in literature and civilization: show me the eras of distinguished artists, orators, and poets, and there will I show you true polish, a love of freedom, a generous public spirit, and a lettered people." To the youthful Cole and Asher Durand, both of whom may have been in the audience—Durand engraved the frontispiece of the published address—the exalted note of national pride may have been as appealing as Ray's comments on painting which followed: "To the Artist in one branch of it, our country affords peculiar advantages: I mean the Landscape-painter. For him extends an unappropriated world, where the glance of genius may descry new combinations of colors, and new varieties of prospect. No matter what species of scenery is best suited to his taste: if vastness and grandeur fill his mind—if he can command the rich and golden hues of colouring, let the new Titian touch his pencil on the Catskill Mount; or let him, another Claude Lorrain, looking upon its laughing scenes of plenty, shed on them the same delicious repose and serenity, which have been claimed for Italy alone. Or if his half-savage spirit, like Salvatore Rosa's, delights in rocks and crags, and mountain fastnesses, an unattempted creation rises at a distance to invite him. There he may lose himself, till a wild scene of cascades, of deep glens, and darkly shaded caverns, is frowning around him: and though, thanks to our equal laws, no bandit is seen issuing from his hiding place, yet there he may plant the brown Indian, with feathered crest and bloody tomahawk, the picturesque and native offspring of the wilderness. Come then, son of Art, the Genius of your country points you to its stupendous cataracts, its highlands intersected with the majestic river, its ranging mountains, its softer and enchanting scenery. There, where Nature needs no fictitious charms, where the eye requires no borrowed assistance from the memory, place on the canvass the lovely landscape, and adorn our houses with American prospects and American skies."

Thomas Cole had anticipated Ray's advice during the late summer of 1825 when he took a sketching trip—his first one—up the Hudson. Cole's biographer Louis L. Noble wrote, "From the moment when his eye first caught the rural beauties clustering round the cliffs of Wehawken, and glanced up the distance of the Palisades, Cole's heart had been wandering in the Highlands and nestling in the bosom of the Catskills." Three of the pictures resulting from the trip were the ones discovered by Trumbull, who complimented Cole: "You surprise me, at your age, to paint like this. You have already done what I, with all my years and experience, am yet unable to do." Cole's great admirer William Cullen Bryant, in his funeral oration on Cole, recalled that thereafter "he had a fixed reputation, and was numbered among the men of whom our country had reason to be proud. I well remember what an enthusiasm was awakened by these early works of his ... the delight which was expressed at the opportunity of contemplating pictures which carried the eye over scenes of wild grandeur peculiar to our country, over our aerial mountain tops with their mighty growth of forest never touched by the axe, along the banks of streams never deformed by culture, and into the depth of skies bright with the hues of our own climate; skies such as few but Cole could ever paint, and through the transparent abysses of which it seemed that you might send an arrow out of sight."

Cole was an unusual combination of writer, poet, philosopher, observer, and painter, not unlike Washington Allston. Cole wrote his ideas on nature down and referred to his writings when he painted, and his observations made while painting found their way into written form. Louis Noble reprinted many of Cole's writings; two of the most interesting refer to Hudson River and Catskill Mountain scenes which he painted as well, revealing to what a great extent Cole was a poet-painter who saw significance in details of nature and painted accordingly: "Sunrise From the Catskill Mountains—The mists were resting on the vale of the Hudson like drifted snow: tops of distant mountains in the east were visible—things of another world. The sun rose from bars of pearly hue: above there were clouds light and warm, and the clear sky was of a cool grayish tint. The mist below the mountain began first to be lighted up, and the trees on the tops of the lower hills cast their shadows over the misty surface—innumerable streaks. A line of light on the extreme horizon was very beautiful. Seen through the breaking mists, the fields were exquisitely fresh and green. Though dark, the mountainside was sparkling; and the Hudson, where it was uncovered to the sight, slept in deep shadow." Treating the same vision poetically, Cole wrote:

The Wild

Friends of my heart, lovers of nature's works,
Let me transport you to those wild, blue mountains
That rear their summits near the Hudson's wave.
Though not the loftiest that begirt the land,
They yet sublimely rise, and on their heights
Your souls may have a sweet foretaste of heaven,
And traverse wide the boundless. From this rock,
The nearest to the sky, let us look out
Upon the earth, as the first swell of day
Is bearing back the duskiness of night.
But lo, a sea of mist o'er all beneath;
An ocean, shoreless, motionless and mute.
No rolling swell is there, no sounding surf;
Silent and solemn all; - the stormy main
To stillness frozen, whilst the crested waves
Leap'd in the whirlwind, and the loosen'd foam
Flew o'er the angry deep.
                              See! now ascends
The lord of day, waking with heavenly fire
The dormant depths. See how his luminous breath
The rising surges kindles: lo, they heave
Like golden sands upon Sahara's gales.
Those airy forms, disparting from the mass,
Like winged ships sail o'er the marvellous plain.
Beautiful vision! Now the veil is rent,
And the coy earth her virgin bosom bare
Slowly unfolding to the enraptured gaze
Her thousand charms.

One of Cole's axioms, not surprisingly, was "To walk with nature as a poet is the necessary condition of a perfect artist." Cole's landscapes, particularly following his first trip from America to England, France, and Italy in 1829–1832, have a freely developed, painterly quality, and rich coloring that go well with the extremely dramatic arrangements of billowing clouds, massive gnarled trees, deep chasms, towering peaks, and golden light that are common in the pictures. Cole acknowledged the role that the mind and interpretation played in his landscapes, writing to Durand: "Have you not found?—I have—that I never succeed in painting scenes, however beautiful, immediately upon returning from them. I must wait for time to draw a veil over the common details, the unessential parts, which shall leave the great features, whether the beautiful or the sublime, dominant in the mind."

As early as 1826 Cole, with his *Garden of Eden and the Expulsion,* devoted himself to allegorical and imaginary scenes as well as to the less imposing pure landscapes. As the years passed before Cole's early death in 1848, he became increasingly devoted to religious thought and painting scenes that held an obvious word message. His most famous allegories include *The Course of Empire,* done in five canvases showing the rise and decay of a great ancient city; *The Departure and the Return,* a medieval romance painted in 1837, showing knights in armor going to and returning from battle; *The Past and Present,* showing the glory and then the decay of an impenetrable medieval fortress, done in 1838; and *The Voyage of Life* in four canvases, done in 1839 and 1840, showing life's religious stages from childhood to youth to manhood and finally old age. The final major series, *The Cross and the World,* showing a pilgrim trekking through the world toward the Cross at the end of the journey, was never completed. Noble, writing his posthumous biography of Cole, pointed out that "Cole's out-door life, corresponding mainly with that of earlier years, is particularly worthy of mention. He watched and sketched the skies, especially at sunset, almost daily, walked, and sketched the landscape, snatching as he walked its choicest details, wandering away through the rich, broken country of the Catskill river,—through the cloves, and up to the peaks of the mountains for the gathering of thoughts, and the kindling of his feelings as well as for making fresh studies." Toward the end of Cole's life, however, "a favorite theme was the Church, in whose welfare his spirit was fast becoming all absorbed." Today's taste for Cole's pure landscapes in preference to his allegorical scenes is understandable but does not change the fact that most of the public Cole worked for preferred the allegories. The art critic for the *New-York Mirror* in 1840 particularly praised *The Course of Empire:* "Suffice it to say that none but a great mind would have dared choose so vast a subject, and few but a Thomas Cole could have accomplished the design so successfully. It required the attributes of a poet and a philosopher, and displays a thorough knowledge of classic literature, and a familiarity with the history of nations." The reviewer got great pleasure from the beautiful handling of the landscape details of all the history pictures, but it was the sentiment and quality of mind of the artist that most attracted him. Bryant, on Cole's death, spoke of him with emotion as "not only a great artist but a great teacher; the contemplation of his works made men better. ... The paintings of Cole are of that nature that it hardly transcends the proper use of language to call them acts of religion."

Jonathan Sturges, partner of Cole's deceased patron Luman Reed, and a collector of note himself, heard Bryant's eulogy to Cole. Deeply moved, he wrote afterward to Bryant that he had "requested Mr. Durand to paint a picture in which he should associate our departed friend and yourself kindred spirits." He gave the picture, today hanging in the New York Public Library, to Bryant "as a token of gratitude for the labor of love performed on that occasion." Even before Cole's death Bryant waxed enthusiastic over Durand's pictures: "There are no landscapes produced in any part of the world which I would more willingly possess than his." Durand easily assumed the leading role among American landscape painters upon Cole's death, and while he occasionally attempted to rival Cole with allegorical series such as *Morning* and *Evening,* he concentrated on painting the landscape as he saw it to be—verdant, shining, and welcoming. In 1855 Durand wrote a characteristic letter to *The Crayon* from North Conway, New Hampshire, noting that in the White Mountains "passages of the sublime and the beautiful are not infrequent, and for those who have the physical strength and mental energy to confront the former among the deep chasms and frowning precipices, I doubt not it would be difficult to exaggerate, and the simple truth would be sufficient to convey the full idea of 'boundless power and inaccessible majesty' presented by such scenes. But to one like myself, unqualified to penetrate the 'untrodden ways' of the latter, the *beautiful* aspect of the White Mountain scenery is by far the predominant feature."

Asher Brown Durand reached his pre-eminence as painter after a long career as America's most successful engraver. Born in 1796 in New Jersey, he learned engraving at home, making plates from hammered copper coins, then in 1812 went to work for Peter Maverick at Newark, who had a thriving business producing plates for calling cards, book plates, illustrations, and most particularly, bank notes. In five years Durand outstripped his master (and, for a while, partner) in skills, and set up his own firm in New York with his brother Cyrus and thereafter dominated the American fine-engraving market. His production included engravings of Trumbull's *Declaration of Independence,* which established his reputation, *Ariadne,* after Vanderlyn, and many portrait plates of famous Americans for Herring and Longacre's *National Portrait Gallery,* published between 1834 and 1839. In 1823 Colonel Trumbull, delighted with Durand's engraving of *The Declaration of Independence,* sent a copy to Lafayette in Paris with the note that it was "by a young engraver, born in this vicinity, and now only twenty-six years old. This work is wholly *American,* even to the paper and printing, a circumstance which renders it popular here, and will make it a curiosity to you, who knew America when she had neither painters nor engravers, nor arts of any kind, except those of *stern utility.*" Tuckerman, at a later date, tells of the American sculptor Horatio Greenough at a foreign artists' cafe in Florence showing around the *Ariadne* print "and with difficulty persuading them of its American origin, so greatly were they all impressed with its mature skill." As New York's leading engraver in the 1820s, Durand played an important role in establishing the National Academy of Design and was, with Cole, an intimate of New York's cultural and intellectual leaders such as Bryant and Gulian Verplanck.

With the founding of the National Academy, Durand began to paint, doing a few landscapes and religious scenes. In the 1830s he did considerably more painting, especially portraits of distinguished men, among them James Madison, John Quincy Adams, and Luman Reed, the wholesale grocer who was a staunch supporter of Cole, Durand, and other New York painters. In 1836 or before, Durand gave up almost entirely the arduous work of engraving, which presumably did not yield artistic satisfaction enough in proportion to the labor involved. Strongly encouraged by Luman Reed, he devoted himself for several years to portraiture and figure painting, producing several illustrations of Cooper's and Irving's stories, among them "The Wrath of Peter Stuyvesant" for Reed. His history and genre paintings were not unsuccessful, but they appeared then to the critics, as they do today, to be rather stiff and lifeless. Fortunately Durand, in love with landscape painting, produced an increasing number of country scenes in the late 1830s. In 1837, for example, he exhibited seven portraits, one religious scene, and three landscapes at the academy, and in 1838 he had reversed the emphasis, exhibiting two portraits, two Irving illustrations, one allegory, and eight landscapes. Thereafter he painted occasional portraits and figure pieces, but almost all his production was landscape, and thus, for a full ten years, he was a colleague in the art with Thomas Cole. Daniel Huntington, himself a landscape painter, who preferred to paint portraits of New York worthies, said in his memorial to Durand that at this juncture he "had been a pioneer in engraving; he was now a pioneer in another very important branch of study, viz., that of painting carefully finished studies directly from nature out-of-doors. Before his day our landscape painters had usually made only pencil drawings or, at most, slight watercolor memoranda of the scenes. . . . Cole, to be sure, lived at Catskill, in full view of magnificent scenery, and was endowed with a wonderful memory, so that he gave an astonishing look of exact truth to many of his pictures of American scenery, but he rarely, if at all, up to that period, painted his studies in the open air."

Durand, the master of detail and observation, wrote a famous series, "Letters on Landscape Painting," for *The Crayon* in 1855. In these eight letters, supposedly directed to an aspiring landscapist, he gave at length his feelings about painting. In the first he promulgated that the aspirant should learn from studying nature, not the work of other artists. "Yes! go first to Nature to learn to paint landscape, and when you shall have learnt to imitate her, you may then study the pictures of great artists with benefit. . . . True Art teaches the use of the embellishments which Nature herself furnishes, it never creates them." The key to Durand's ideas and drive lay in his own deep religious absorption in nature and its reflection in his art, and certainly not in hopes for financial success: "It is better to make shoes, or dig potatoes, or follow any other honest calling to secure a livelihood, than seek the pursuit of Art for the sake of gain. . . . I would sooner look for figs on thistles than for the higher attributes of art from one whose ruling motive in its pursuit is money. . . . it is only through the religious integrity of motive by which all real Artists have been actuated, that it still preserves its original purity, impressing the mind through the visible forms of material beauty, with a deep sense of the invisible and immaterial, for which end all this world's beauty and significance, beyond the few requirements of our animal nature, seems to be expressly given." Although Durand's methods and finished pictures differed from Cole's, both men agreed in their puritan transcendentalism that art must be a vision of God through nature and never a thoughtless whim or attempt by the artist to be technically exciting or picturesque. "Although painting is an imitative Art, its highest attainment is representative, that is, by the production of such resemblance as shall satisfy the mind that the *entire* [italics added] meaning of the scene represented is given." Claude Lorrain, whose works Durand closely inspected and often followed, was remarkable for "truthfulness of representation in his light and atmosphere, and moving waters," but it was Turner "who has gathered from the previously unexplored sky alone, transcripts of Nature, whose mingled beauty of form and chiaroscuro have immortalized him, for the sole reason that he has therein approached nearer to the representation of the infinity of Nature than all that have gone before him." Durand in his final letter made specifically clear that Idealism and selective Realism were the same in Art. "That is a fine picture which at once takes possession of you—draws you into it—you traverse it—breathe its atmosphere—feel its sunshine, and you repose in its shade without thinking of its design or execution, effect or color."

Durand's green and gold vision had an army of admirers and imitators, but when he died in 1886 at the age of ninety, his example had also been set in his ideas, recommendations, and Jovian presence among his fellows. In 1872, seven years before he painted his last picture, Durand was given a surprise visit at his house at South Orange, New Jersey. Bryant, McEntee, Erastus Palmer, Eastman Johnson, Kensett, Sanford Gifford, Whittredge, and many others gathered to show their "veneration for the old man."

One of the few youths who persuaded Durand to take him as a pupil and assistant was John Casilear, who in 1831 joined his studio after having been trained in engraving by Peter Maverick. Casilear himself became an important bearer of influence, if only for the fact of his later pictures and his personal influence on Kensett. For several years Casilear stuck to engraving and exhibited his vignettes at the Academy, but in 1836 he exhibited two landscapes. From then on, he sought little else but release in landscape painting. In 1838 he sent his old shopmate at

Maverick's, Kensett, a letter saying he was getting ready for a summer outing to the Catskills where he could say "goodbye for a season at least to my 'graven employments.' The fields shall be my workshop and 'everlasting hills' and the leafy denizens my only study. With what real pleasure ... do we dwell on the future, especially when it is arched by the bow of providence and presents a picture wrought ... by the fancy fingers of imagination." In 1840 Casilear, who previously had tried unsuccessfully to get Kensett a place in Durand's shop, talked the very willing Kensett into joining himself, Durand, and Thomas Rossiter on a trip to Europe. Leaving Kensett and Rossiter behind in England, Casilear and Durand went on with the grand tour, combining landscape painting in Switzerland and Italy with copying after the Old Masters in the major galleries of France and Italy.

Casilear returned to New York and continued to engrave while he painted his pictures. His landscapes, quite often of Lake George and the Hudson Valley, were done very much under the ideological influence of Durand—they are detailed and modest in conception. His pictures did not demand attention, as one writer noted: "Casilear's work is marked by a peculiarly silvery tone and delicacy of expression, which is in pleasant accord with nature in repose and of his own poetically inclined feelings." It is interesting that Durand, who recommended painting "green," cautioned the student recipient of his letters against hiding nature in grayish tones. Casilear, who occasionally criticized Durand's work as too elaborate, was more interested in catching the delicate effects of atmosphere and summer mists. His developed work is closely related to the more skilled Kensett's and to luminism or "air-painting," as Gifford called it. The Luminists, as they have come to be called, painted during the middle decades of the century, concentrating on capturing weather, light, and air effects. Kensett and Gifford, among the New York group, are counted among them, while elsewhere in New England such important figures as Fitz Hugh Lane and Martin Johnson Heade worked.

John Frederick Kensett, another of the youthful tribe of engravers, was born the son of an engraver in 1816 at Cheshire, Connecticut. He worked in New Haven, New York, and Albany, making bank-note and postage-stamp vignettes in the years before he finally decided to follow Casilear into painting. In 1838 he exhibited his first landscape at the National Academy, where it met with mild interest as "a very fair production from a young engraver; a little too green, however, to be a good representation of nature." Kensett may have been overimpressed by one of Durand's usually green works. Kensett eagerly joined Durand's party going to Europe, and, once settled in Paris in late 1840, he wrote to an English uncle: "I am painting and engraving alternately—have completed a couple of landscapes which I shall send to the National Academy of Design New York for their next exhibition. They are much the best of my performances. . . . R. [Rossiter] and self are drawing every night in the week at the Ecole Préparation des Beaux Arts. . . . we see plainly now what application is necessary to fit us to that standing in our professional labours which we are both seeking honestly to obtain."

Kensett's plucky spirit is one often seen in the younger, or "second generation," Hudson River School painters. They knew, and often said, they had to work hard to get recognition for their art, and prestige for the United States. Kensett returned to New York in 1847 after having painted and traveled widely in England, France, Germany, Switzerland, and Italy. Everything began to go perfectly for Kensett, who had remarkable gifts for socializing. He sold pictures with ease; he met the right people, joined their clubs, became a leader in New York art politics, and, in general, rode the crest of the growing wave of enthusiasm for art. The sarcastic George Templeton Strong, a New York social leader and diarist, described a "respectable" party he gave for people like himself: "Rossiter, Kensett . . . and other artists assisted, whom it's not only creditable but aesthetic and refined to have at one's parties." The artists had indeed come a long way from 1825, when the gentry refused them equal membership in the American Academy of the Fine Arts.

Kensett scoured the picturesque parts of the northeast, the Great Lakes, and Colorado during his subsequent short career in search of mountains, woodlands, waterways, and ocean shores, producing hundreds of sketches and finished oil "rock portraits," as Tuckerman termed them. A conscientious and thoughtful follower of Durand, Kensett selected and painted what he saw and never concerned himself with ideal or allegorical compositions. Like Durand, Kensett carted his oils, canvases, and trappings into the field in order not to miss a thing. His early pictures, done before returning to America, were often dark and tortured attempts at woods interiors, but his mature production was uniform in its conscientious attention to American nature. Using his small brushes like chisels, Kensett built up his rocks, trees, waters, and skies touch by tiny touch. He painted the quiet, serene, rather ordinary aspects of nature, paying particular attention, like Casilear and Gifford, to the air and its effects. He wrote at one point, "Bright colors are sparingly distributed throughout the natural world. The white, red, blue and yellow blossoms of plants, shrubs, and trees are not prominent even in their season of bloom; while the main masses are made up of cool greens, grays, drabs and browns intermingled, and are always harmonious and agreeable." Unlike Cropsey, who almost invariably painted in an autumnal blaze of red, yellow, and purple, Kensett presumably stayed in his studio during the fall, harmonizing his summertime studies. Kensett did not write lengthy descriptions of his ideas on art, but his tireless work at catching the countryside on canvas without any tricks shows his adherence to the primary precepts of Durand. Had he produced allegorical series or historical landscapes, it is doubtful that his posthumous studio sale in 1873 of almost six hundred pictures would have netted $132,312, as it did. He was widely admired as a charitable person, and his pictures were highly influential, as many people, among them Casilear and David Johnson, attempted to approximate his effects.

The inspiration of both Cole and Durand came together to act upon certain of the "second generation" figures, just as certain of them chose to ally themselves and pattern their work after only one of the "founding fathers." The Durand following, if painting precise and nondramatic views of nature qualifies an artist for this group, could include the already discussed Casilear and Kensett, plus David Johnson, Sanford Gifford, Worthington Whittredge, and William Stanley Haseltine, among an army of lesser figures.

David Johnson, a master of richly painted sketches and close-ups of rocks and trees, was born in New York in 1827. He studied with Jasper Cropsey, "but was a close student of Nature, looking upon her as his teacher and master." He had his biggest success in the 1860s and 1870s, exhibiting numerous Hudson River, Adirondack, and New England views. His larger pictures are carefully painted in a manner like Kensett's, although they tend to be somewhat drier in finish. His work today is still not well known but is rapidly regaining recognition.

Sanford Gifford, born in 1823, son of wealthy and cultured parents, was raised in Hudson, New York, a neighbor of Cole at Catskill. After a false start at Brown University, and encouraged by his family, Gifford entered the New York drawing school of John Rubens Smith in 1845. While learning to draw the human figure, Gifford found the appeal of landscape painting: "During the summer of 1846 I made several pedestrian tours among the Catskill Mountains and the Berkshire hills, and made a good many sketches from nature. These studies, together with the great admiration I felt for the works of Cole, developed a strong interest in Landscape art, and opened my eyes to a keener perception and more intelligent enjoyment of Nature. Having once enjoyed the absolute freedom of the Landscape painter's life, I was unable to return to portrait painting. From this time my direction in art was determined."

Gifford's early landscapes show a natural affinity with the early, rather dry and liney works of Cole, but he rapidly moved in the direction of a different style. By the mid-1850s he had discovered his own style in generally small-scale, minutely painted atmospheric views of mountains, placid stretches of water, and glowing sunsets. Gifford's technique in achieving his completed "air paintings" was given by the art critic George Sheldon in 1879: "Mr. Gifford varnishes the finished picture so many times with boiled oil, or some other semi-transparent or translucent substance, that a veil is made between the canvas and the spectator's eye—a veil which corresponds to the natural veil of the atmosphere." Gifford received considerable criticism for this method, the opening shot coming from *Harper's Weekly* in 1860: "Why should that admirable painter, Mr. Gifford, with so sensitive an eye, with so delicate a touch, with so felicitous a fancy—why should he steep every scene he paints in that vague, shimmering, sandy hue, until the spectator believes he sees only a mirage, and not the fair, substantial reality of earth and sky and sea?" Every good artist has an enthusiasm or special interest which he puts into his work, and Gifford saw the landscapes he painted—American, European, Mediterranean—in relation to light and air. His paintings could be seen almost as simple weather researches if they were not so carefully and well arranged. In his devotion to researching and capturing what he saw in nature, Gifford belongs spiritually more to Durand than to his chosen model, Cole, in spite of the fact that Durand himself might have rejected Gifford's supercharged shimmer as mannered. As John Weir said at Gifford's memorial service in 1880, "Gifford loved the light."

Frederic E. Church, during the heyday of his greatest popularity in the late 1850s and 1860s, was probably America's best known landscape painter at home and abroad. Albert Bierstadt was the only possible competitor for the title. Church was born in Hartford, Connecticut, in 1826. He studied painting with two local painters for a short while before going to Catskill in 1844, where Thomas Cole took him as a student for two years, and Church learned his use of the loaded brush and dark colors to paint highly charged landscape scenes. Tuckerman wrote that "here he observed, under singularly favorable auspices, the permanent traits of indigenous vegetation, the characteristic phases of atmosphere, and the evanescent phenomena of skies, trees and herbage ... all the essential features of Nature in her wild and primeval haunts, he there faithfully studied, and thus laid the foundation of that breadth and executive skill whereby he subsequently represented, with such marvelous truth, her less familiar traits...." Church left Cole in 1846, settled in New York in 1847, and began producing a few allegorical and historical scenes, but primarily numerous well constructed views with names like *Storm in the Mountains; Kauterskill Clove, Catskill; View near Stockbridge; West Rock, New Haven;* and *Ira Mountain, Vermont.* He felt secure enough to accept his first pupil, William Stillman, in 1848.

From the first, Church was a great eye and a keen technician with the oils and traveled more widely than most of his colleagues in search of demanding subjects. In 1851, for example, he traveled to Virginia, possibly North Carolina, Kentucky, and the Upper Mississippi in June. In July he was at work in the Catskills, and August found him at Grand Manan and the Bay of Fundy. In October he was on Mount Desert Island. The following year he restrained himself and went only to Grand Manan, Maine, and the Catskills; but in 1853 Church, in the company of Cyrus Field, later the proponent of the trans-Atlantic telegraph cable, made an extended trip to Colombia, Ecuador, and Panama. This trip proved the turning point of Church's career since thereafter he appropriated the unfamiliar mountainous South American scene as his primary subject matter and went on to travel to far-flung places such as Jamaica, Newfoundland, Labrador, Europe, Egypt, Syria, Lebanon, Turkey, Greece, Russia, and, in his latter days, Mexico.

Church's great fame came from the "full-length" showpiece landscapes, especially his *Niagara* and *Heart of the Andes*, which stood the art world and the general public on their ears when first shown in the late 1850s. Church's remarkable ability as a painter of detailed sketches served him perfectly as he compiled the massive landscapes, bringing together a mind-boggling variety of minutiae in vast panoramas. By removing emphasis on foreground detail, but accumulating detail throughout the rest of the picture and thrusting the viewer into the picture, Church achieved an encyclopedic wrap-around art that fascinated and riveted the attention of a surprised public. Inspired by the original mind and thirst for exploration of Von Humboldt and a deep personal religiosity, Church created his fantastic scenes, believing that they expressed in their scale and beloved detail his most profound ideas of man's intimate but minor relationship to the marvels of nature. He delivered, as it were, Cole's and Durand's ideas with a showman's flourish.

Tuckerman described Church's working methods, which were akin to those of the other landscapists of the period. "It is Church's habit to devote the summer to observation and reflection; then he gathers the materials, and thinks over the plan and scope of his pictures, seeking at the same time, by life in the open air . . . [to] lay up a stock of strength as well as ideas for work during the winter. That season he passes in the city, resolutely shut up several hours daily in his studio, concentrating his mind upon some long-contemplated task, to which his time and thoughts are given with a rare and exclusive devotion."

Among the most beautiful works by Church are the fluently executed oil sketches on paper and canvas which are preserved at his fantastic pseudo-Moorish country home, Olana, and in the Cooper-Hewitt Museum, New York. His large works were often, particularly at the end of his life, criticized for being mechanical, over brilliant, and too technical in their vision, "rather scientific than artistic," but the extraordinary looseness and bravura of the oil sky-sketches alone are enough to establish Church as one of the finest Hudson River School masters. In the long thirty years at the end of his life when his pictures were unwanted and depreciated, he worked on such sketches in large numbers, maintaining his habit described by Tuckerman. "It has long been his daily custom to ascend a hill, near his country home, to observe the sunset; and in his landscapes 'the earth is always painted with reference to the skies' which is one reason for their truth to nature."

Jasper Cropsey was born on Staten Island in 1823, of "poor but very respectable parents." He entered a New York architect's office and worked for five years before taking up landscape painting in 1841, a few years after Casilear and Kensett had made similar decisions. Like them, he went to Europe, spent two years in Italy from 1847 to 1849, living in Thomas Cole's old Roman studio. Having painted landscapes of the nearby New York and New Jersey countryside before his European sojourn, Cropsey added Italian and Scottish scenes to his repertoire when he returned to New York in 1849. Working very much in the shadow of Cole's work, Cropsey produced stormy mountain scenes and allegories such as *Spirit of War* and *Spirit of Peace*. His early works are remarkably similar to Cole's in color, handling, mood, and conception. Until he went to England in 1856, Cropsey made the usual rounds— the White Mountains, New York State, Massachusetts, Newport, and Niagara Falls, which he painted in obvious imitation of Church who had done so the previous year. Cropsey lived in London and the Isle of Wight until 1863, when he returned to the United States because of the Civil War. During his residence in London he painted and exhibited in 1860 what has ever since been regarded as one of his greatest works, *Autumn on the Hudson*. Cropsey had seen the *Heart of the Andes* by Church when it was shown in London during July 1859, and his response was to produce a picture almost as large but of a typically North American subject, the Hudson Valley in its brightest coloration. The London *Times* commented on the painting: "American artists are rapidly making the untravelled portion of the English public familiar with the scenery of the great Western continent. Mr. Church's *Niagara Falls*, and the *Heart of the Andes*, recently exhibited, have found a companion picture in Mr. Cropsey's *Autumn on the Hudson River*, now on view. The painting is a perfectly faithful view of the locality. ... The point of view is well chosen for variety of effect. It comprises a lake-like inlet of the river, the distant river itself, mountains, and an undulating foreground of forest and wood. The singularly vivid colors of an American autumnal scene, the endless contrast of purples and yellows, scarlets and browns, running into every conceivable shade between the extremes, might easily tempt a painter to exaggerate, or revel in variety of line and effect, like a Turner of the forest. But Mr. Cropsey has resisted the temptation, and even a little tempers the capricious tinting of nature; his autumn is still brilliant, but not quite lost to sobriety, as we have sometimes, we think, seen it in the Western World. The result is a fine picture, full of points that are new, without being wholly foreign and strange to the European eye. It will take the ordinary observer into another sphere and region, while its execution will bear any technical criticism."

Cropsey's success was considerable, as he sold the nine-foot canvas to an Englishman and was presented to Queen Victoria in recognition of his new prominence. Although the picture was probably the main reason for Cropsey's subsequent specialization as a painter of autumn coloring, he produced a number of more sober English views such as *Richmond Hill—Midsummer* and *Corfe Castle, Dorset*, as well as several large gothic romances such as *The Olden Time*, which are obvious references to Cole's imaginary scenes. In 1865 Cropsey painted his massive *Wyoming Valley, Pennsylvania*, which is a remarkably bright, spacious, and atmospheric handling of an incredible amount of rural detail. The picture sold for $3500, which was part of his $9000 income that year, the high financial point of his career. Impressed by his progress in the world, and probably envious of his colleagues Church and Bierstadt, Cropsey built a gigantic house-*cum*-studio, Aladdin, in Warwick, New York. In 1884 he had to give up the house because of the expense involved, and he bought a more modest place on the Hudson at Hastings. Cropsey spent the rest of his career painting a large number of oil and watercolor views of the river. The production tended to be repetitious in its reliance on hot colors depicting superdramatic weather conditions, and he suffered for lack of patronage. While Cropsey had been an important continuer of the Cole tradition, he was indeed a mannerist, albeit a charming one, who outlived his artistic prime.

Cole, Church, and Cropsey all constructed very large and impressive landscapes of foreign and East Coast locations, but it was the German-born and -trained Albert Bierstadt who chose to explore and depict the scenic wonders of the American West on a truly epic scale. His timing was perfect—during the 1860s and 1870s, when the popular press here and abroad gave considerable attention to the opening of mountainous regions of the West which were indeed our last frontier. His fame approached or equaled that of his contemporary Church, and his subject matter has guaranteed him a lasting national reputation. The West was big and Bierstadt painted it gigantic in such crushing masterpieces as *The Rocky Mountains, Storm in the Rocky Mountains,* and *The Domes of the Yosemite.*

Bierstadt was born near Düsseldorf in 1830, grew up in New Bedford, Massachusetts, and in 1853 returned to study at the Düsseldorf Academy at the time the grandiose and careful Düsseldorf style had its greatest following here and in Europe. Like Church, Bierstadt was a fluent and gifted draftsman and oil sketcher who turned out countless preparatory pieces for his large machines, ranging from pencil sketches to finished medium-scale canvases. Perhaps from his friend Gifford, also at Düsseldorf, Bierstadt gained his understanding of how to paint the shimmering, glowing light of clouds and moisture-laden air. Bierstadt entered the landscape competitions of the United States in 1857 when he returned here following training and travel through Germany, Switzerland, and Italy. In 1859 at the National Academy of Design, he displayed eight pictures of a familiar, cultured type, such as *View near Newport, The Bernese Alps, The Temple of Paestum,* and *Mt. Washington from Shelburne, New Hampshire.*

In April 1859 Bierstadt set off on his first trek westward, joining Col. Frederick Lander's army expedition in Nebraska and Wyoming, along the North Platte and Sweetwater Rivers, the purpose of which was, in Lander's words, to "proceed to the frontier and thence to the south pass of the Rocky Mountains; to go over the road opened last year, make such improvements on it as might be necessary . . ." and to obtain "a continuous survey over the whole road and further information of a route said to exist north of [the Humboldt river]." His report included mention of Bierstadt and a fellow artist named Frost, who took "sketches of the most remarkable of the views along the route, and a set of stereoscopic views of emigrant trains, Indians, camp scenes, etc., which are highly valuable and would be interesting to the country." Bierstadt, whose brother was a professional photographer, used photographs and any other technique necessary to capture the accuracy and dramatic mood of his pictures. The paintings of the Wyoming Rockies that began issuing from his studio in 1860 established Bierstadt as *the* painter of our West, and in following quests he covered thousands of miles, sketching the mountains of Wyoming, Colorado, Utah, Nevada, California, Oregon, Washington, and Alaska. Rich collectors such as James Lenox, Marshall Roberts, Robert L. Stuart, Leland Stanford, Collis Huntington, and a variety of titled Englishmen, including Lord Dunraven, paid up to $35,000 for his major works. The United States Congress paid $10,000 each for *The Landing of Hendrick Hudson at Manhattan Island* and *Entrance into Monterey.*

The bottom went out of Bierstadt's market, just as it did for Church and Cropsey, in the late 1870s and the 1880s. After having astounded and pleased the public for twenty very lucrative years, Bierstadt must have found it devastating to read Yale Professor John Weir's *Official Report of the American Centennial Exhibition* of 1876: "The earlier works of this artist showed a vigorous, manly style of art, that had its undeniable attractions. His pictures exhibited at Philadelphia indicate a lapse into sensational and meretricious effects, and a loss of true artistic aim. They are vast illustrations of scenery, carelessly and crudely executed, and we fail to discover in them the merits which rendered his earlier works conspicuous." Bierstadt's style had not changed so much as critical attitudes toward panoramic art. The bloom was definitely off the rose. Perhaps the best appreciation of Bierstadt came from the not wholly enthusiastic Tuckerman in 1867: "The qualities which strike us in Mr. Bierstadt, as an artist, are, first, a great audacity, justified by perfect ability to accomplish all that he intends. He is not a mere copyist of nature, but an artist having definite artistic intentions, and carrying them out with care and resolution." Bierstadt's enthusiastic vision of nature at its grandest is one that will guarantee the lasting popularity of his work.

Church, Bierstadt, and Cropsey, as they declined into obscurity and repetitiousness during the 1880s, proved the point that art is not and cannot be a static thing. The public and the artist get bored with sameness, and the fatigued eye begins to look around for new exercises. Every art movement has within it individuals who are capable of moving on to the new ideas and new styles—the Hudson River School was no exception to the rule.

Among those who worked in a detailed naturalistic style from the late 1840s through the 1860s was George Inness. Inness, who was born on the Hudson at Newburgh in 1825, became an engraver but gave it up in 1840 to study landscape painting with the French immigrant snowscapist Régis Gignoux, who painted in a precise academic style that won approval of the New York critics. Inness stayed only long enough to learn the basics of painting, but the most important event in his development was seeing Old Master prints and some originals by Cole and Durand. He said, "There was a lofty striving in Cole, although he did not technically realize that for which he reached. There was in Durand a more intimate feeling of nature. 'If,' thought I, 'these two can only be combined! I will try!' " One of the most thoughtful artists painting at that time, Inness propounded that "the true use of art is, first, to cultivate the artist's own spiritual nature, and, second, to enter as a factor in general civilization. . . . Every artist who, without reference to external circumstances, aims truly to represent the ideas and emotions which come to him when he is in the presence of nature is a benefactor of his race. . . . the true artistic impulse is divine." Inness went to Europe several times in the late 1840s and the 1850s and spent the years 1870 to 1874 in Italy and France. He early discovered the Barbizon painters of France and moved away from his earlier admiration for Cole and Durand. He told his son that "as landscape-painters I consider Rousseau, Daubigny, and Corot among the very best. Daubigny particularly and Corot have mastered the relation of things in nature one to another. . . . Rousseau was perhaps the greatest French landscape-painter. . . . the trouble with Rousseau was that he has too much detail." The Innesses returned to New York from Paris in 1854, and he began painting in earnest for the local market. His woodland, meadow, and twilight scenes, which today seem so respectable and handsome, were apparently not acceptable to the buyers. His son wrote, "For several years he struggled for recognition, but New York still held to the old school and would have none of him; so we moved to Boston. . . . We then took up our residence in Medfield, a suburb of Boston, and times became better." Inness remained in Medfield from 1859 to 1864, then he lived in Eagleswood, New Jersey, and Brooklyn before his four-year stint in Europe during the 1870s. Upon his return to the United States, Inness worked in New York and Montclair, New Jersey. He died in 1894. According to his son, Inness usually worked in a barn as a studio when he was not out of doors. "Out of doors he was quiet, rational, and absorbed. I have seen him sit in the same spot every day for a week or more studying carefully and minutely the contours of trees and composition of the clouds and grass, drawing very carefully with painstaking exactness. But in his studio he was like a madman. He seldom painted direct from nature. He would study for days, then with the most dynamic energy, creating the composition from his own brain, but with so thorough an underlying knowledge of nature that the key-note of his landscapes was always truth and sincerity and absolute fidelity to nature."

Varying considerably from previous Hudson River School example, Inness said, "Never put anything on your canvas that isn't of use, never use a detail unless it means something." As Inness developed his style, it became freer, almost impetuous, more atmospheric, and remarkable for the nearly palpable atmosphere of light and air that he created. He increasingly moved away from repetitiousness and drudgelike copying of nature. His conviction was that "the true end of Art is not to imitate a fixed material condition, but to represent a living motion." Inness had, in fact, applied the broad techniques of the Barbizon painters to his own highly mystical view of nature. Writing in 1879, S. G. W. Benjamin, author of *Art in America*, commented that "the first landscapes of George Inness . . . properly belong in style to the early and distinctively American school of landscape, while his recent method has identified him with the later graduates of the ateliers of Paris." Benjamin was one of the critical holdouts in favor of the Hudson River School and felt uneasy about the invasion of French style into American art. He makes little mention of the fact that from Cole onward the American landscapists absorbed English, German, and Italian art quite freely without feeling that they were debasing American artistic currency. If we grant that all American art grew to greater or lesser extent out of European impulses, then the example of Inness and those he influenced, like Homer Martin, Wyant, and the Hart brothers, shows the influence of Paris winning over the influence of Rome and Düsseldorf in New York's studios. Inness was an early warning of this major change of taste that shook the American art world and put the Hudson River School out of business.

In 1875 a critic in a review of the annual exhibition of the National Academy of Design, fifty years old that year, greeted "with joy unfeigned an exhibition in which landscape art [holds] a somewhat subordinate rank instead of that place of supremacy which was formerly the dread of the ordinary visitor, and which some years reached a point so absolute that walking through the Academy seemed like exiling oneself among wildernesses where the human form was unknown."

In 1888 Clarence Cook wrote his massive survey *Art and Artists of Our Time*, and from him one would get the idea that Cole, Durand, Church, Kensett, and their various colleagues and followers were almost forgotten history. About Durand's painting he said, "It was patient, minute, and founded on an affectionate study of nature, but unfortunately subjected in his finished pictures to rules purely conventional. . . . He gave great impetus to this minute and scientific study of natural forms, and influenced many of the younger men of his time in this direction." He depreciated Cole for painting "many pictures intended to convey moral teaching in a would-be poetical symbolism." Of Church he merely commented that he "made himself a national reputation by a succession of pictures that are rather to be praised as records of famous places than as works of art in the higher sense." Cosmopolitanism had overtaken the American art scene as a host of new artists, particularly portrait, figure, and genre painters, displaced the old guard that had become crusty and snappish like Daniel Huntington. Huntington, repeating history for New York City, drove the younger men away from the National Academy, as Cole's generation had been driven away from the American Academy of the Fine Arts. The younger artists wanted to pursue new avenues, working in the Barbizon and even impressionist styles, combining technical freedom and painterly bravura with poetic vision. In landscape, names like Martin, Homer, Hunt, Ryder, Wyant, and Chase replaced Church, Cropsey, Bierstadt, *et al.* on the gallery walls. Collectors put off the old style and on the new like a suit of clothes, and auction sales of Hudson River School pictures were numerous in the 1880s. There is no question that America's art vision had broadened and gained vitality as a result of the new tastes. The critics of the 1880s, 1890s, and after looked on Cole, Durand, and their progeny as naïve, saying they "looked on nature with an eye at once too wiggling and too comprehensive." The later men preferred to see paint used for its own sake, as a surface with a life somewhat independent of the subject depicted. Technique assumed a role of being as beautiful and admirable as the content. Today such an attitude is a commonplace, and taste is perceptibly swinging back in favor of the romantic vision of the mid-nineteenth century. Today we can congratulate and admire the landscape pioneers who worked in the studios of New York for their remarkable contributions to American art as well as for their sympathetic presentation of a simpler world, of the beautiful "unappropriated world" of America that Richard Ray had recommended to them in 1825. Their vision is fortunately one that will not pass away.

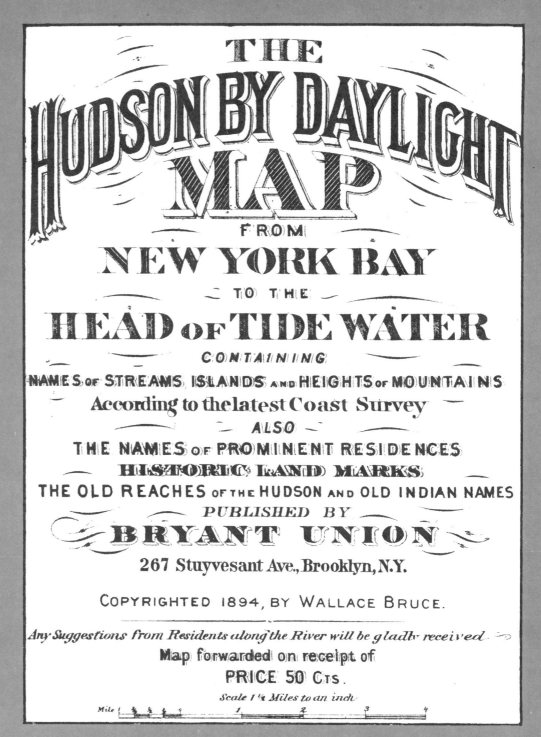

THE
HUDSON BY DAYLIGHT
MAP
FROM
NEW YORK BAY
TO THE
HEAD OF TIDE WATER
CONTAINING
NAMES OF STREAMS, ISLANDS AND HEIGHTS OF MOUNTAINS
According to the latest Coast Survey
ALSO
THE NAMES OF PROMINENT RESIDENCES
HISTORIC LAND MARKS
THE OLD REACHES OF THE HUDSON AND OLD INDIAN NAMES
PUBLISHED BY
BRYANT UNION
267 Stuyvesant Ave., Brooklyn, N.Y.

COPYRIGHTED 1894, BY WALLACE BRUCE.

Any Suggestions from Residents along the River will be gladly received
Map forwarded on receipt of
PRICE 50 Cts.
Scale 1½ Miles to an inch

The Hudson River is a tidal estuary as far north as Troy. Maps of the nineteenth century, delightfully detailed, portray the river and its banks from New York City to slightly north of Troy, since this was the route of normal navigation for the ocean-going vessels and the famous "Dayliners."

The forty miles from Troy to Fort Edward, the real head of navigation, is a domesticated stretch of locks and dams which is now used largely by barges and pleasure boats but was originally the link to the west and the north. Above Fort Edward the proportions of the river change. For a hundred miles it becomes an unnavigable mountain stream. Maps of these headwater areas are more land oriented and, in the nineteenth century, descriptions of the Adirondack wilderness had the loose quality common to early records of "territory." In fact, Lake Tear of the Clouds, highest source of the Hudson River, was not discovered until 1872. For this reason, we have chosen not to use just one map of the river from its source to the sea, but have included two, roughly contiguous and of the same era, on which to follow the artistic journey.

At approximately the same point as the geographical change in the river, the paintings inspired by it begin to reflect a shift in emphasis and flavor.

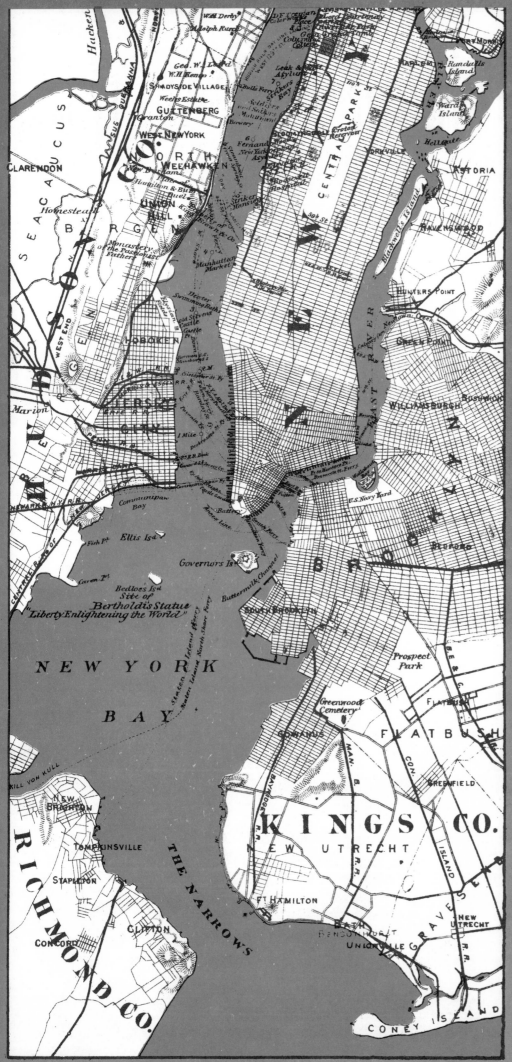

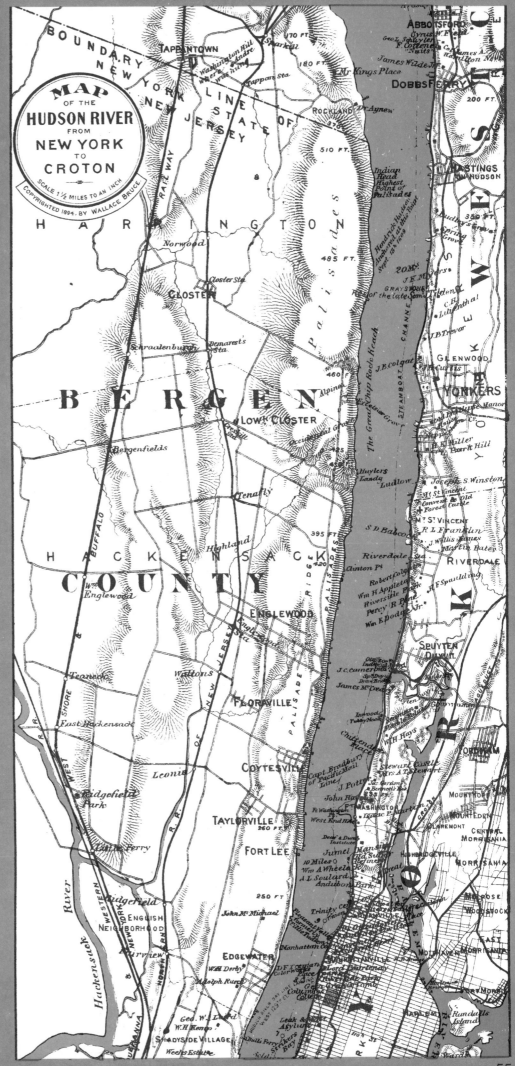

MAP
OF THE
HUDSON RIVER
FROM
NEW YORK
TO
CROTON
SCALE 1½ MILES TO AN INCH
COPYRIGHTED 1894, BY WALLACE BRUCE.

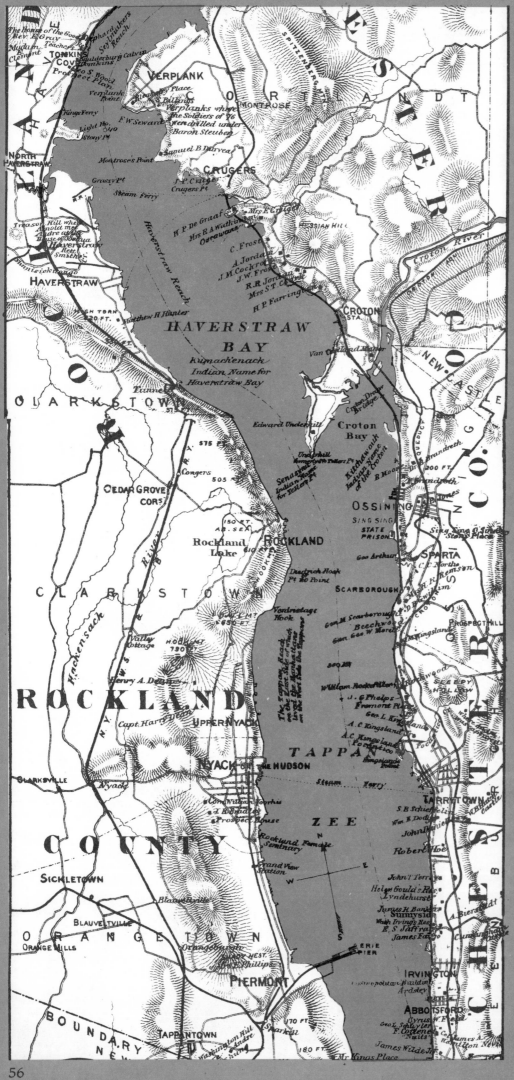

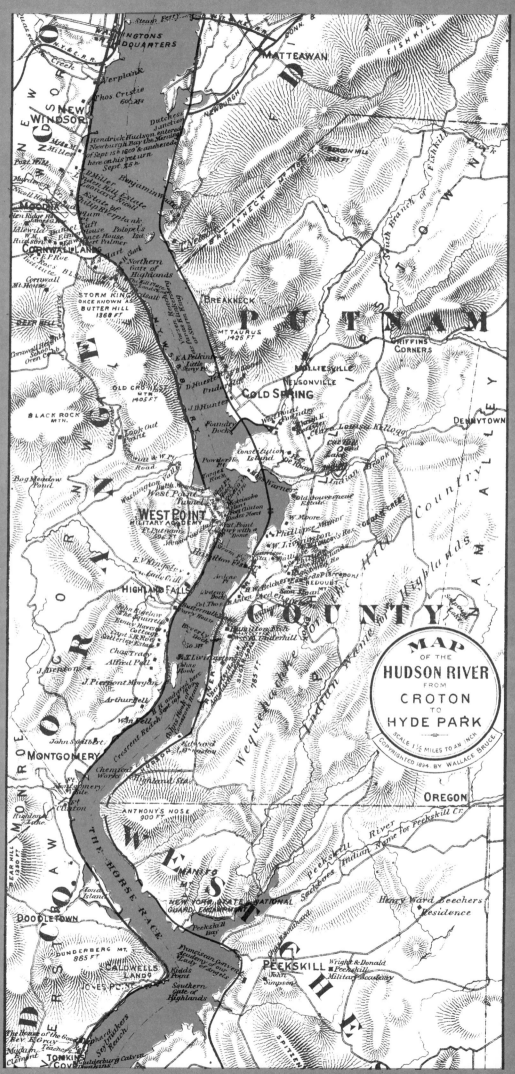

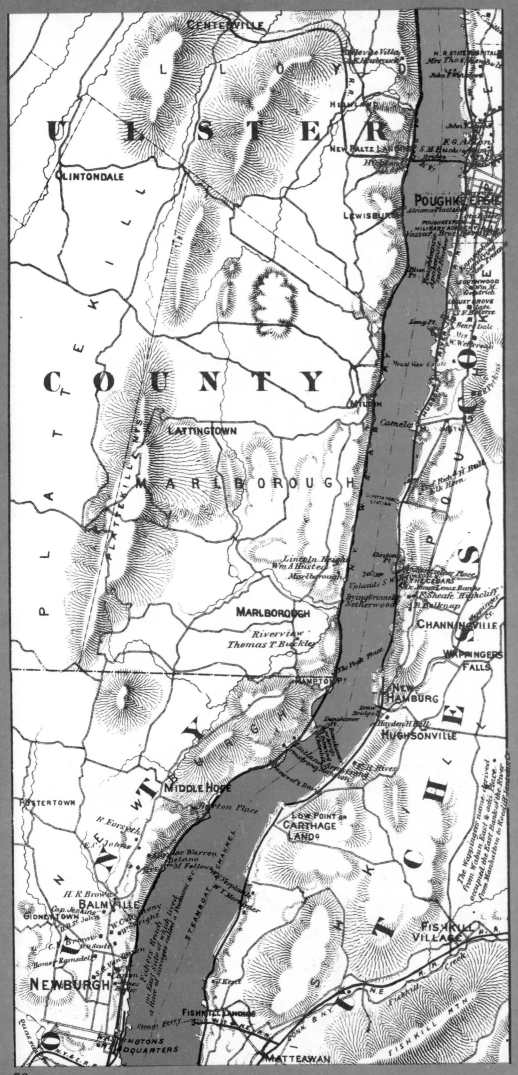

58

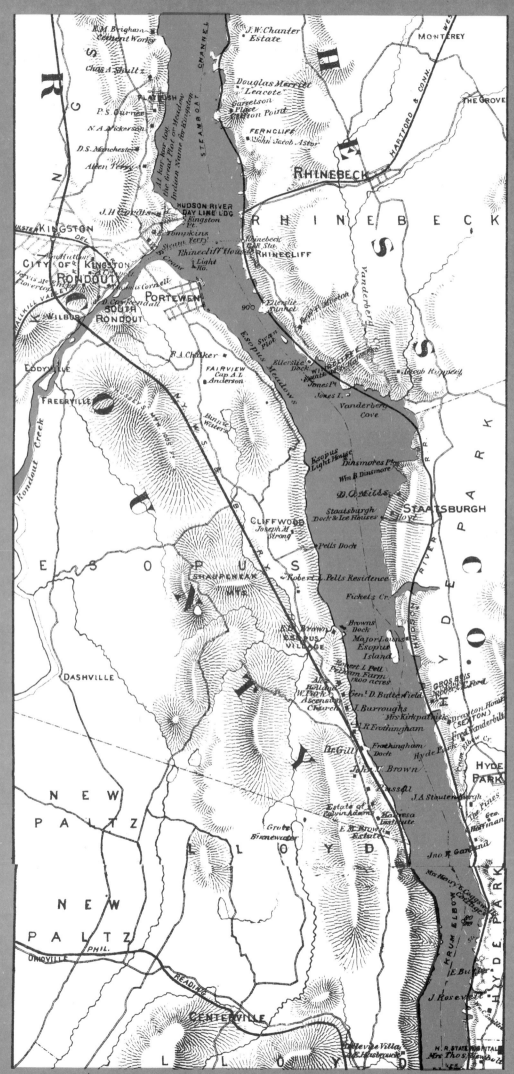

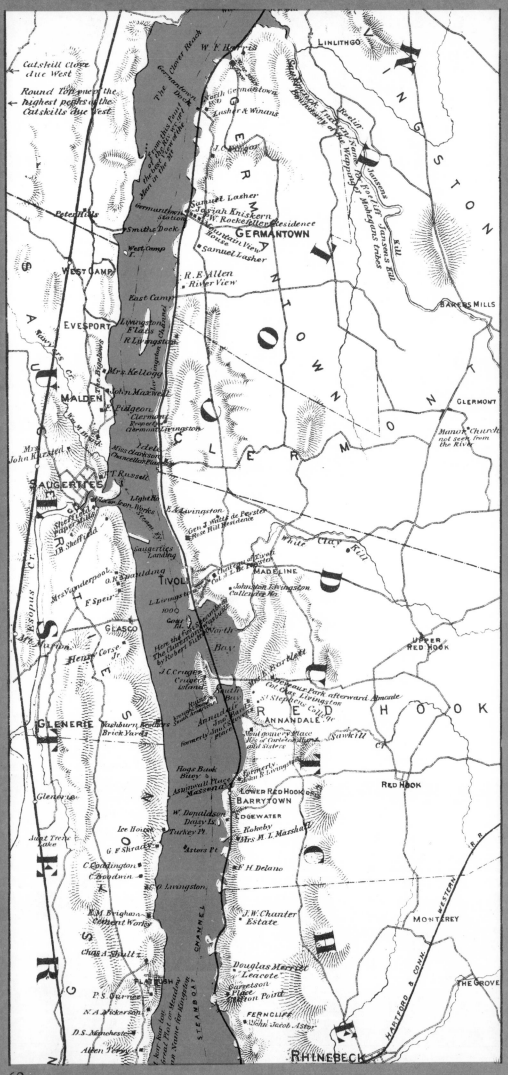

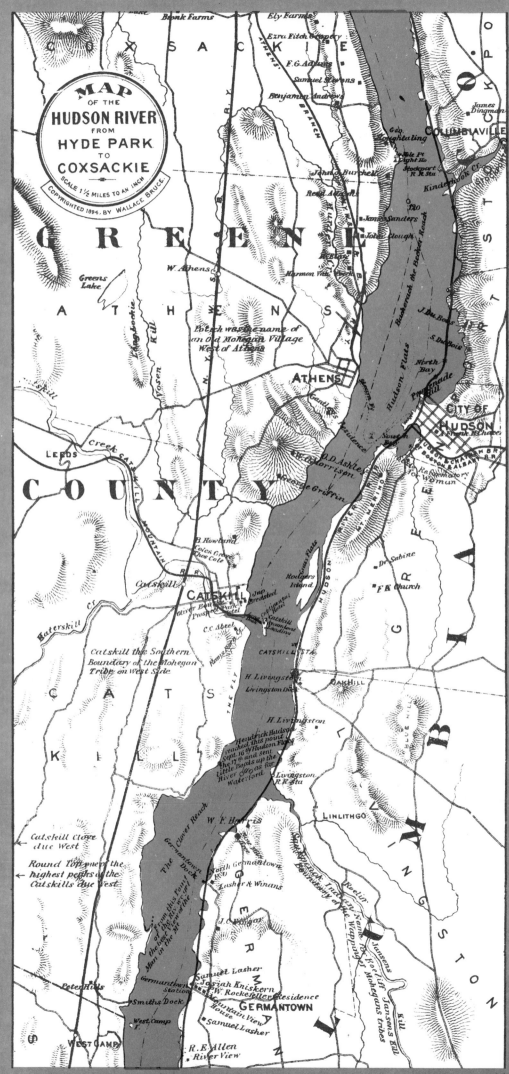

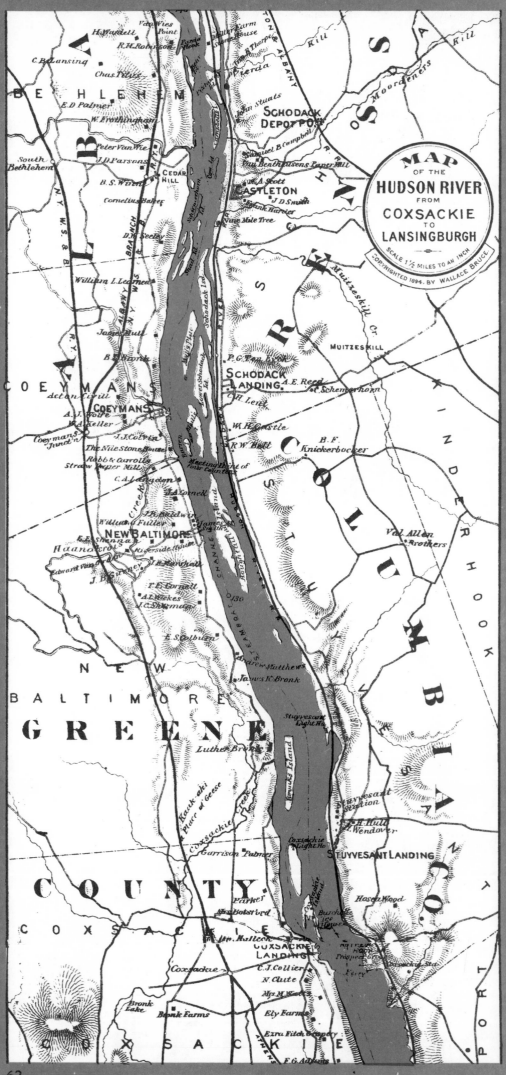

MAP
OF THE
HUDSON RIVER
FROM
COXSACKIE
TO
LANSINGBURGH
SCALE 1½ MILES TO AN INCH
COPYRIGHTED 1894. BY WALLACE BRUCE.

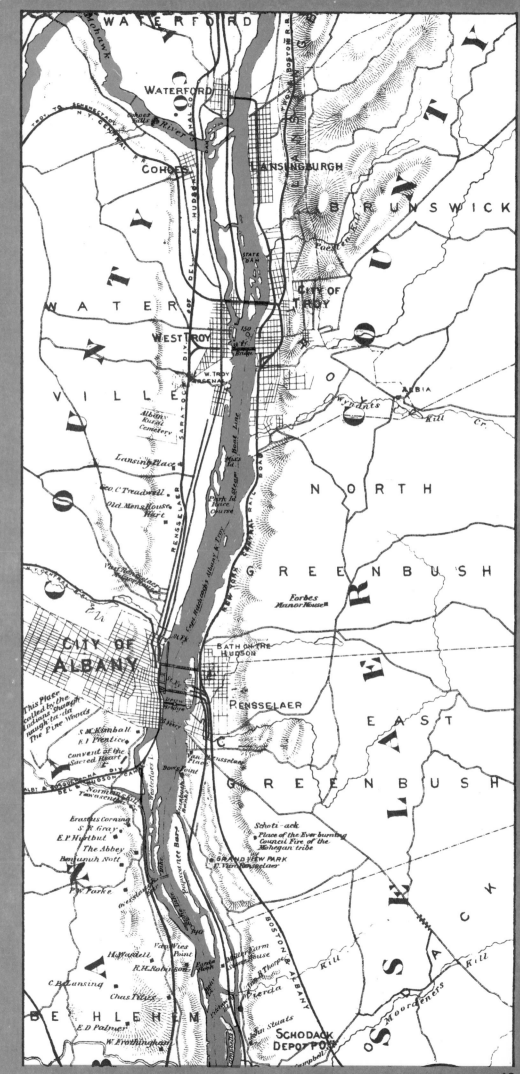

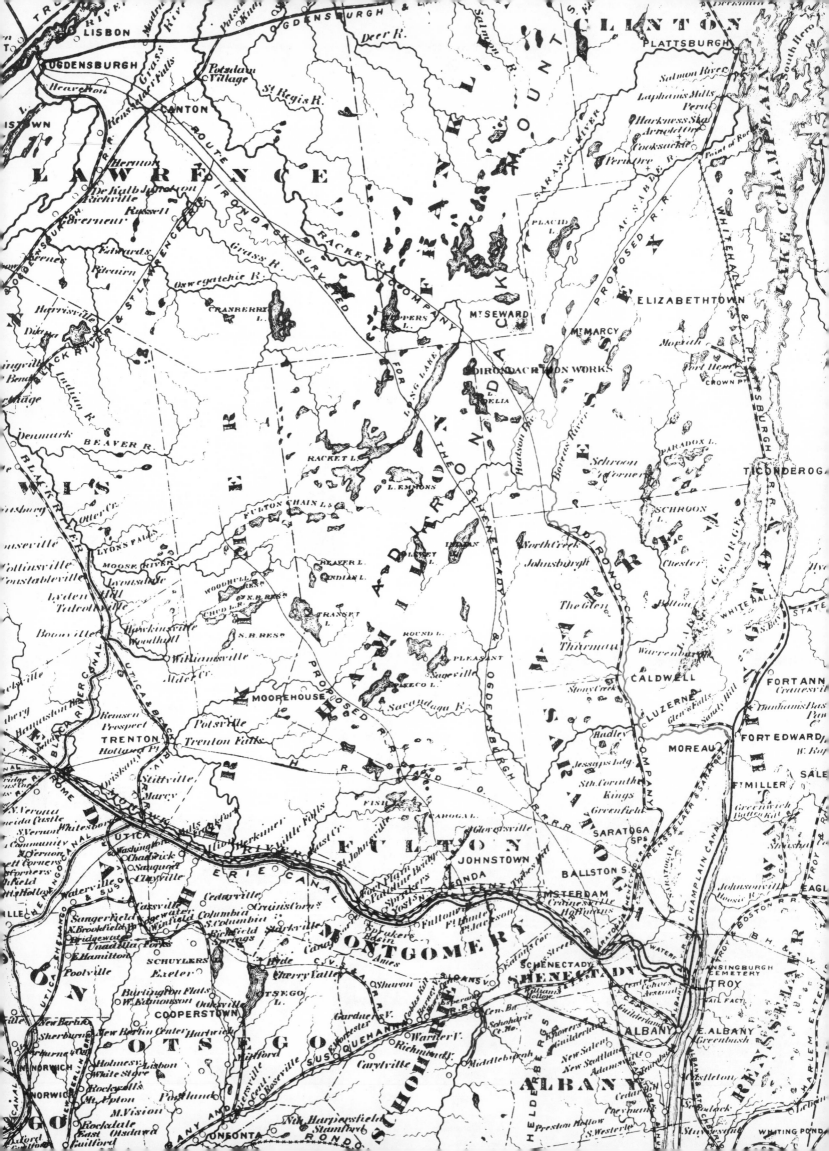

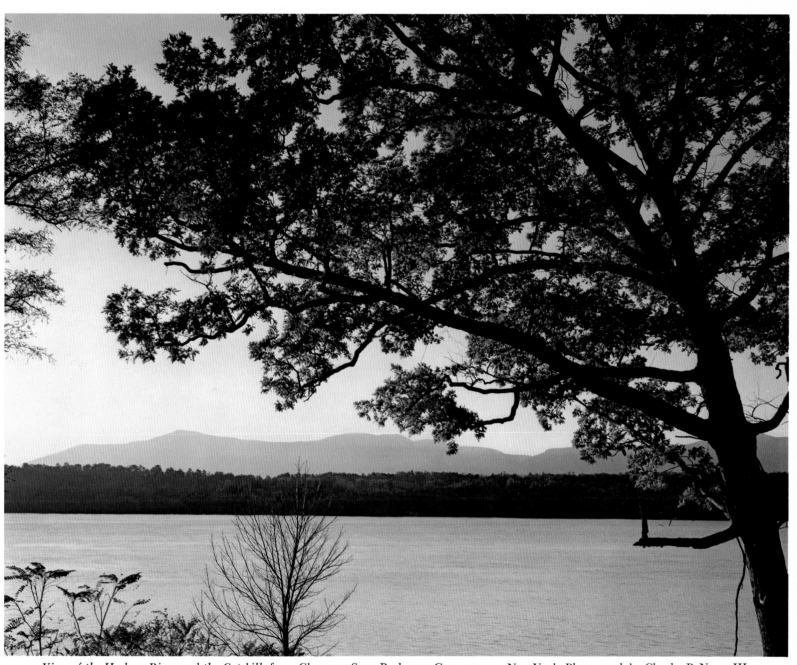

View of the Hudson River and the Catskills from Clermont State Park near Germantown, New York. Photograph by Charles P. Noyes III.

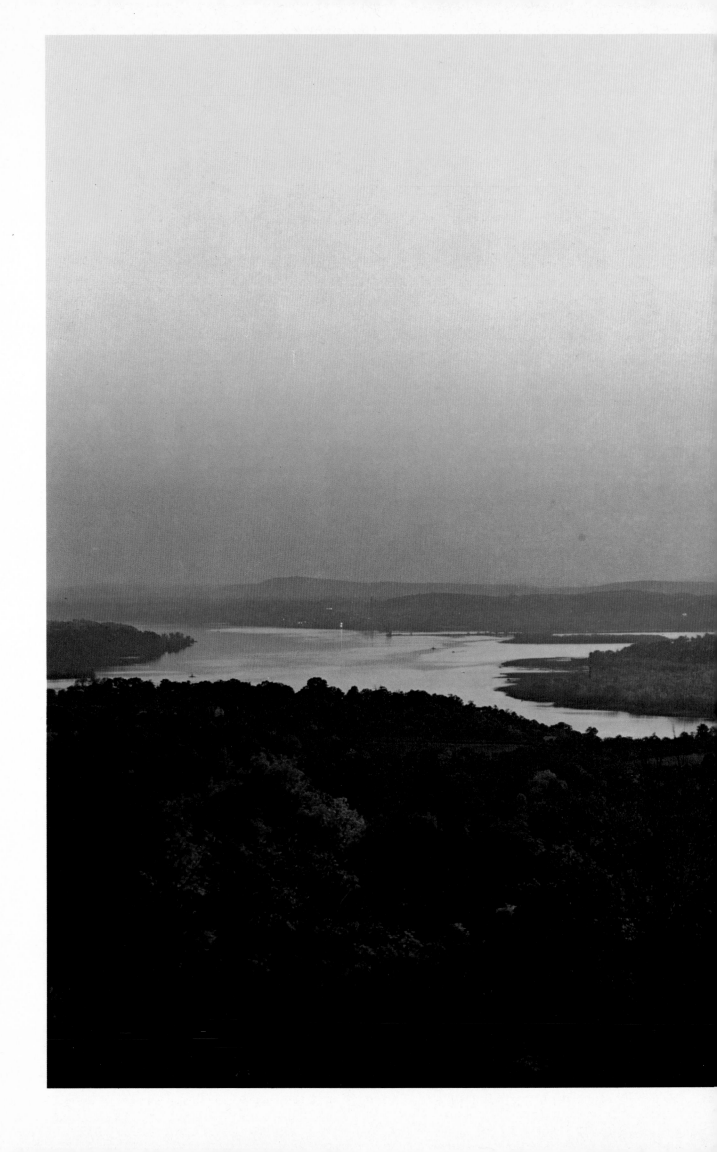

The Hudson River and the Catskills from Olana, Frederic Church's home near Hudson, New York. Photograph by Charles P. Noyes III.

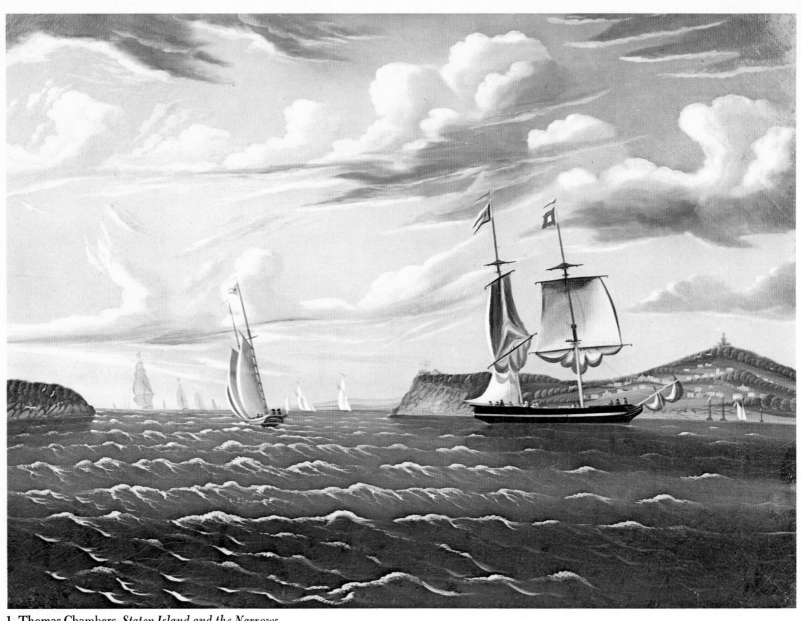

1. Thomas Chambers, *Staten Island and the Narrows*

2. William Henry Bartlett, *View of the Bay and Harbor of New York from Gowanus Heights, Brooklyn*

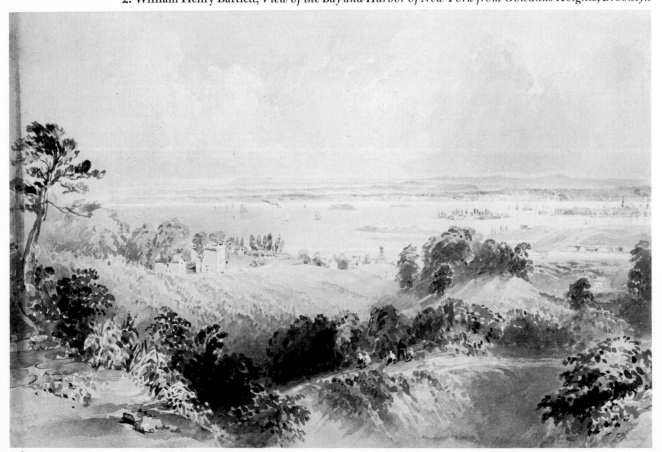

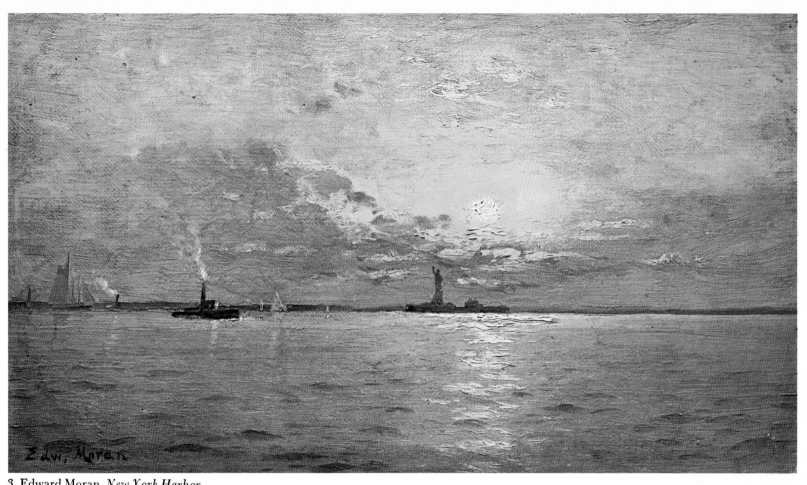

3. Edward Moran, *New York Harbor*

4. Sanford Robinson Gifford, *Sunset over New York Bay*

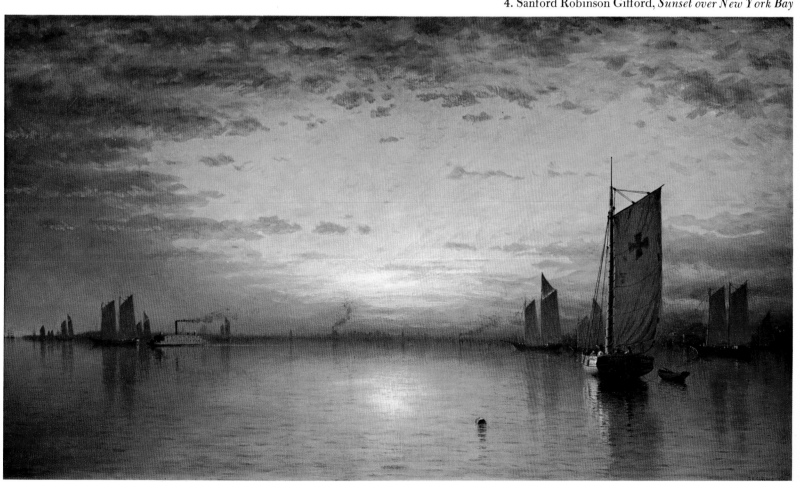

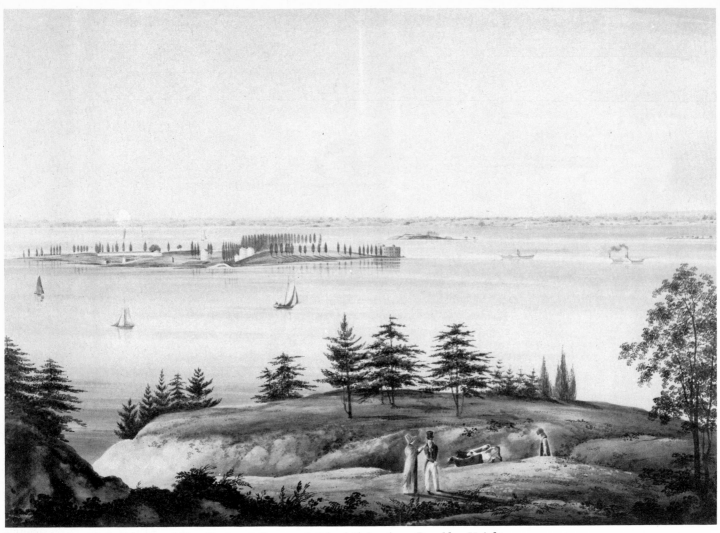

5. William Guy Wall, *The Bay of New York and Governor's Island Taken from Brooklyn Heights*

6. Anonymous (after Thomas Kelah Wharton), *New York from Brooklyn Heights*

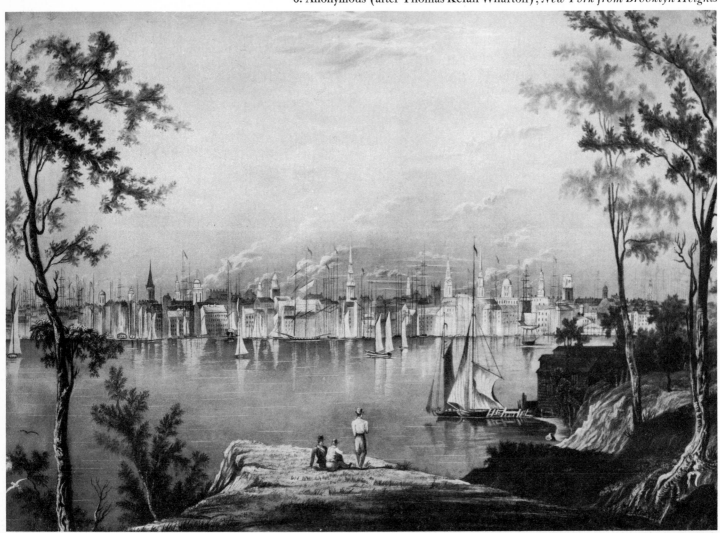

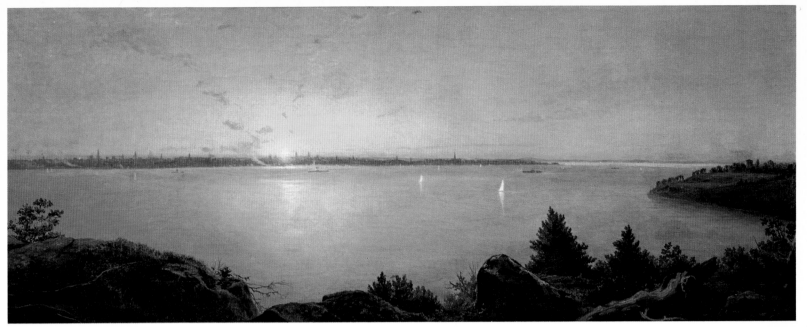

7. Charles Herbert Moore, *Morning over New York*

8. Thomas Chambers, *Villa on the Hudson near Weehawken*

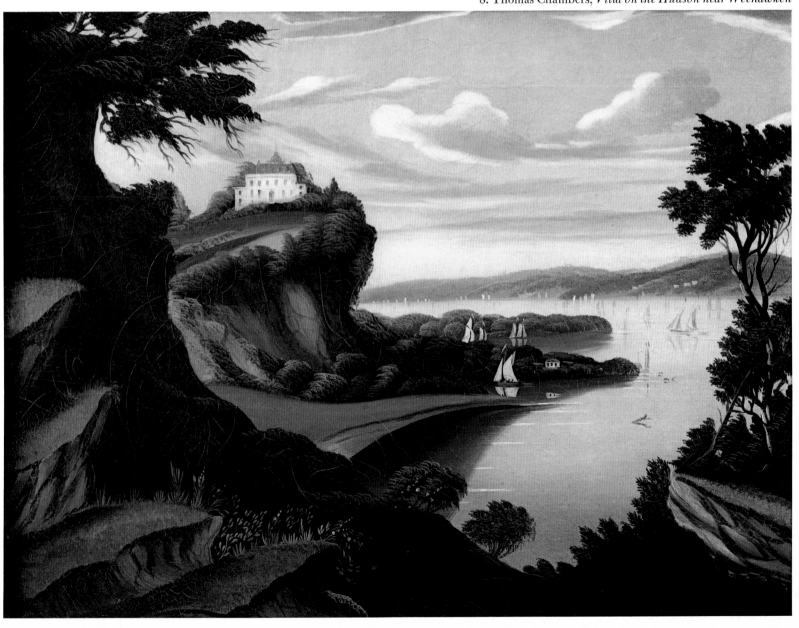

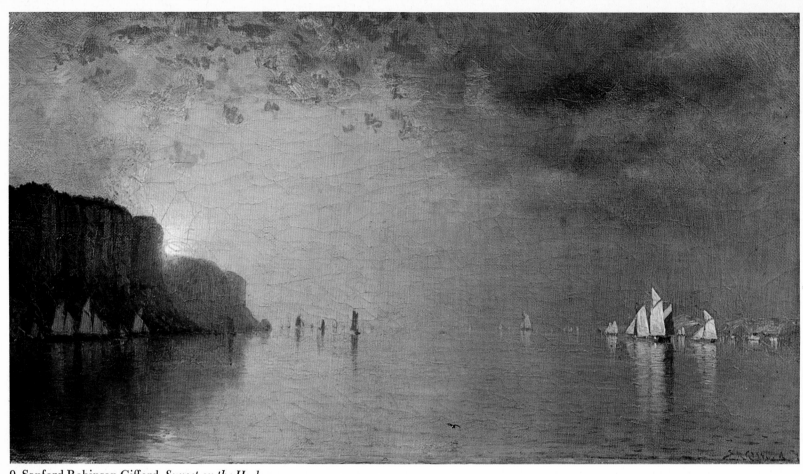

9. Sanford Robinson Gifford, *Sunset on the Hudson*

10. Jasper Francis Cropsey, *Shad Fishing on the Hudson*

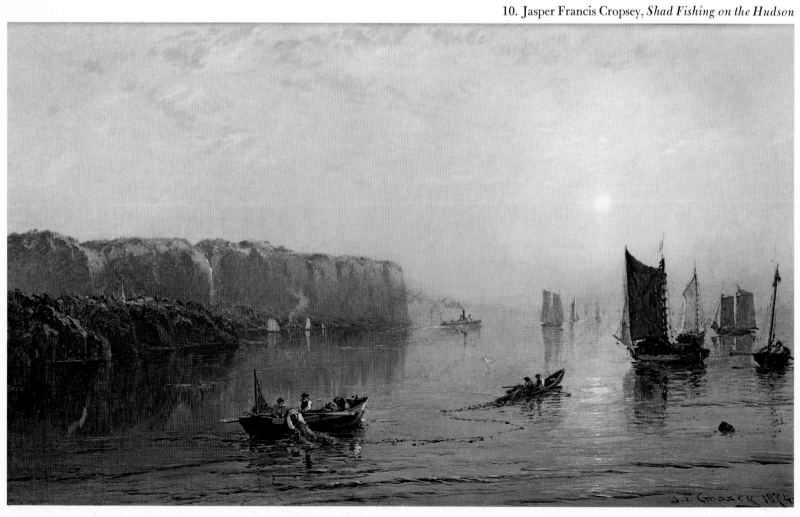

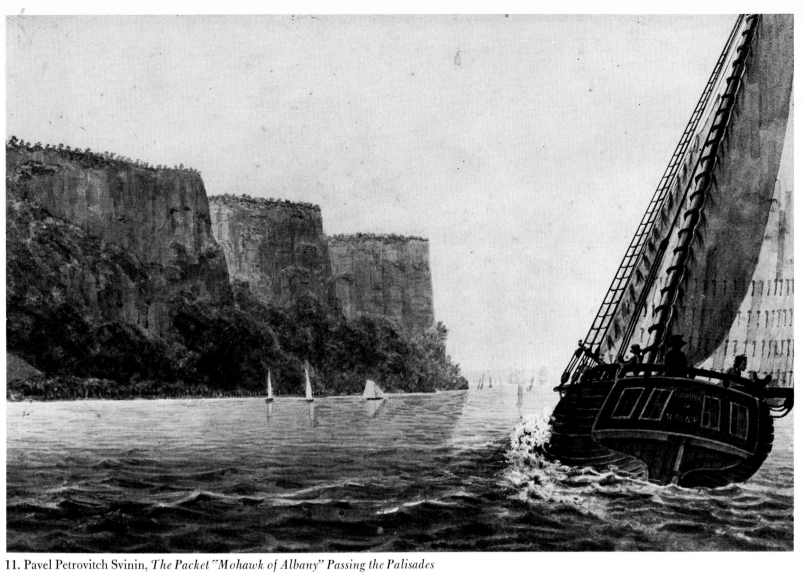

11. Pavel Petrovitch Svinin, *The Packet "Mohawk of Albany" Passing the Palisades*

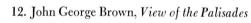

12. John George Brown, *View of the Palisades*

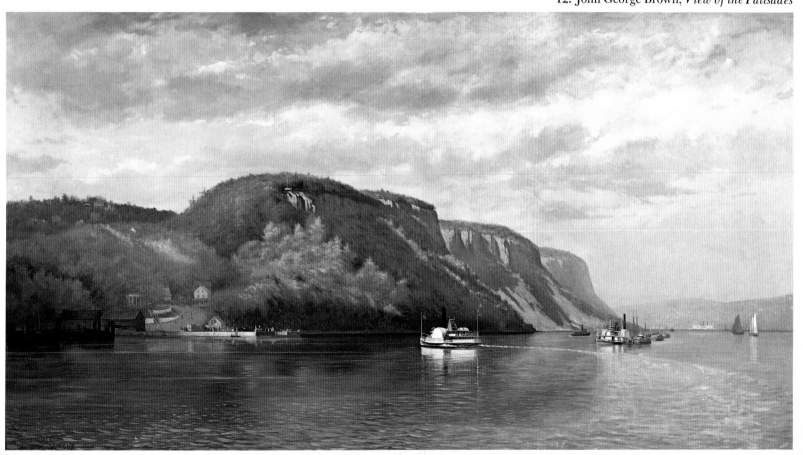

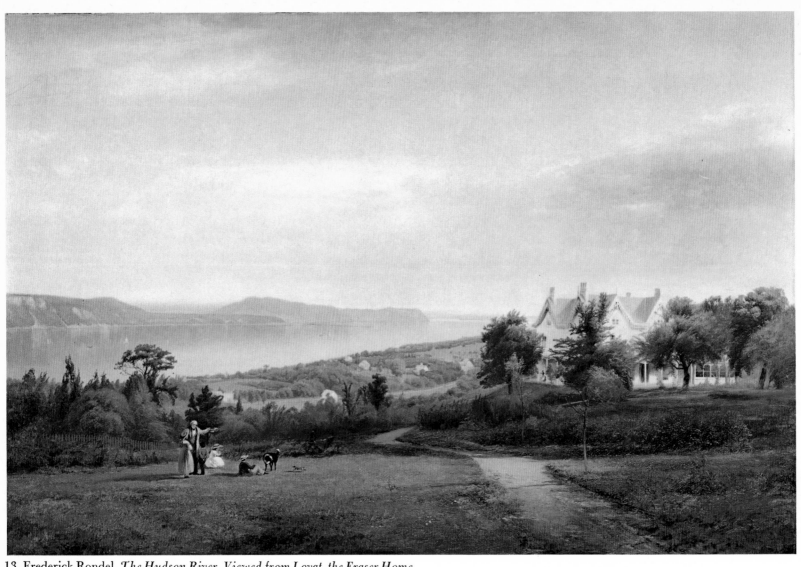

13. Frederick Rondel, *The Hudson River, Viewed from Lovat, the Fraser Home*

14. Anonymous nineteenth-century American artist, *Mill, Philipse Manor and Church, Tarrytown*

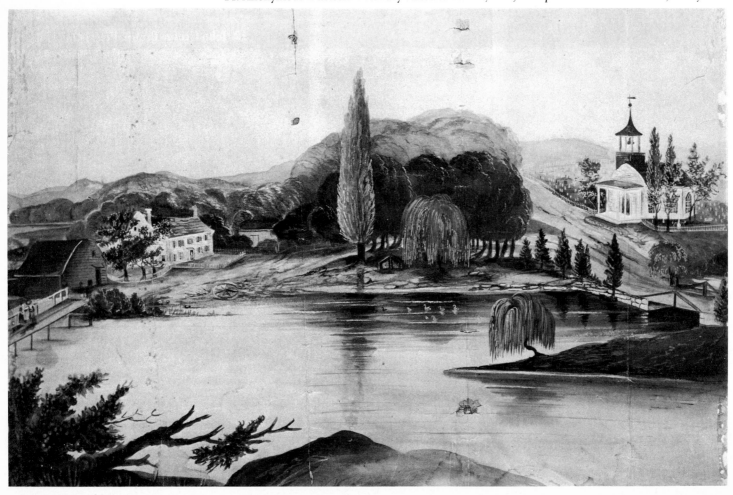

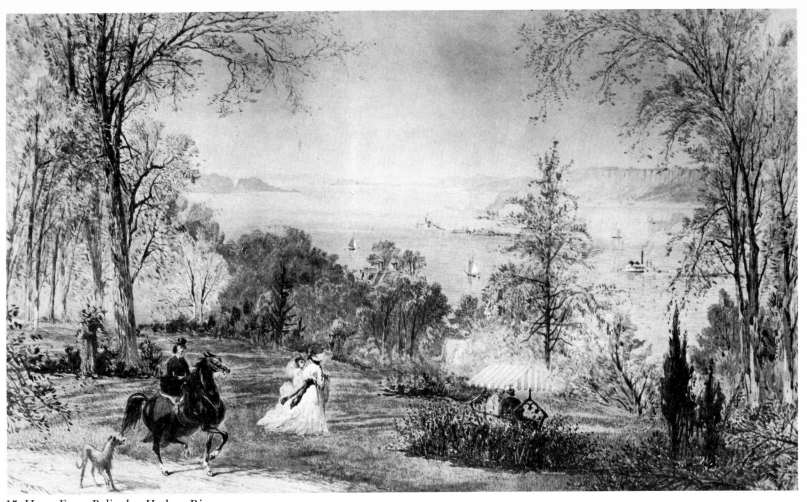

15. Harry Fenn, *Palisades, Hudson River*

16. Francis A. Silva, *The Hudson at Tappan Zee*

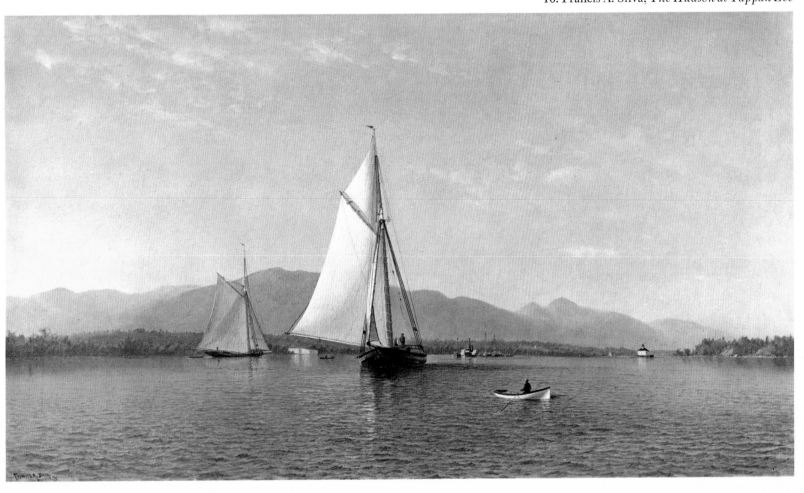

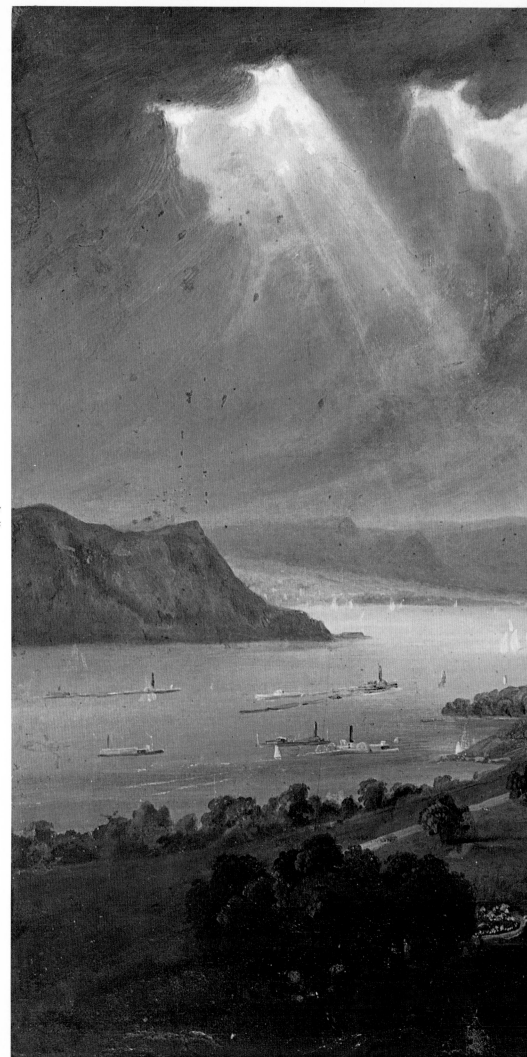

17. Robert Havell, Jr., *View of the Hudson from Tarrytown Heights*

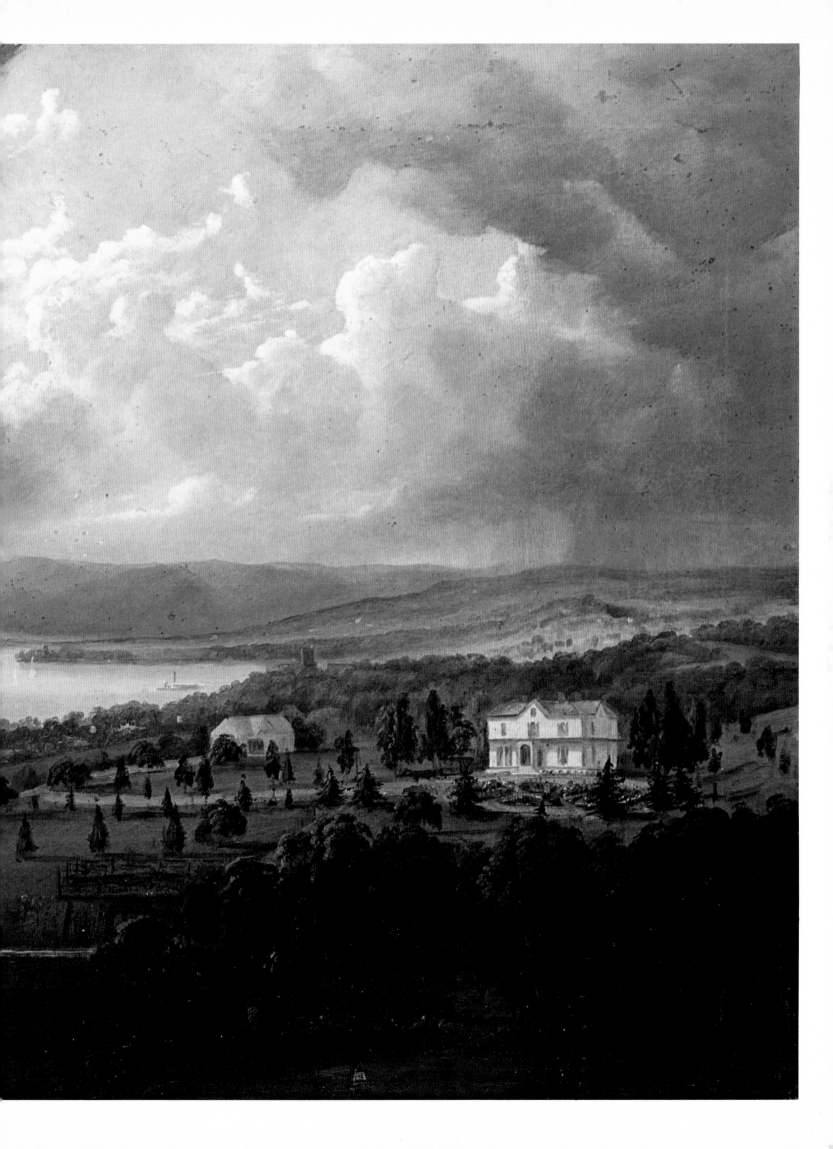

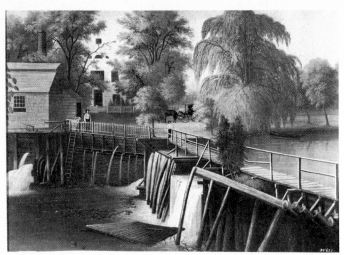

18. Anonymous nineteenth-century American artist, *Old Mill of Sleepy Hollow*

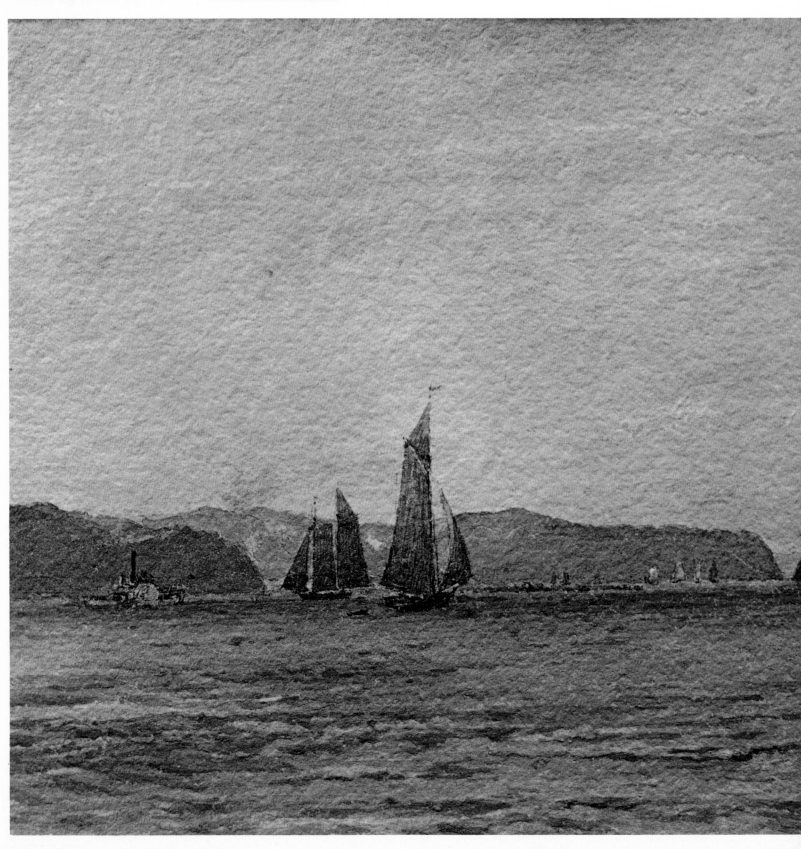

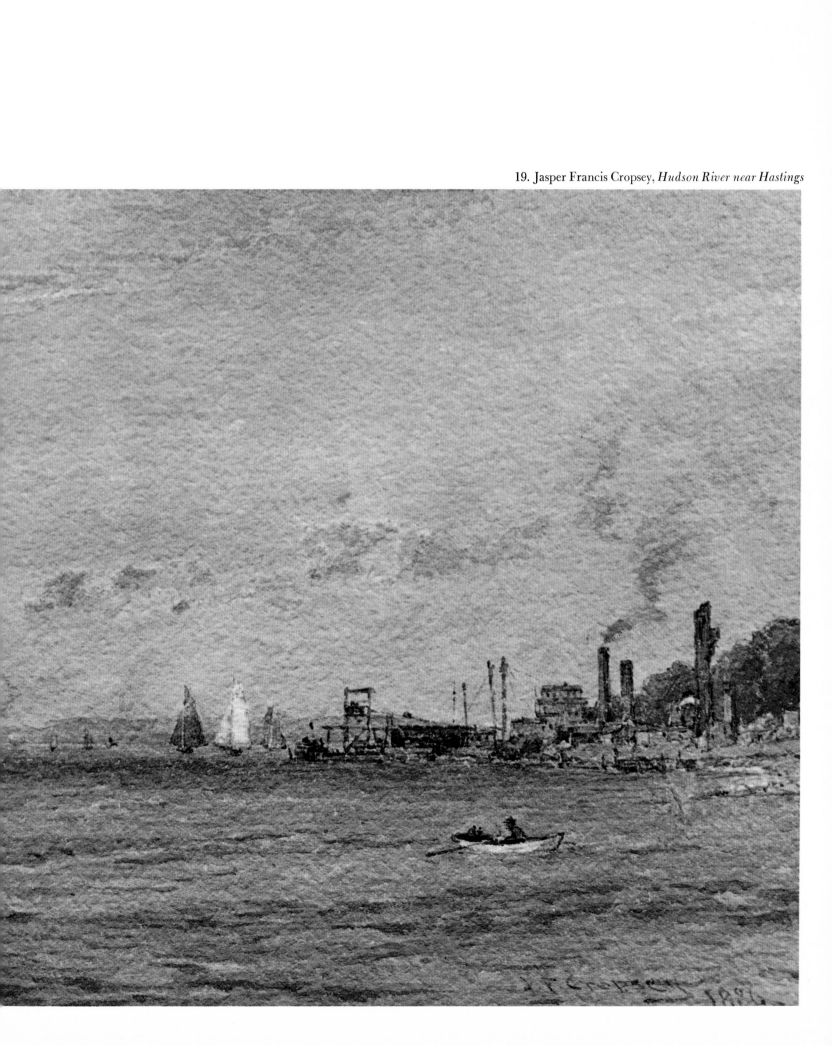

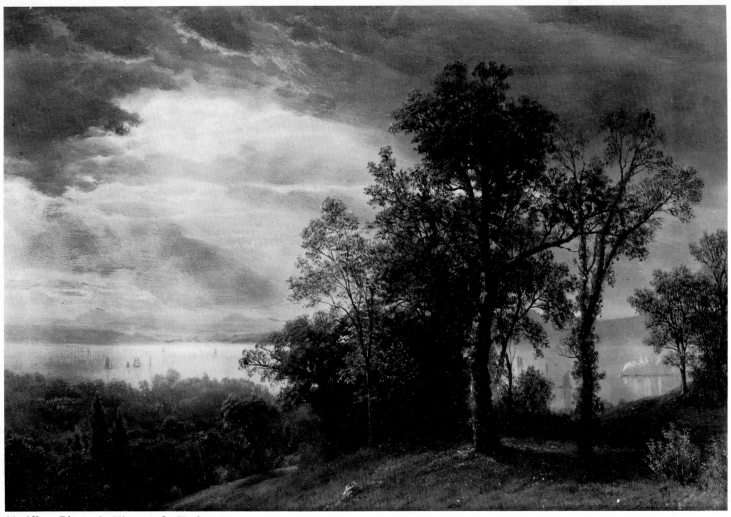

20. Albert Bierstadt, *View on the Hudson*

21. Robert Havell, Jr., *Key to the View of Haverstraw Bay from Sing Sing*

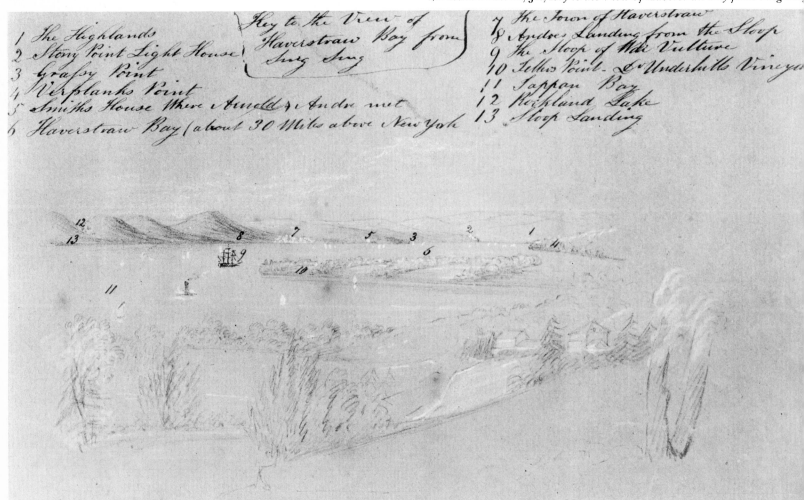

1 The Highlands
2 Stony Point Light House
3 Grassy Point
4 Verplanks Point
5 Smiths House where Arnold & Andre met
6 Haverstraw Bay (about 30 Miles above New York

Key to the View of
Haverstraw Bay from
Sing Sing

7 The Town of Haverstraw
8 Andres Landing from the Sloop
9 The Sloop of War Vulture
10 Tellow Point - & Underhills Vineyard
11 Tappan Bay
12 Rockland Lake
13 Sloop Landing

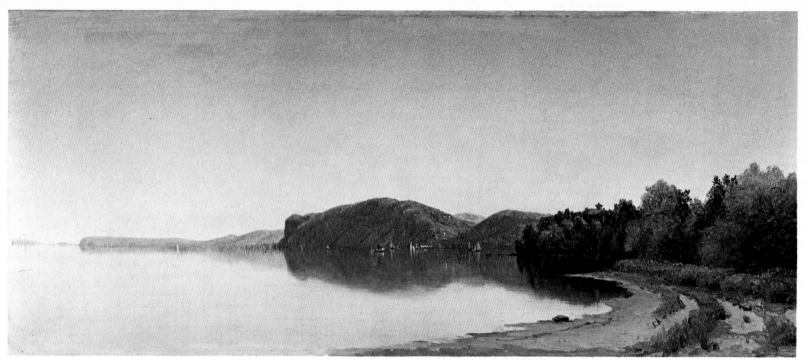

22. Sanford Robinson Gifford, *Hook Mountain, near Nyack, on the Hudson*

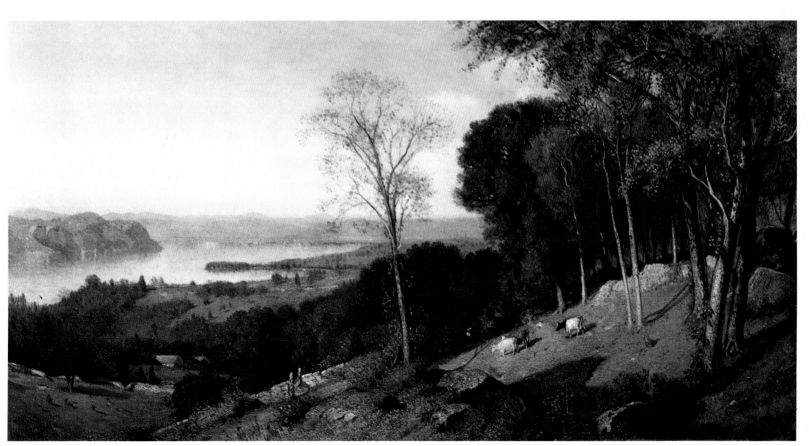

23. Samuel Colman, *Looking North from Ossining, New York*

24. Pavel Petrovitch Svinin, *Shad Fishermen on the Shore of the Hudson River*

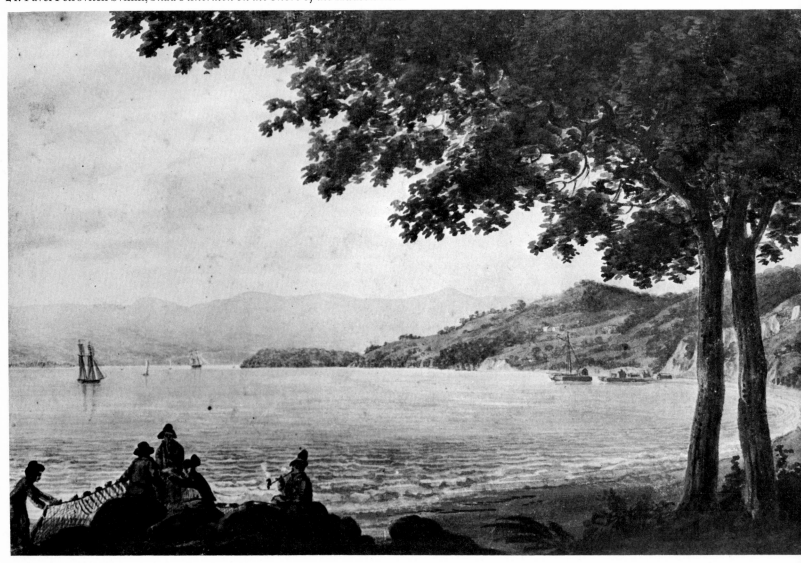

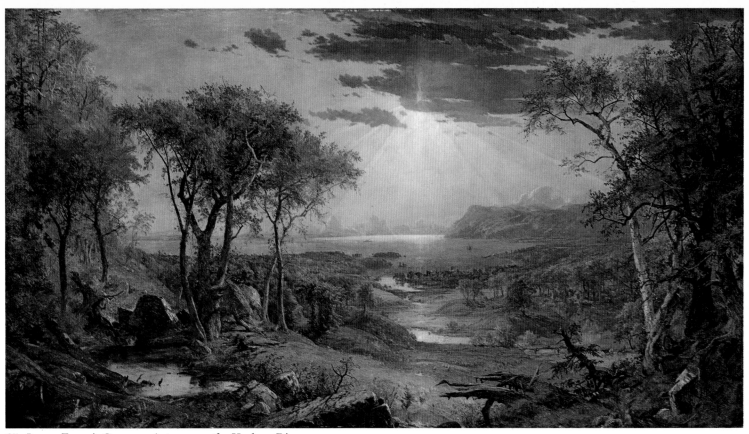

25. Jasper Francis Cropsey, *Autumn on the Hudson River*

26. Asher Brown Durand, *River Scene*

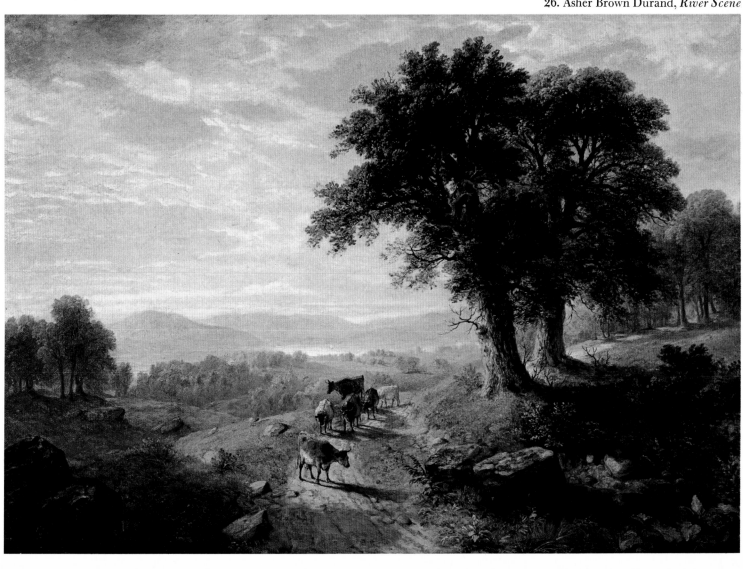

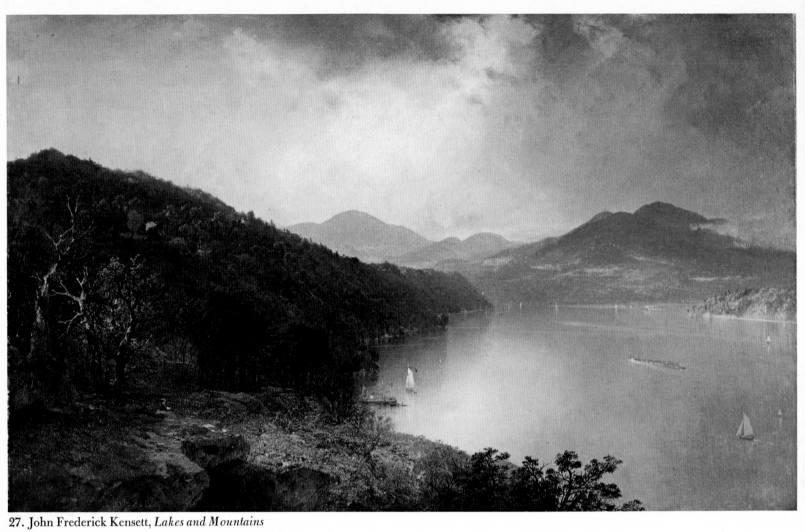

27. John Frederick Kensett, *Lakes and Mountains*

28. William Guy Wall, *View near Fort Montgomery*

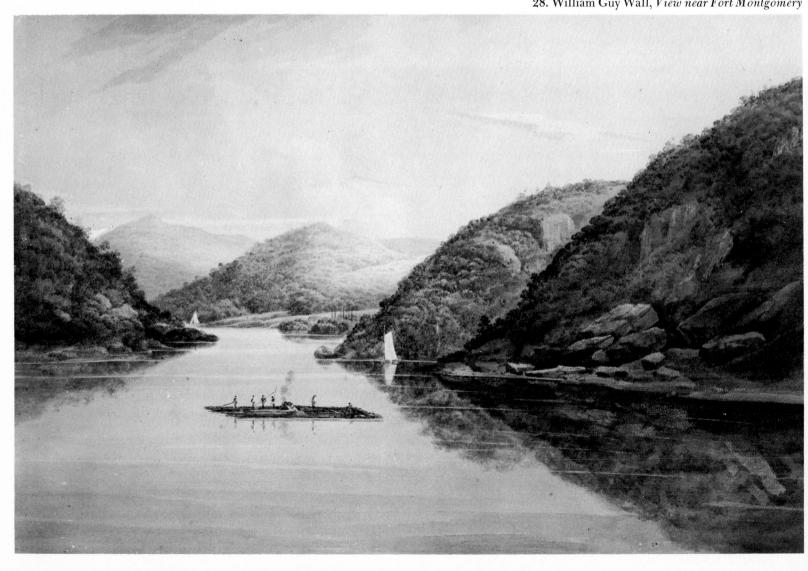

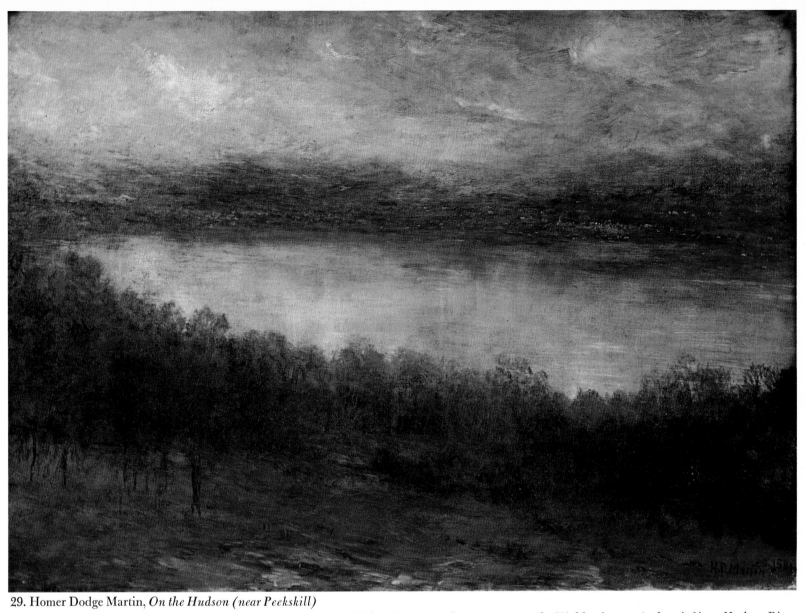

29. Homer Dodge Martin, *On the Hudson (near Peekskill)*

30. William Henry Bartlett, *Entrance to the Highlands near Anthony's Nose, Hudson River*

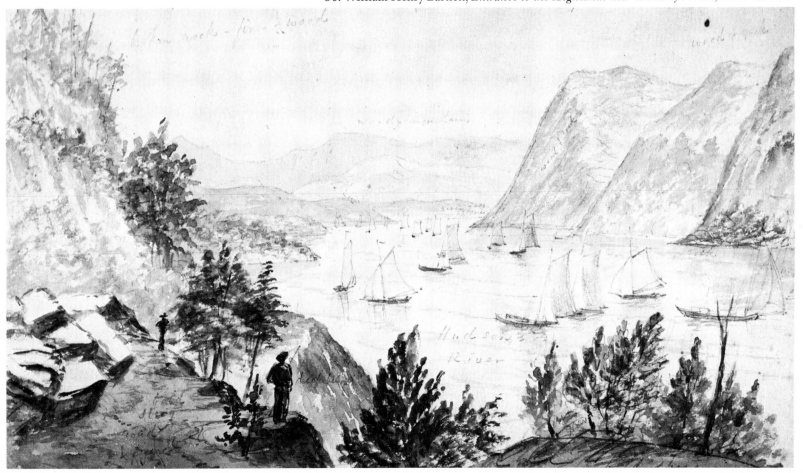

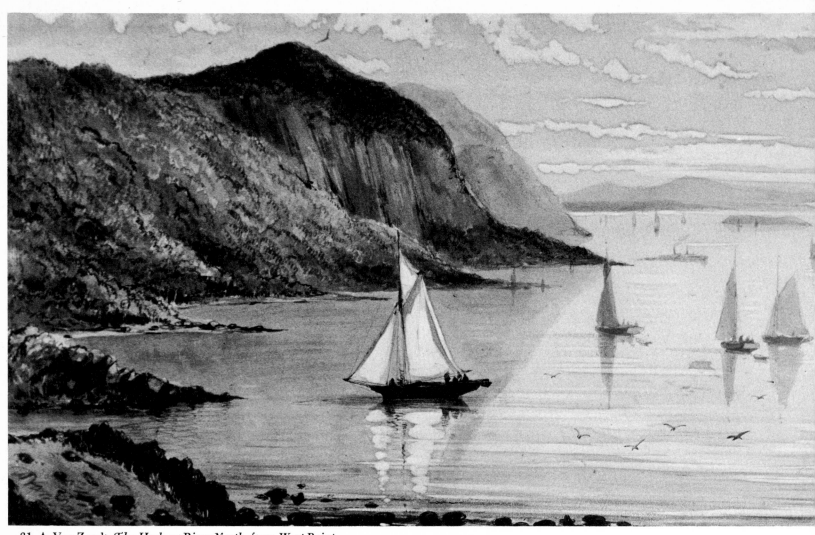

31. A. Van Zandt, *The Hudson River North, from West Point*

32. John Frederick Kensett, *View near Cozzens Hotel from West Point*

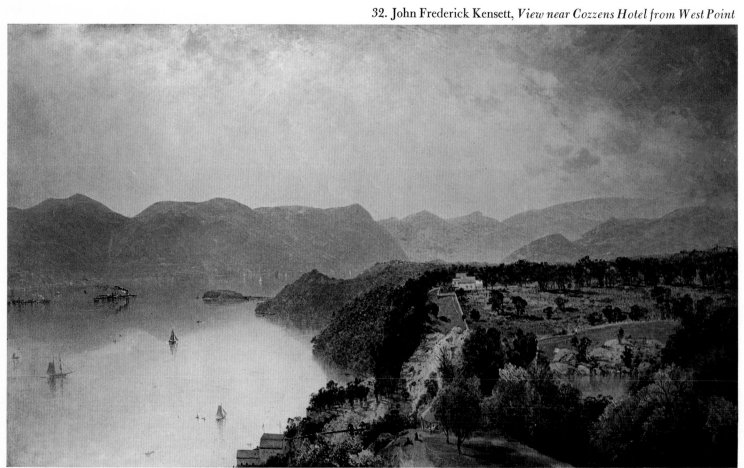

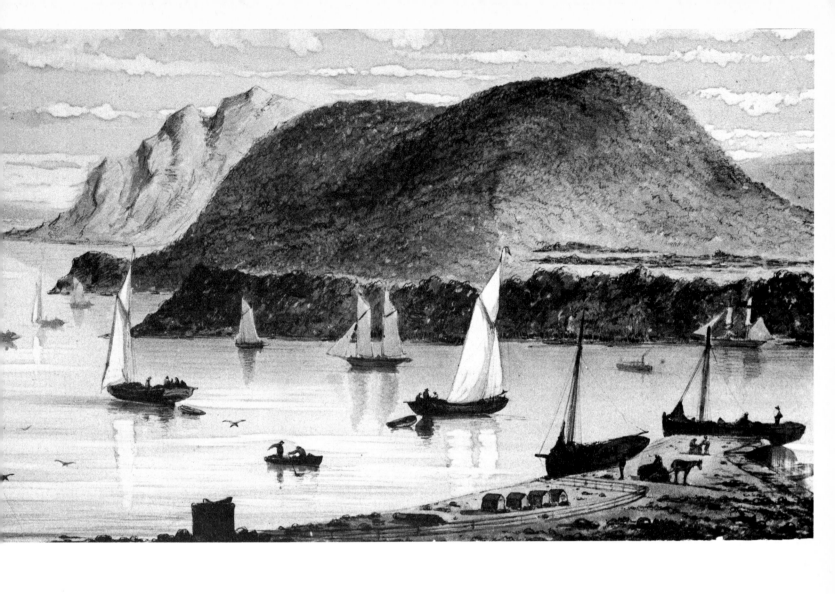

33. David Johnson, *West Point from Fort Putnam*

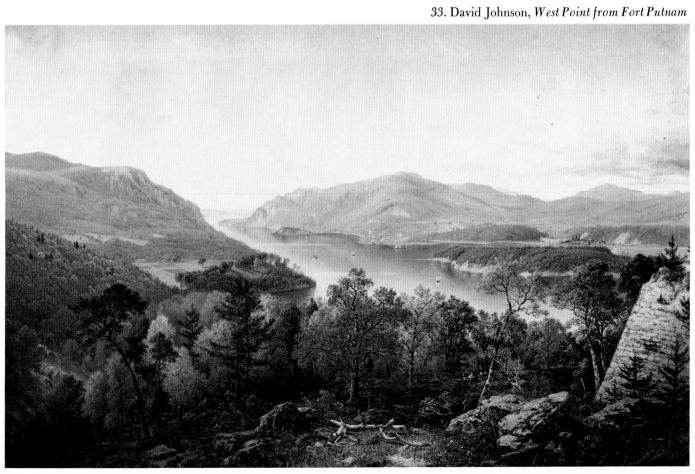

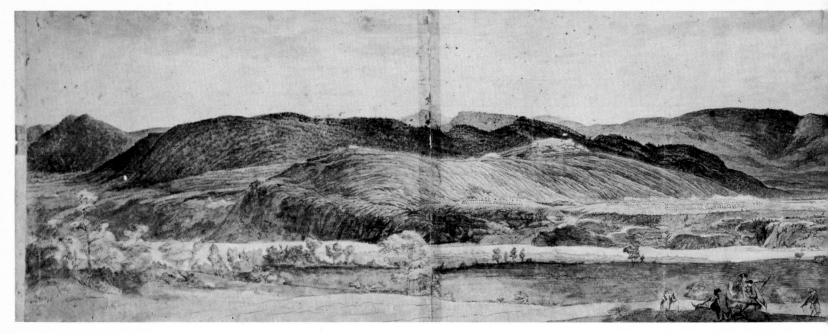

34. Pierre Charles L'Enfant, *West Point*

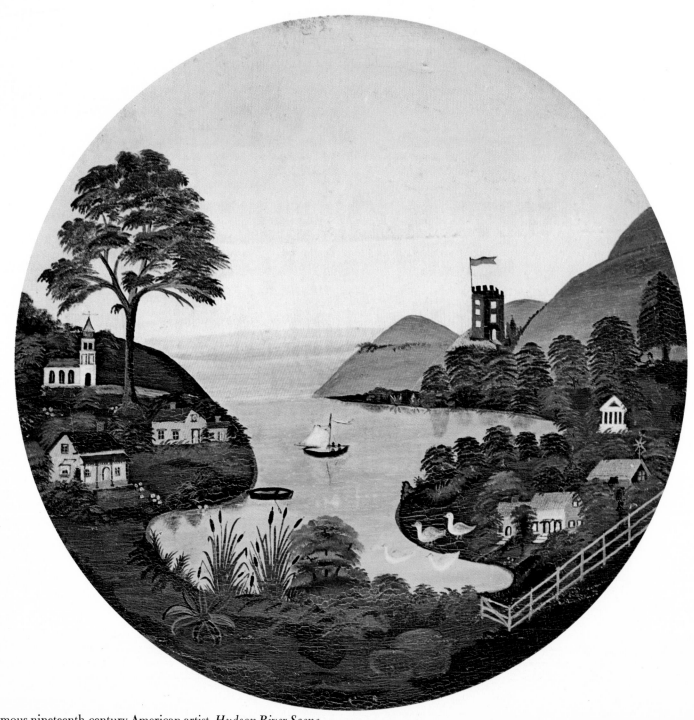

35. Anonymous nineteenth-century American artist, *Hudson River Scene*

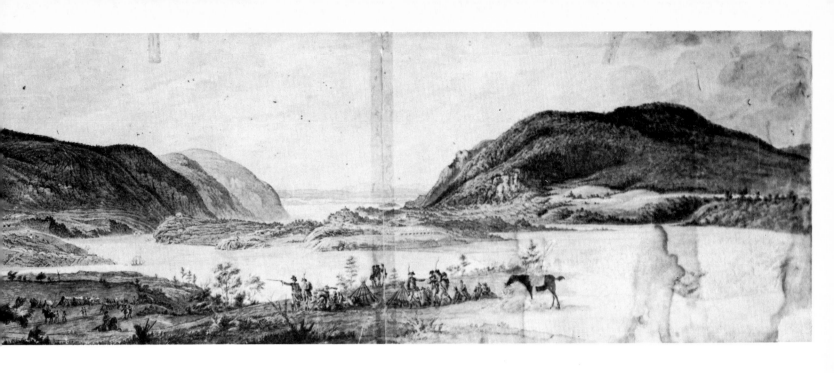

36. Thomas Chambers, *View from West Point*

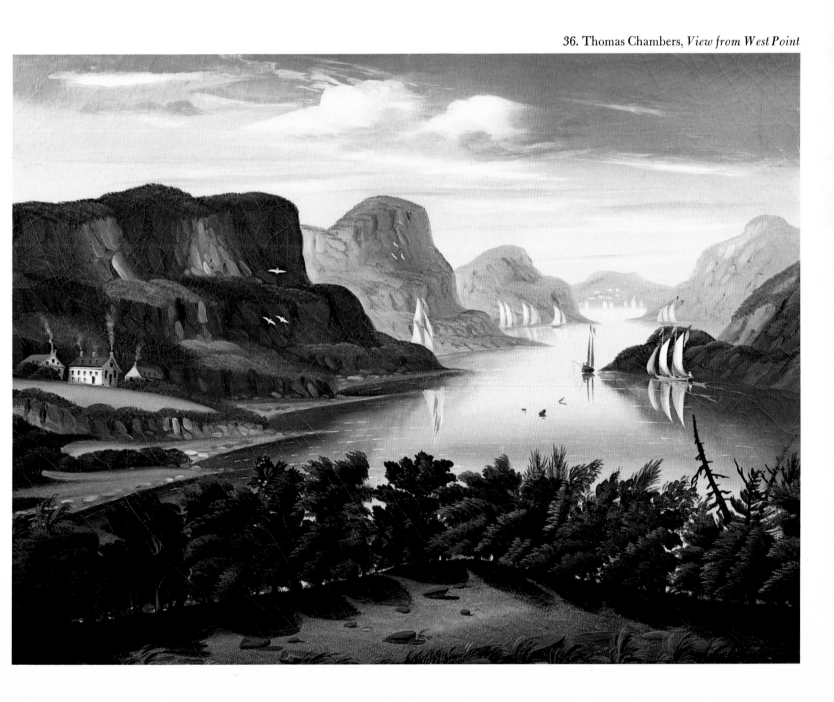

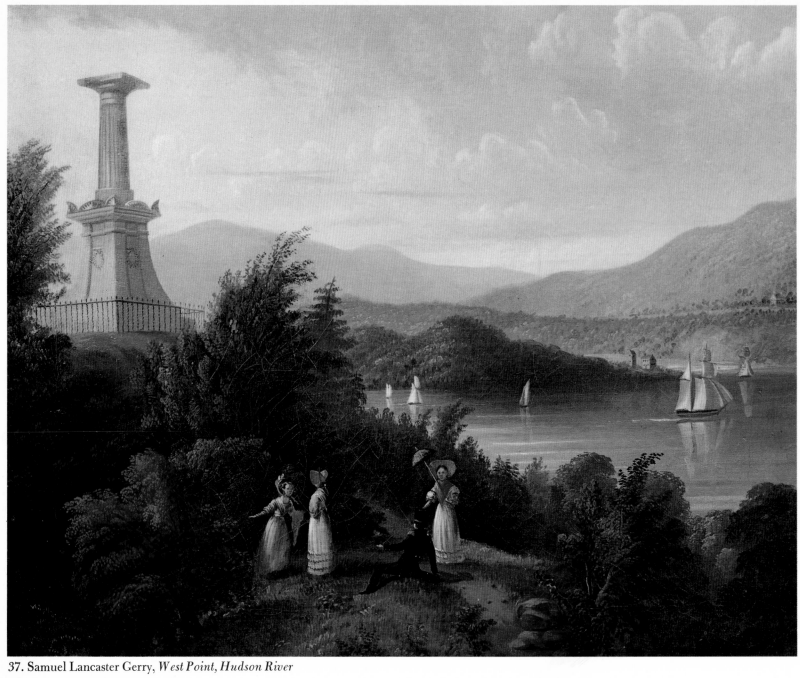

37. Samuel Lancaster Gerry, *West Point, Hudson River*

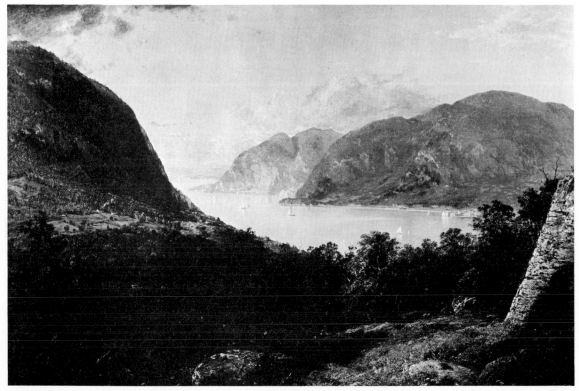

38. John Frederick Kensett, *View of Storm King from Fort Putnam*

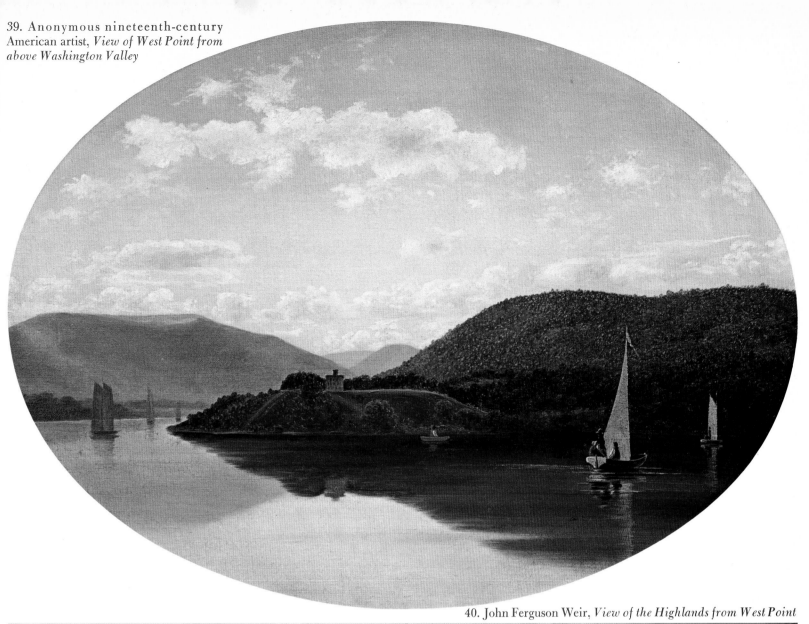

39. Anonymous nineteenth-century American artist, *View of West Point from above Washington Valley*

40. John Ferguson Weir, *View of the Highlands from West Point*

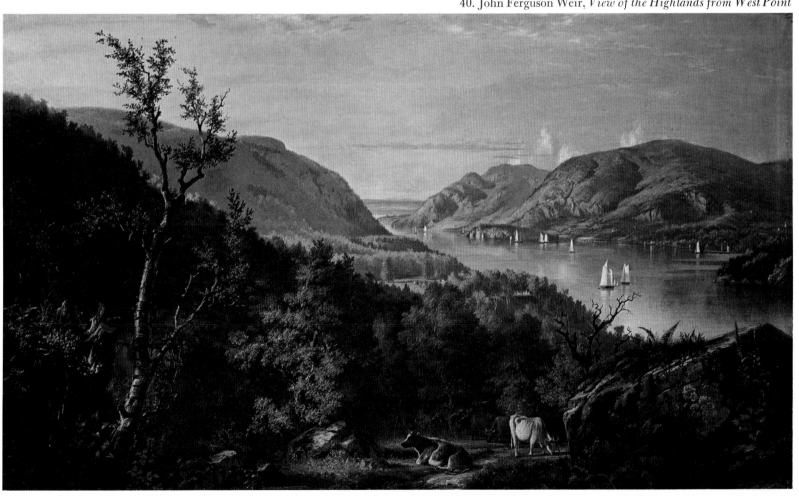

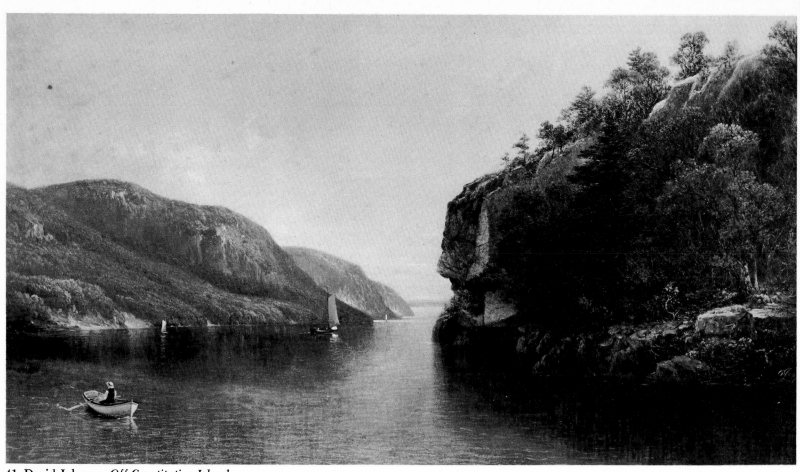

41. David Johnson, *Off Constitution Island*

42. David Johnson, *Foundry at Cold Spring*

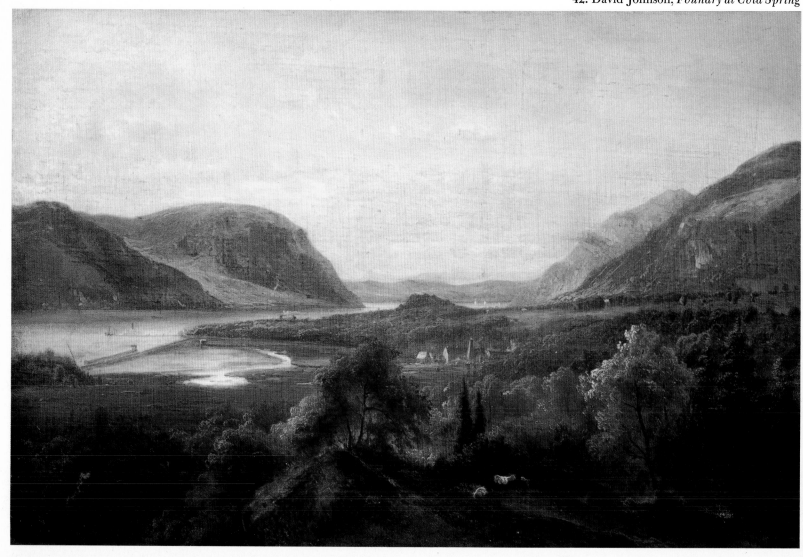

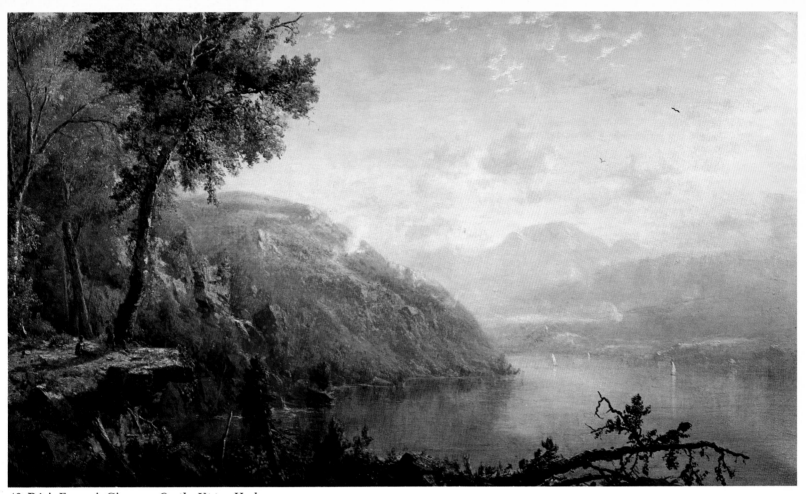

43. Régis François Gignoux, *On the Upper Hudson*

44. Anonymous nineteenth-century American artist, Untitled (*Storm King*)

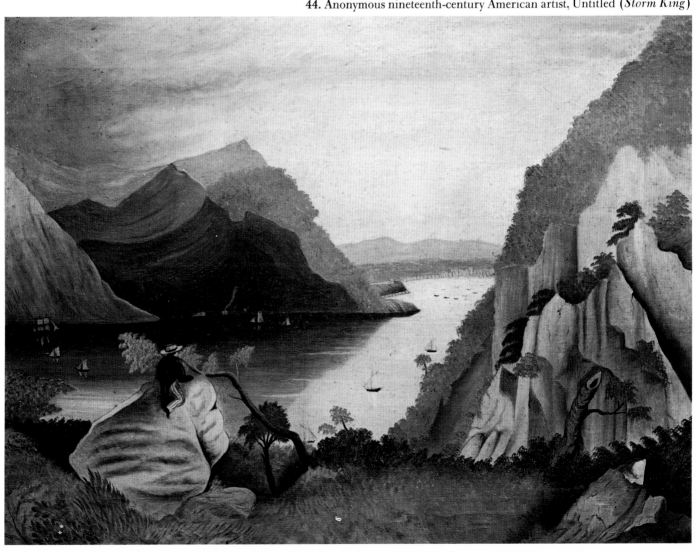

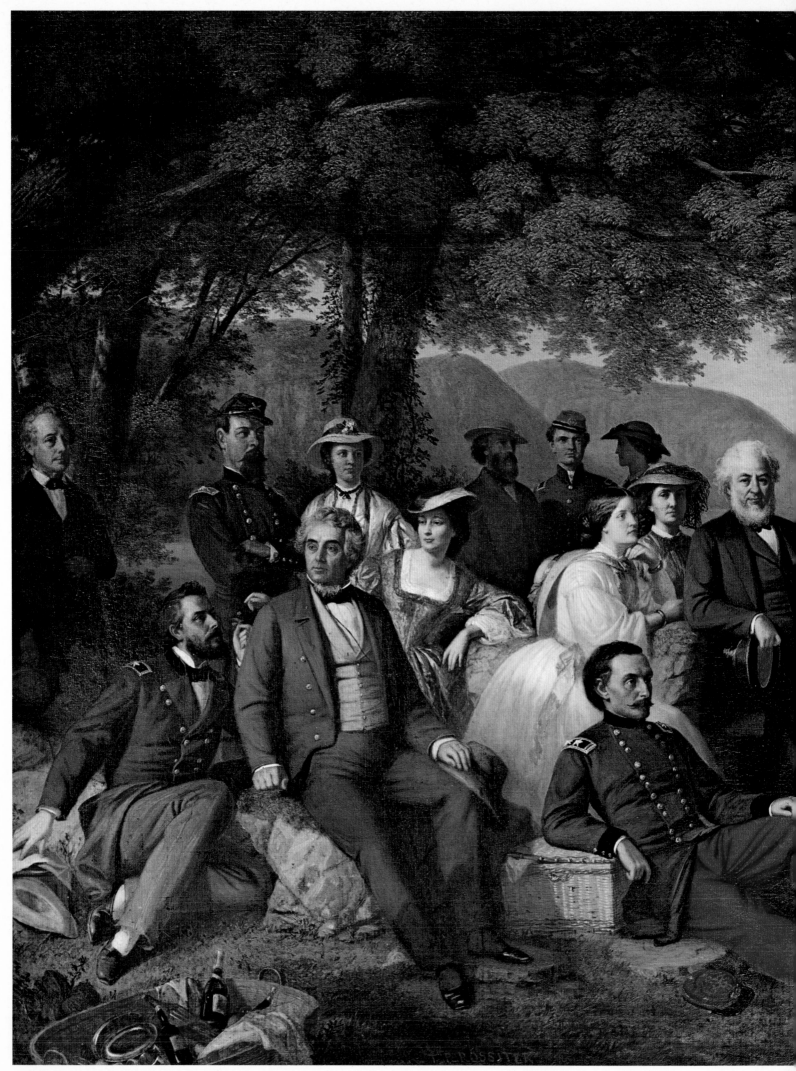

45. Thomas Prichard Rossiter, *A Pic-Nic on the Hudson*

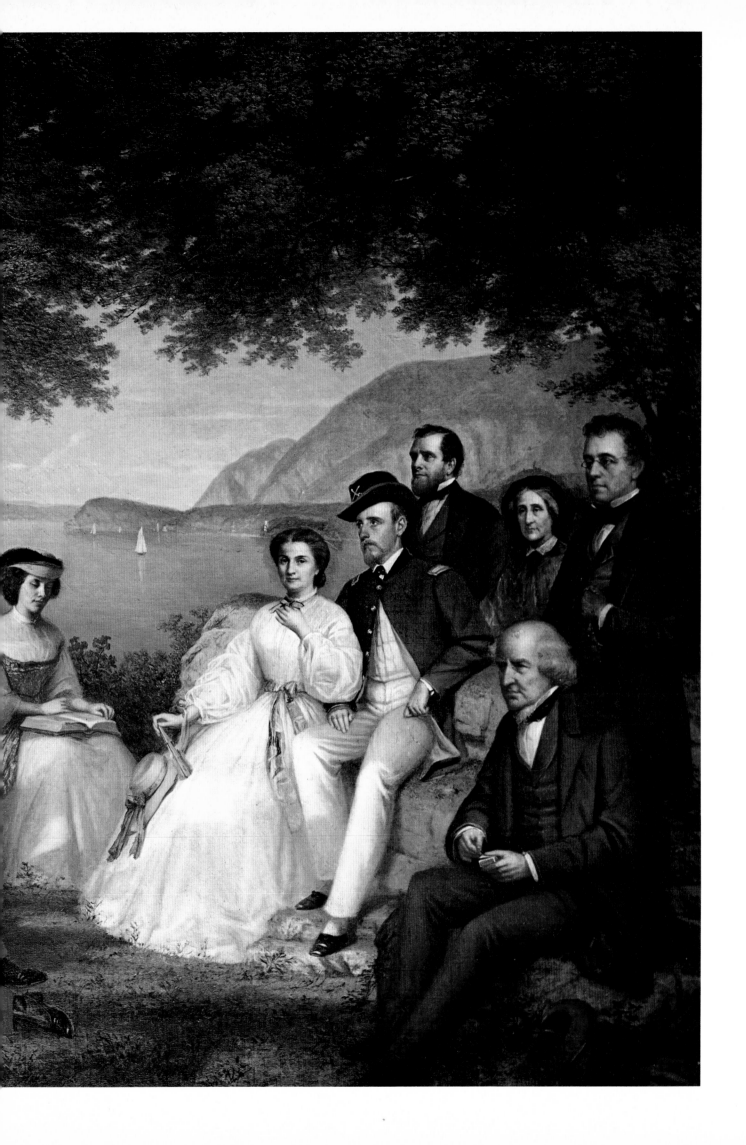

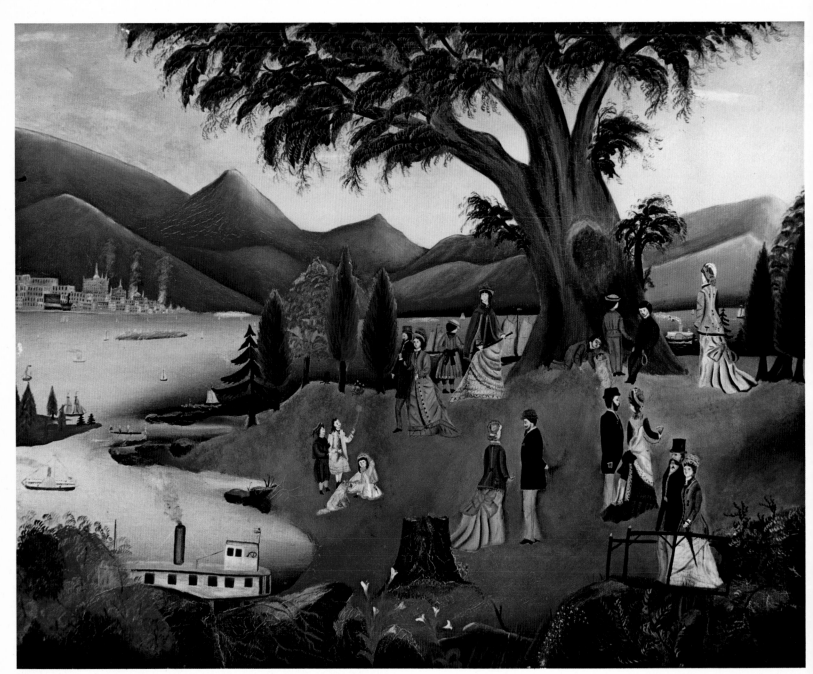

46. Anonymous nineteenth-century American artist, *Outing on the Hudson*

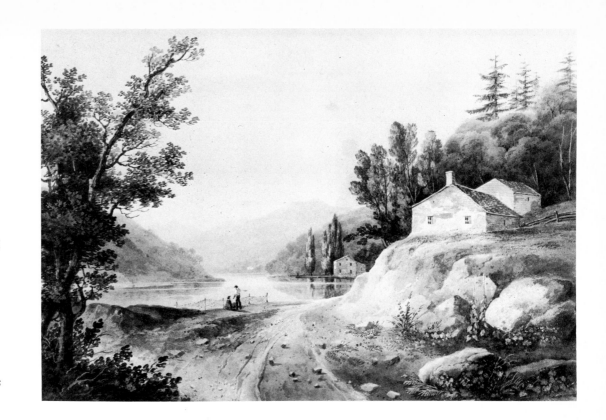

47. William Guy Wall, *View near Fishkill*

48. Thomas Doughty, *View of Highlands from Newburgh, New York*

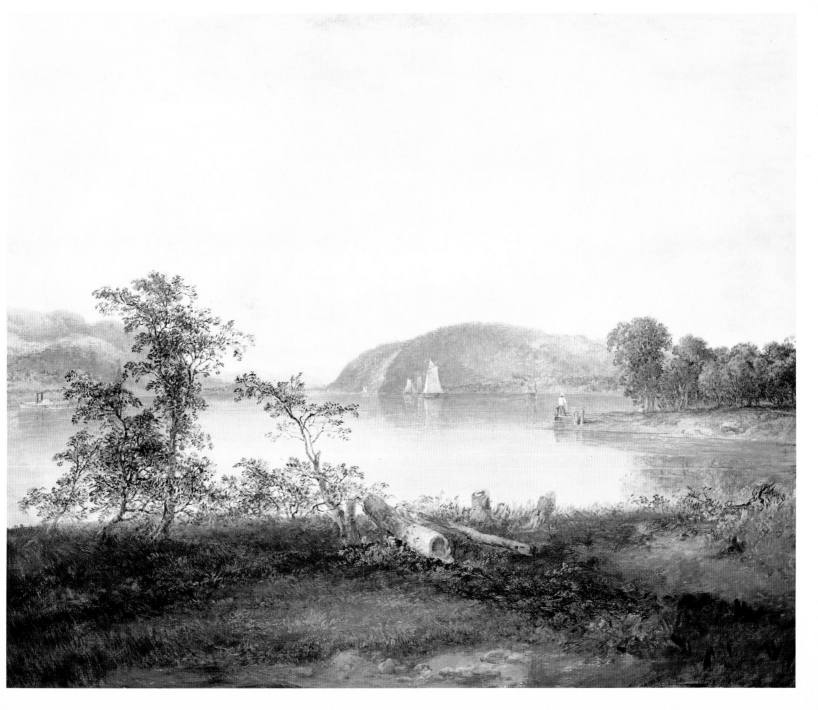

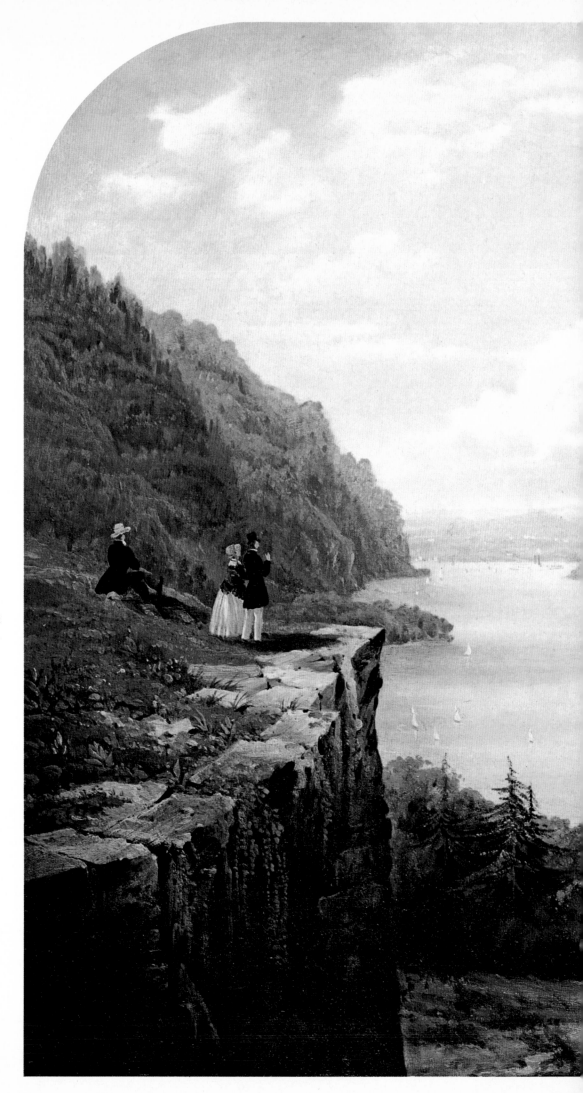

49. Robert Havell, Jr., *West Point from Fort Putnam*

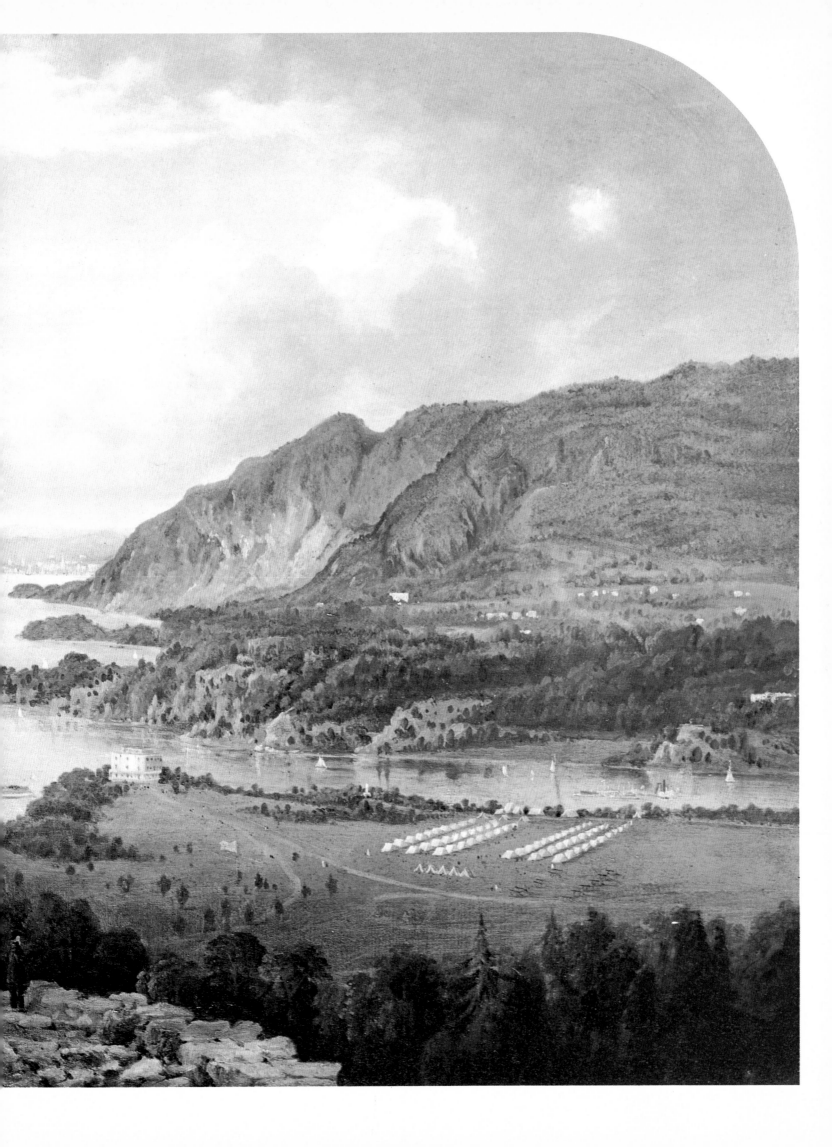

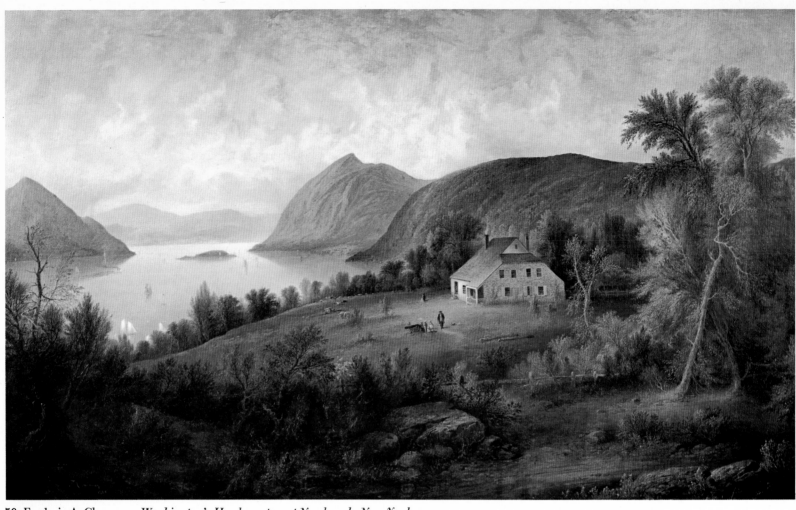

50. Frederic A. Chapman, *Washington's Headquarters at Newburgh, New York*

51. Edmund C. Coates, *Washington's Headquarters at Newburgh*

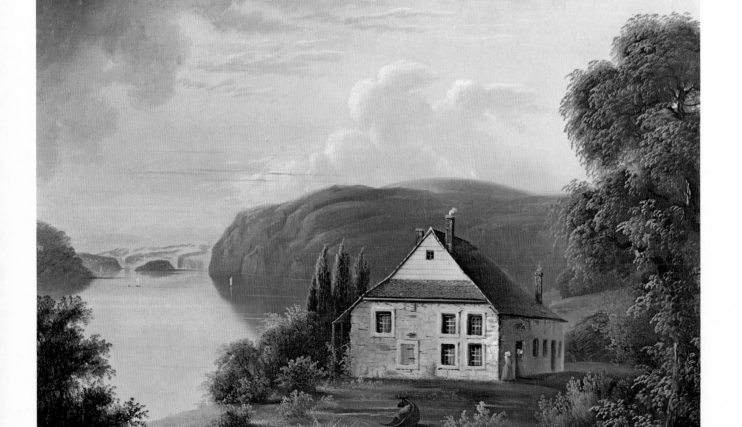

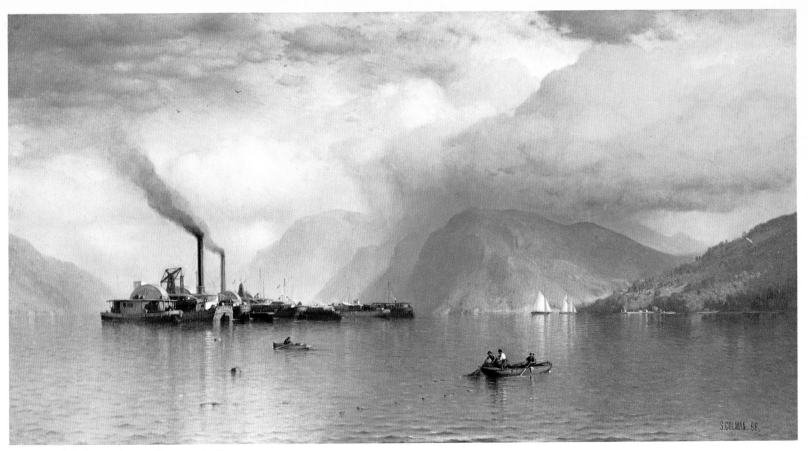

52. Samuel Colman, *Storm King on the Hudson*

53. Anonymous (after William Guy Wall), *View of Highlands Looking South from Newburgh Bay*

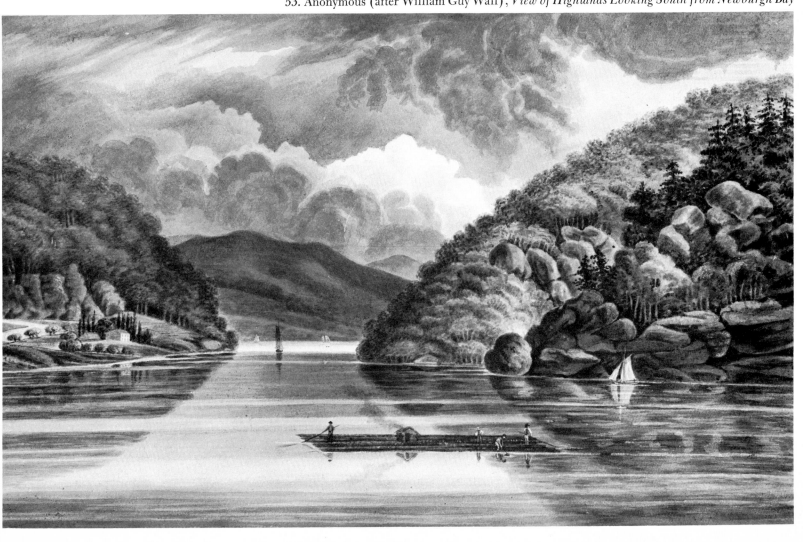

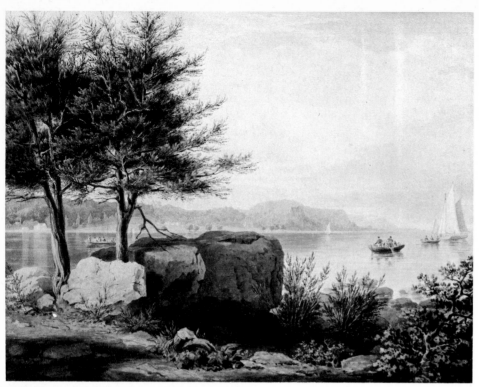

54. William Guy Wall, *View on the Hudson River*

55. Clinton W. Clapp, *Marlborough from New Hamburg*

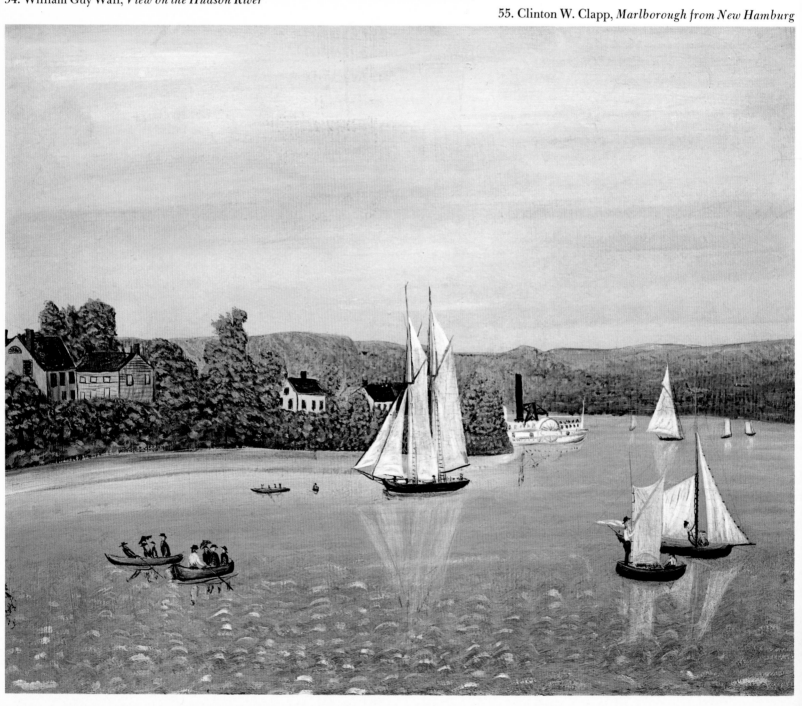

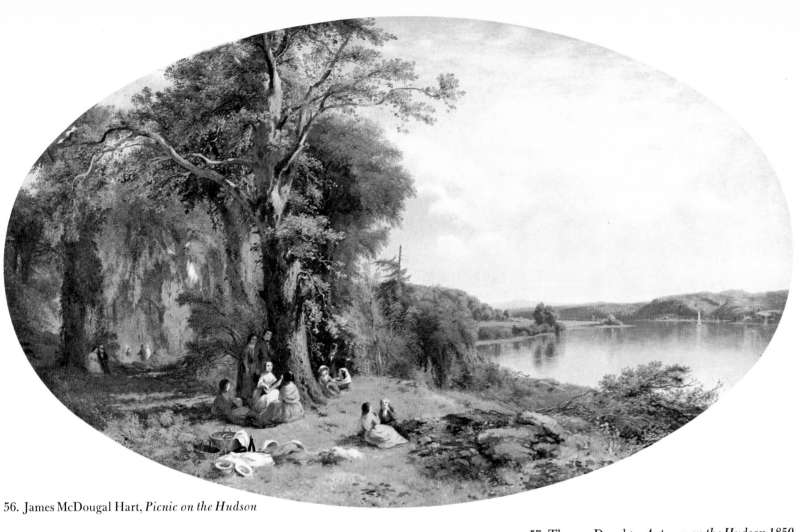

56. James McDougal Hart, *Picnic on the Hudson*

57. Thomas Doughty, *Autumn on the Hudson 1850*

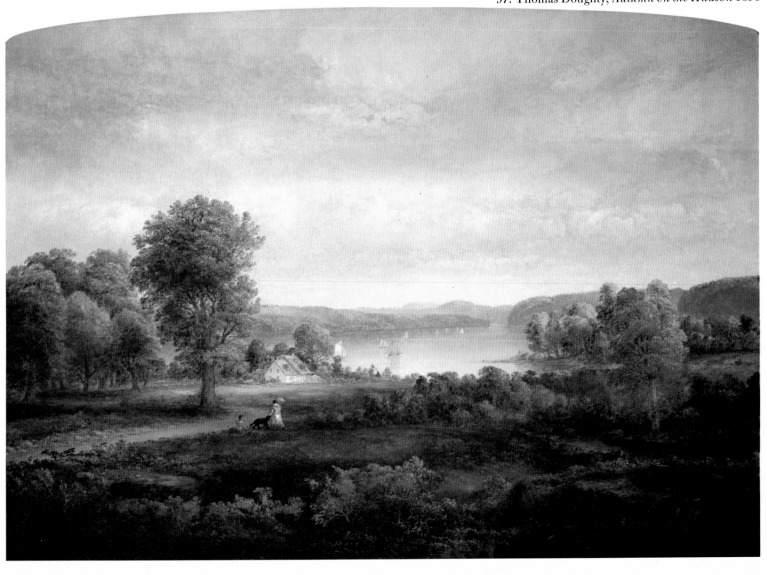

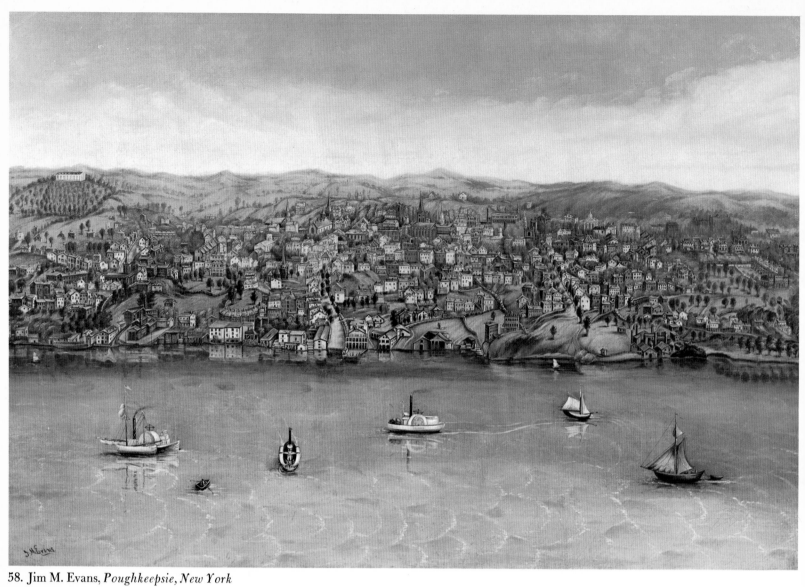

58. Jim M. Evans, *Poughkeepsie, New York*

59. Jasper Francis Cropsey, *Upper Hudson*

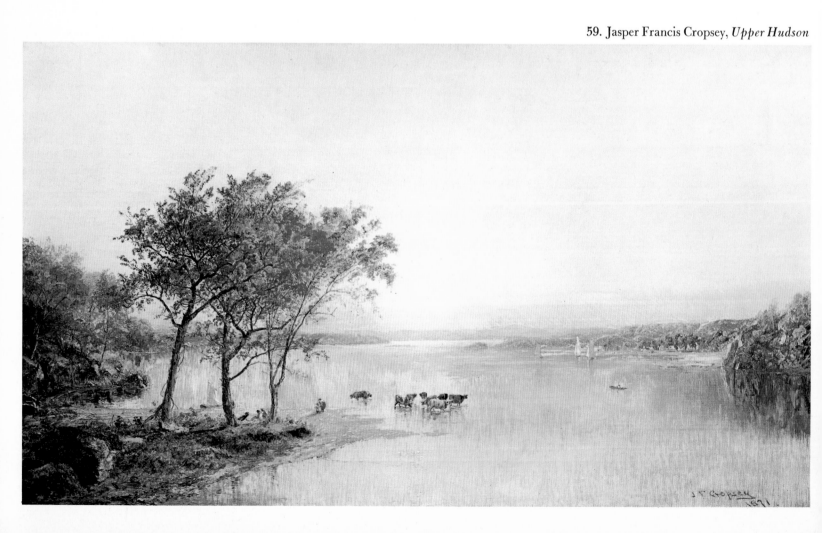

60. William Stanley Haseltine, *Near Hyde Park, Hudson River*

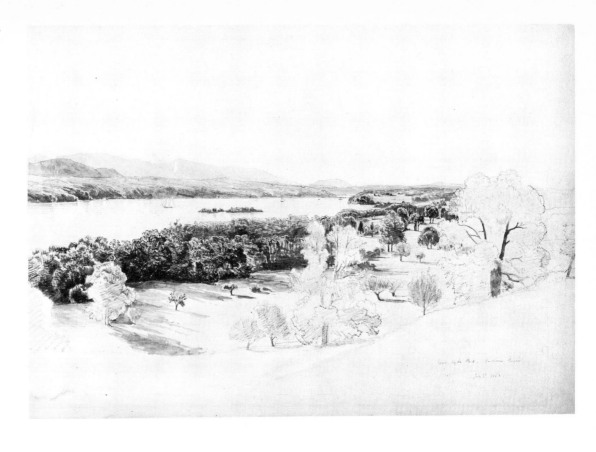

61. Johann Hermann Carmiencke, *Hyde Park, New York*

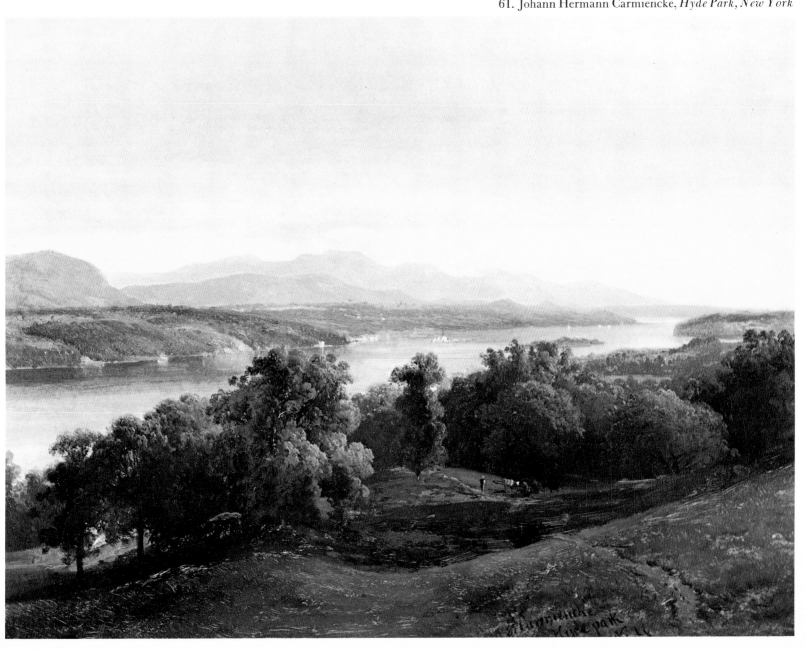

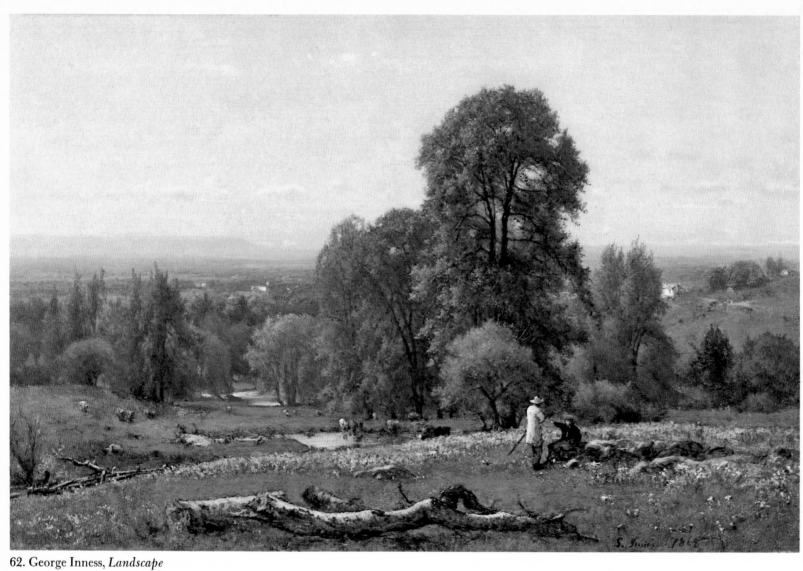

62. George Inness, *Landscape*

63. George Inness, *Landscape, Hudson Valley*

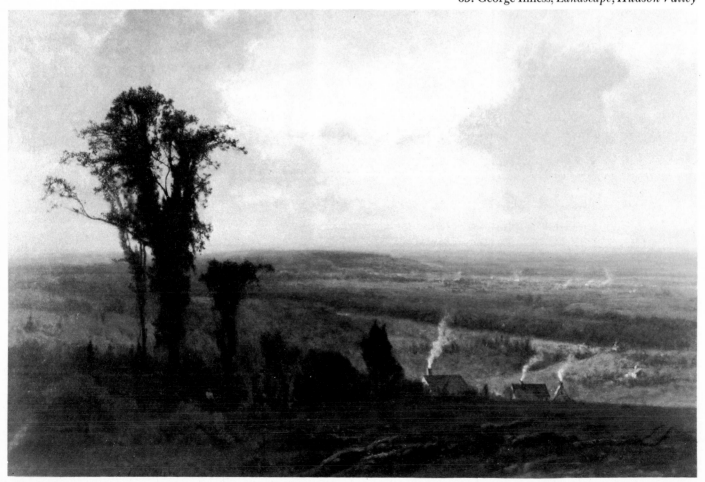

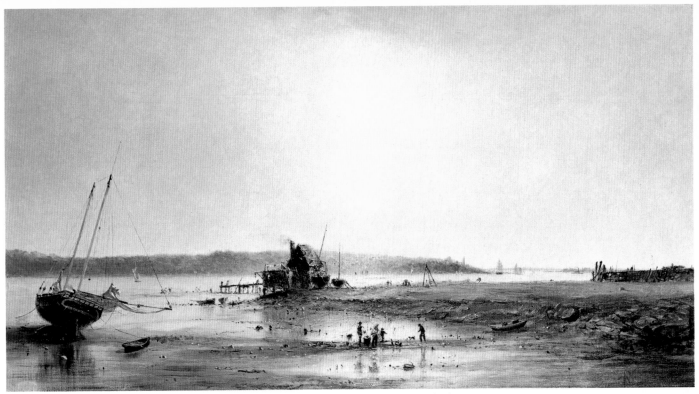

64. Andrew W. Warren, *Red Hook Point on the Hudson, opposite Kingston, New York*

65. Asher Brown Durand, *Hudson River Looking towards the Catskills*

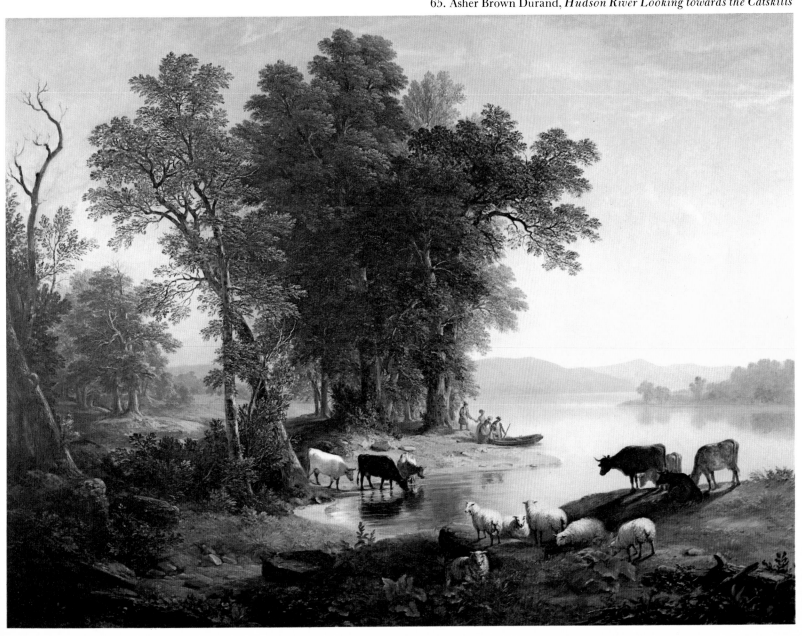

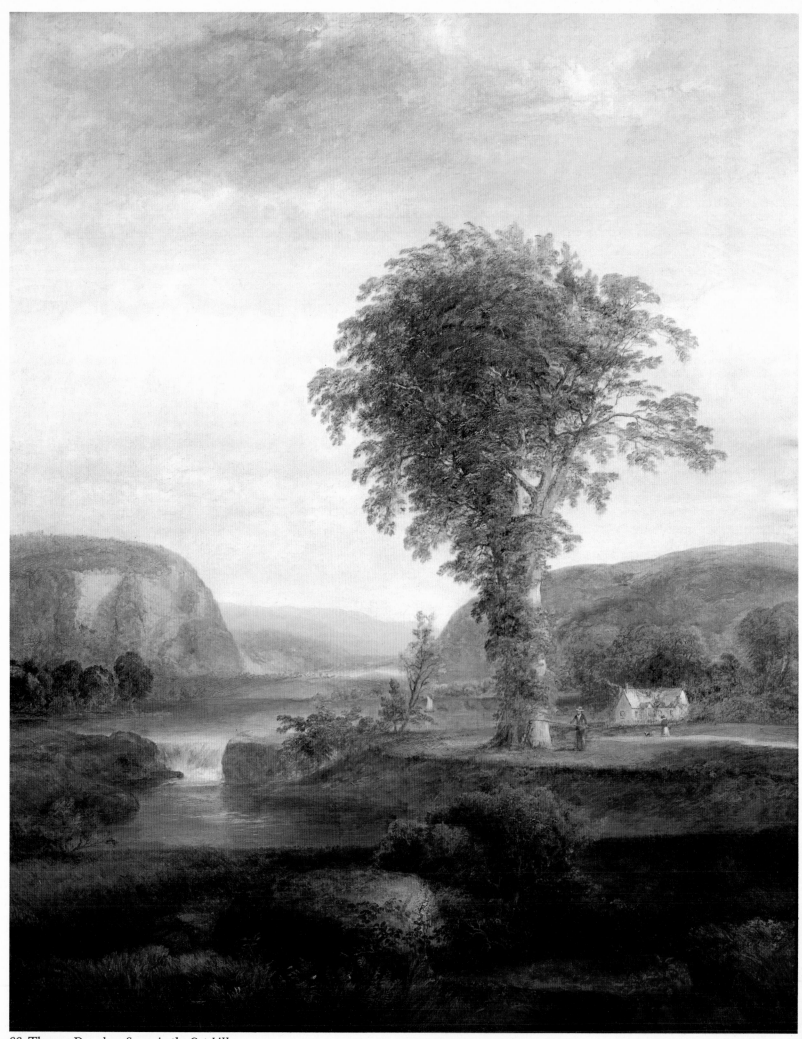

66. Thomas Doughty, *Scene in the Catskills*

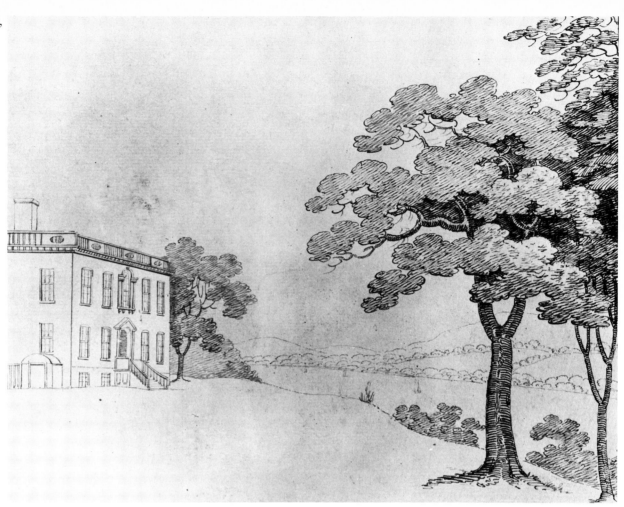

7. Archibald Robertson, *Clermont, the Seat of Mrs. Livingston*

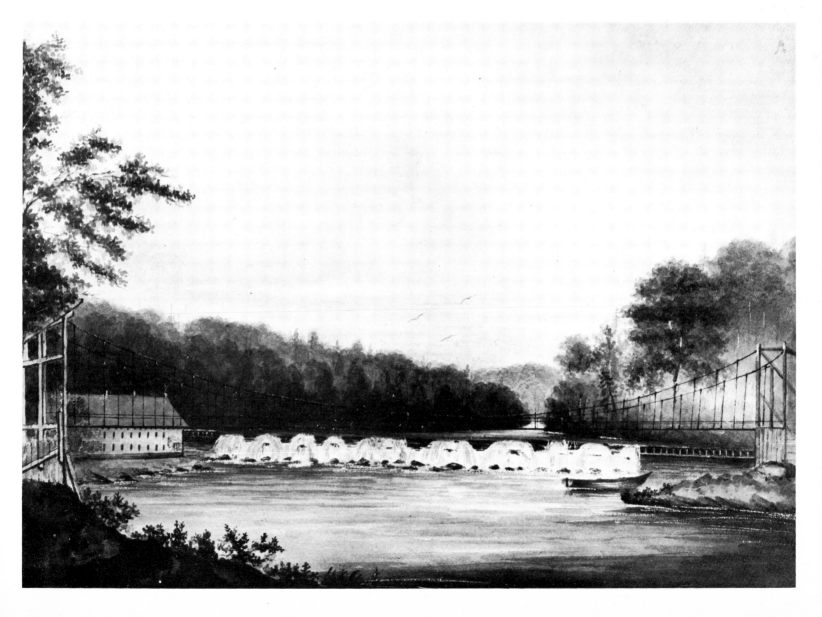

8. William Guy Wall, *Esopus Creek, Saugerties, New York*

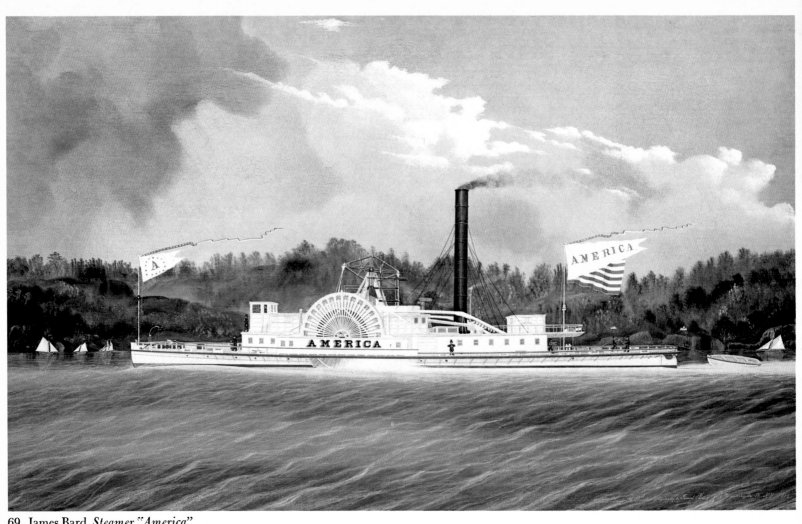

69. James Bard, *Steamer "America"*

70. Jasper Francis Cropsey, *View of Catskills across Hudson*

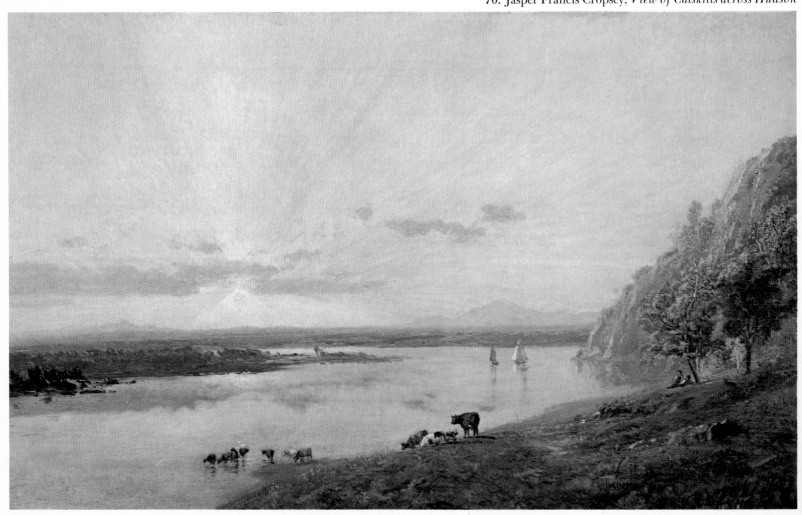

71. Thomas Cole, *Catskill Mountain House*

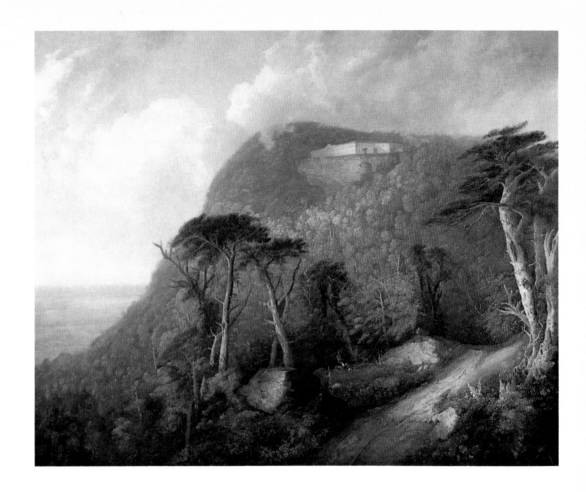

72. Anonymous (after William Henry Bartlett), *Catskill Mountain House*

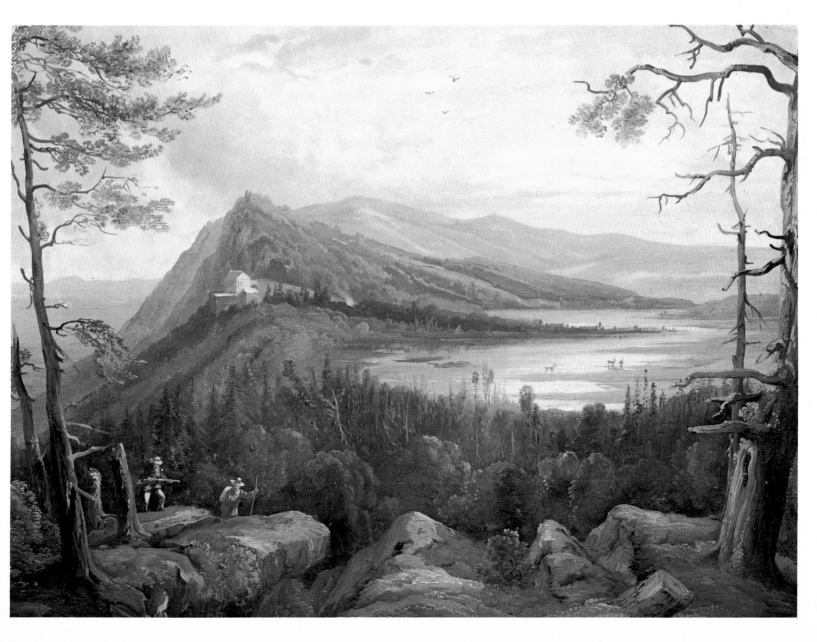

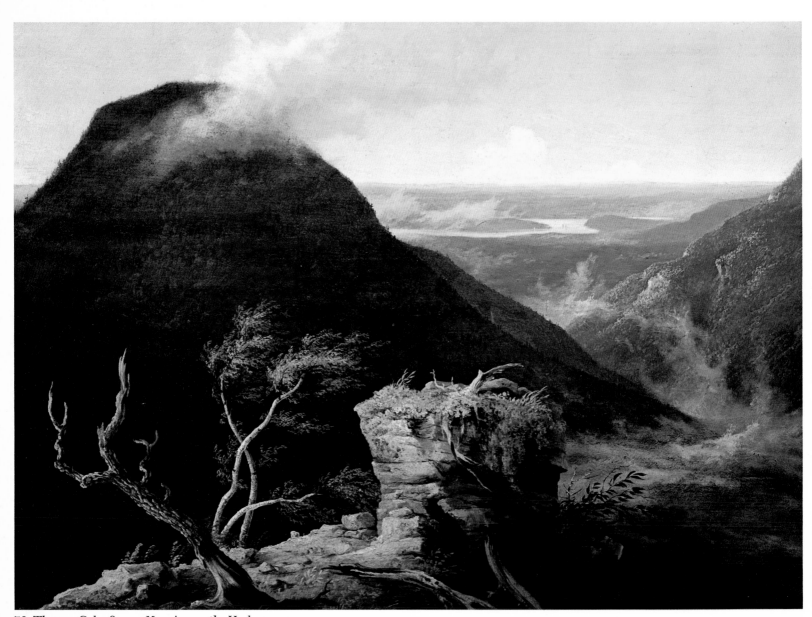

73. Thomas Cole, *Sunny Morning on the Hudson*

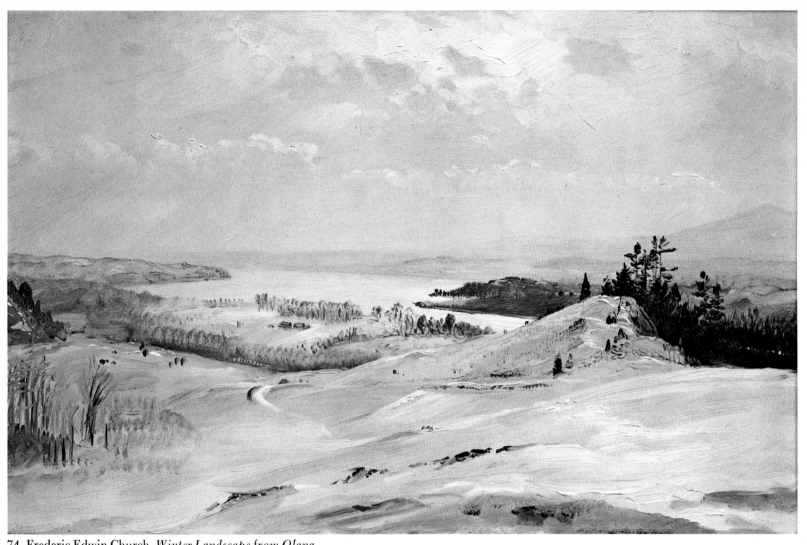

74. Frederic Edwin Church, *Winter Landscape from Olana*

75. Frederic Edwin Church, *Autumn View from Olana*

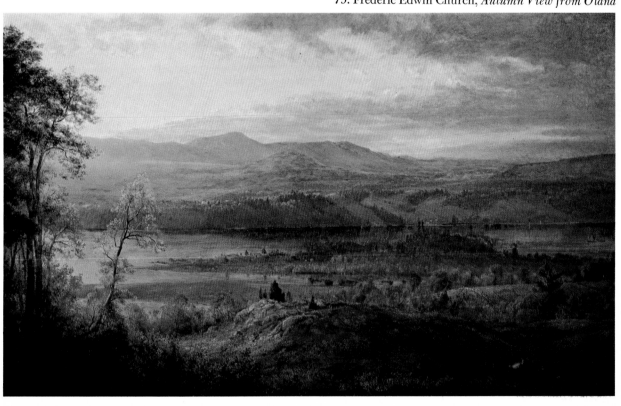

76. Frederic Edwin Church, *Oil Sketch*

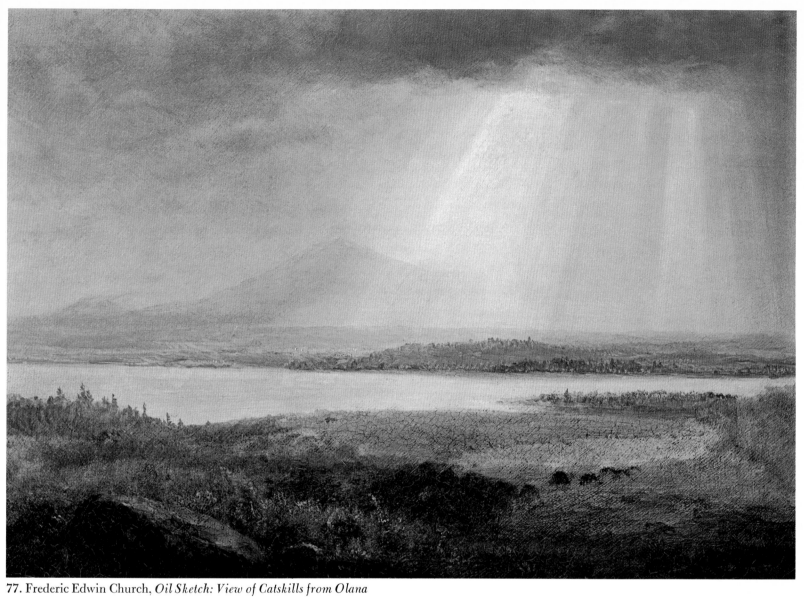

77. Frederic Edwin Church, *Oil Sketch: View of Catskills from Olana*

78. William Louis Sonntag, Untitled

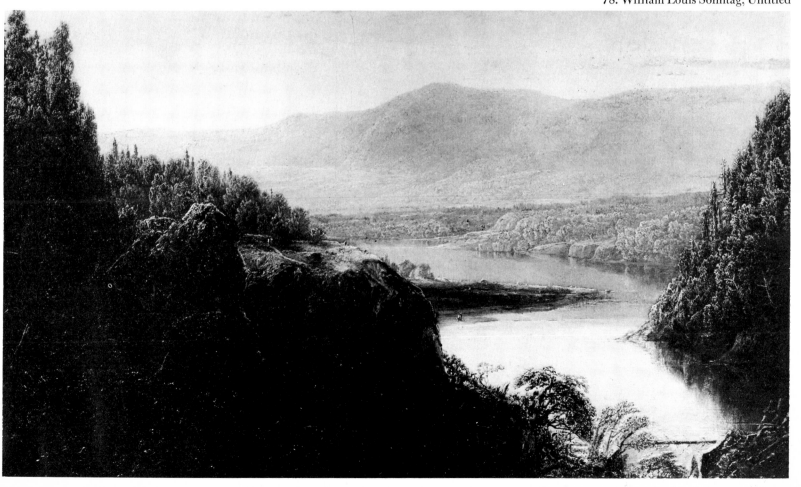

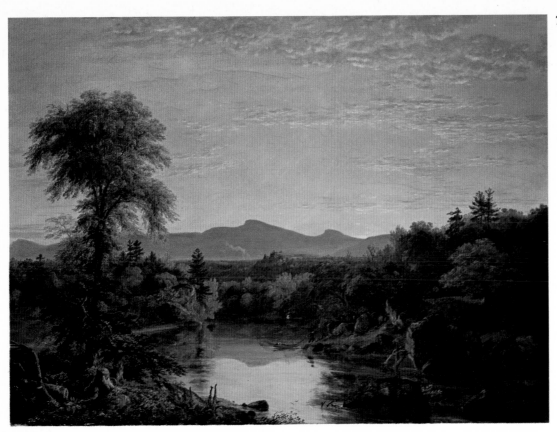

79. Thomas Cole, *Catskill Creek*

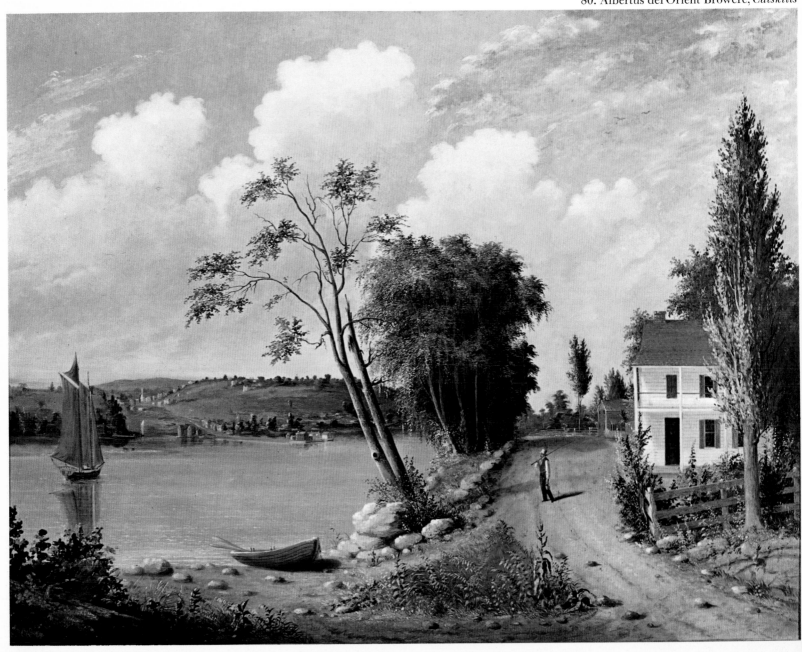

80. Albertus del Orient Browere, *Catskills*

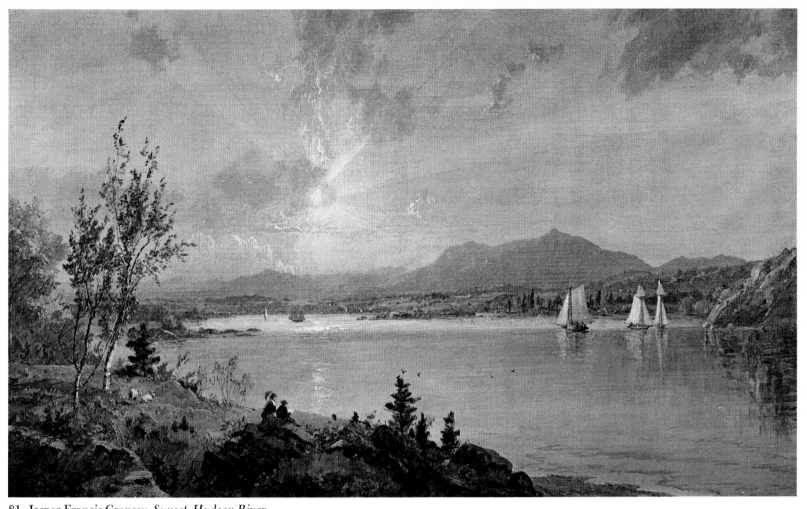

81. Jasper Francis Cropsey, *Sunset, Hudson River*

82. William Guy Wall, *Hudson, New York*

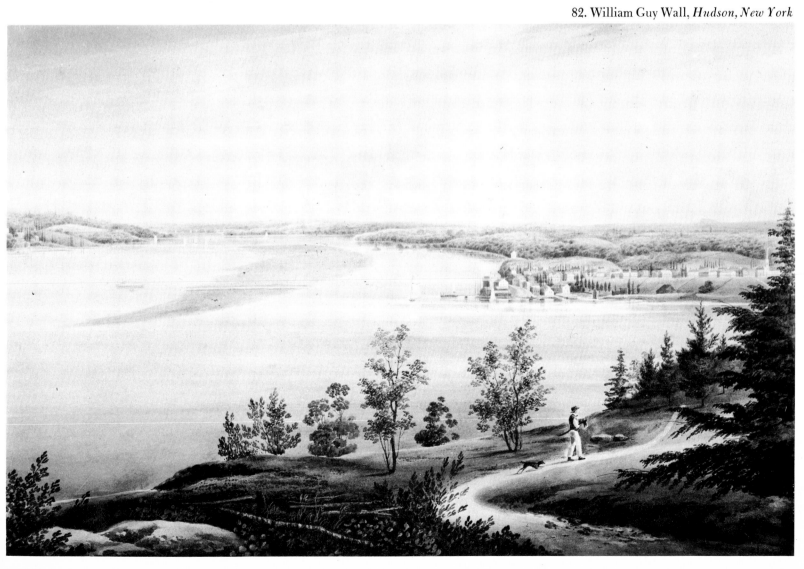

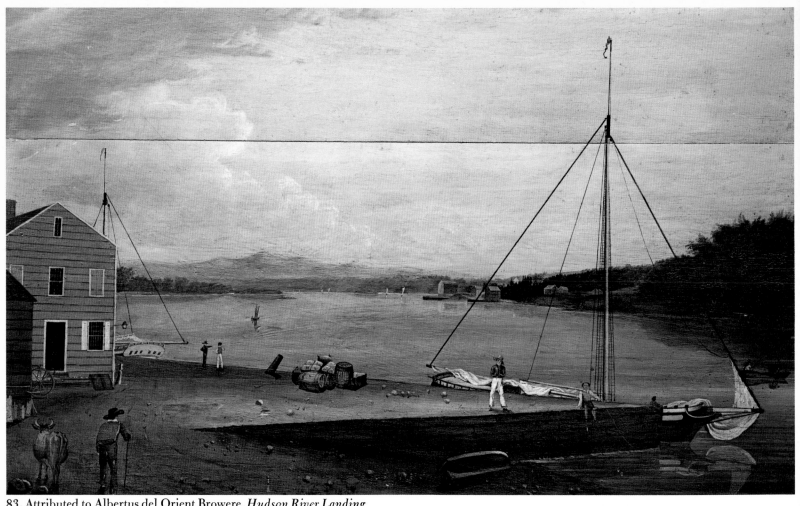

83. Attributed to Albertus del Orient Browere, *Hudson River Landing*

84. Victor Gifford Audubon, *Landscape along the Hudson*

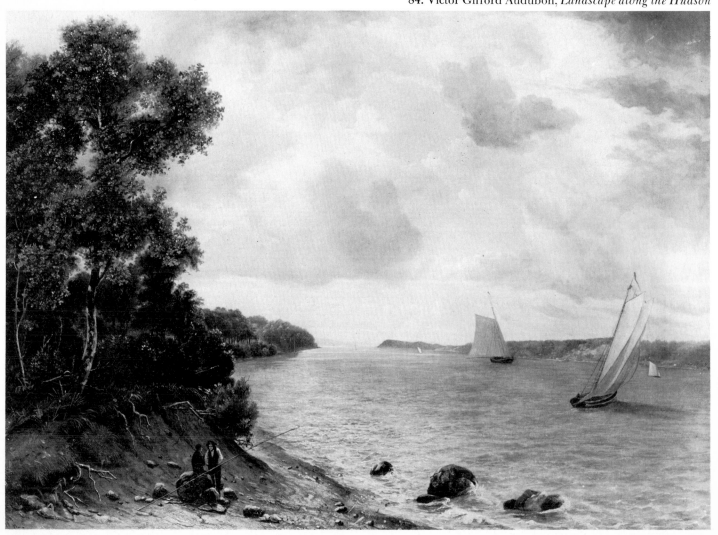

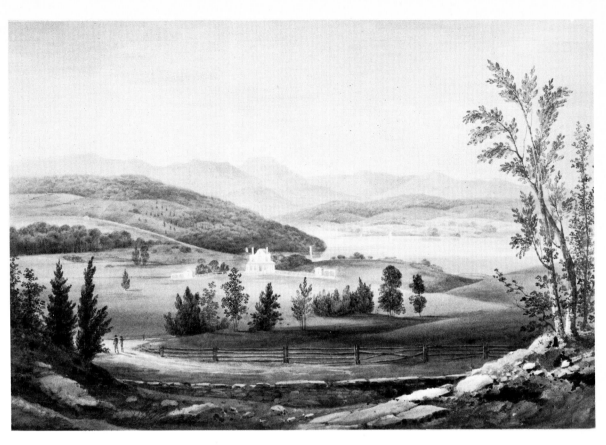

85. William Guy Wall, *View near Hudson Looking Southwest to Mount Merino and the Catskills*

86. William Hart, *Albany, New York, from Bath*

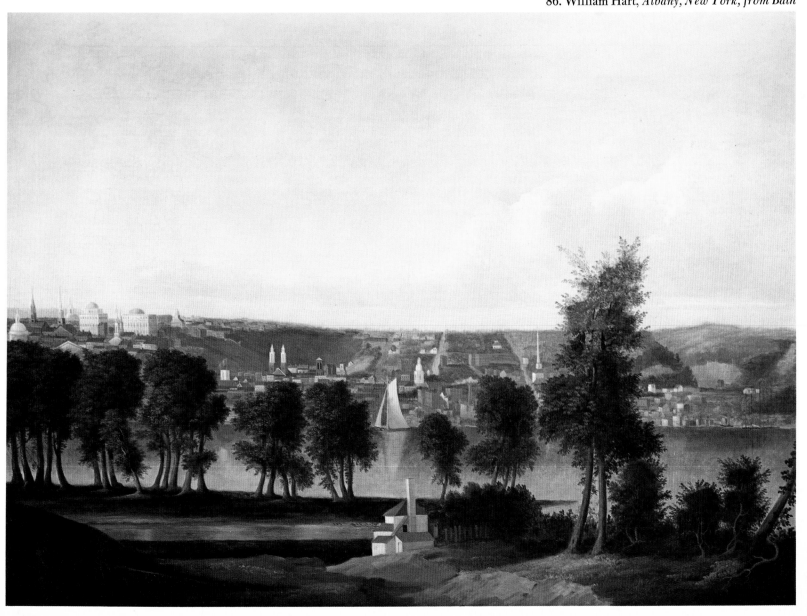

87. James McDougal Hart, *View from Hazelwood, Albany in the Distance*

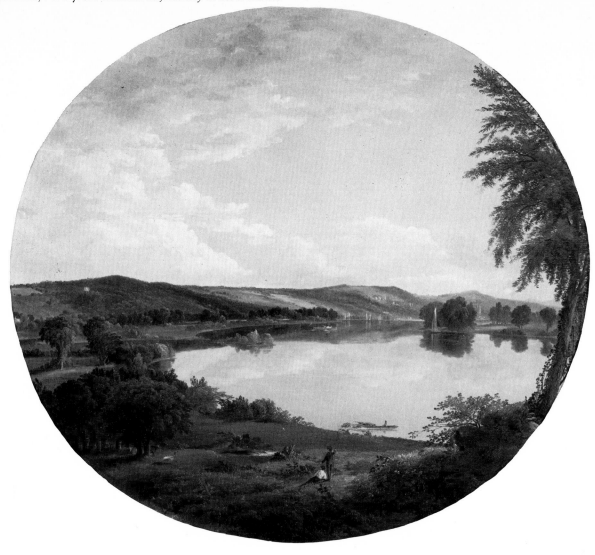

88. Asher Brown Durand, *View of Troy, New York*

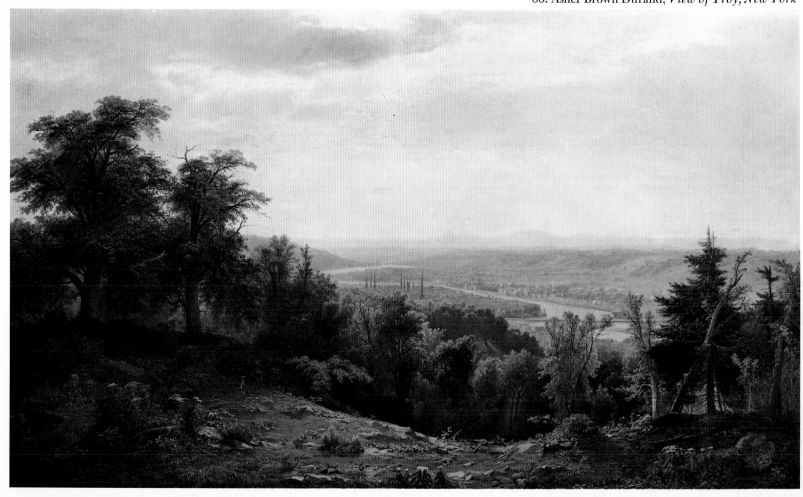

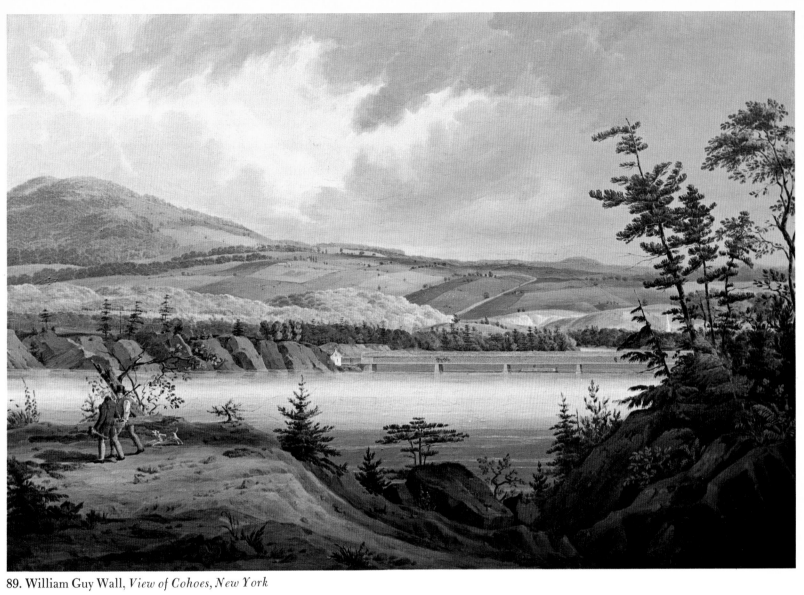

89. William Guy Wall, *View of Cohoes, New York*

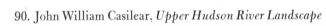

90. John William Casilear, *Upper Hudson River Landscape*

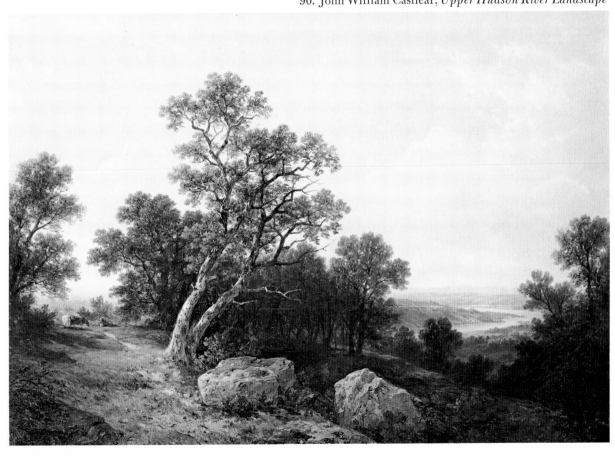

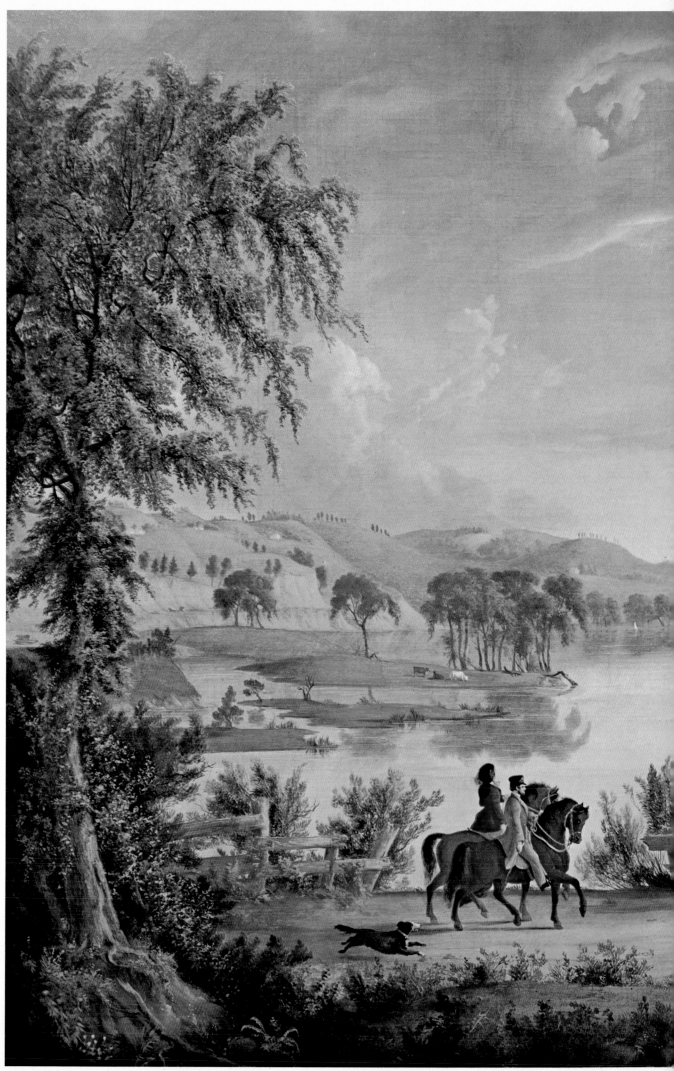

91. Anonymous nineteenth-century American artist, *View of the Hudson River near Troy*

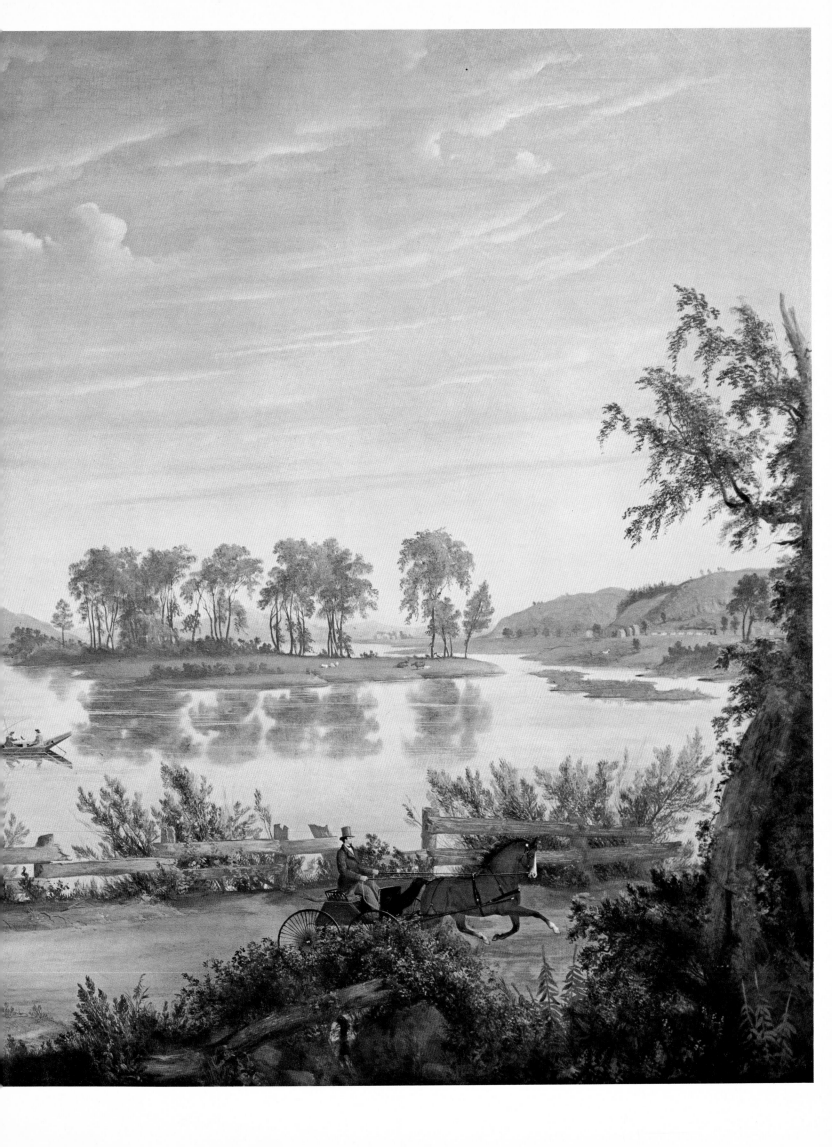

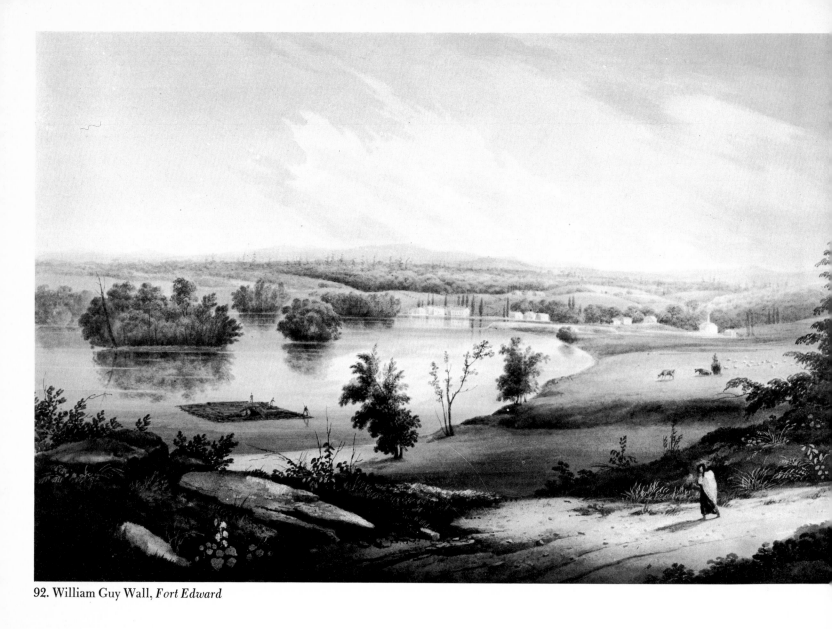

92. William Guy Wall, *Fort Edward*

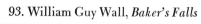

93. William Guy Wall, *Baker's Falls*

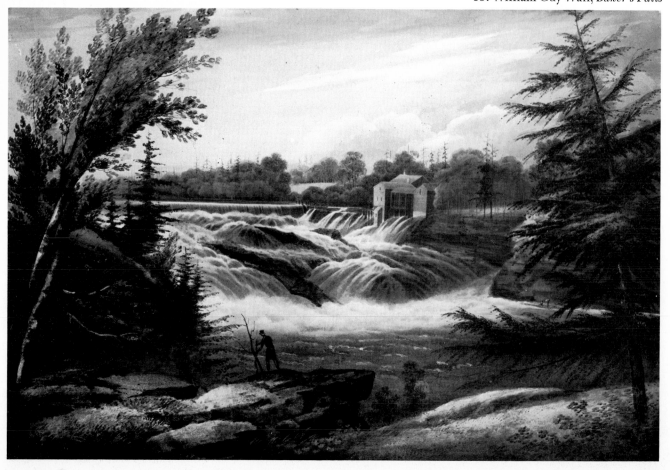

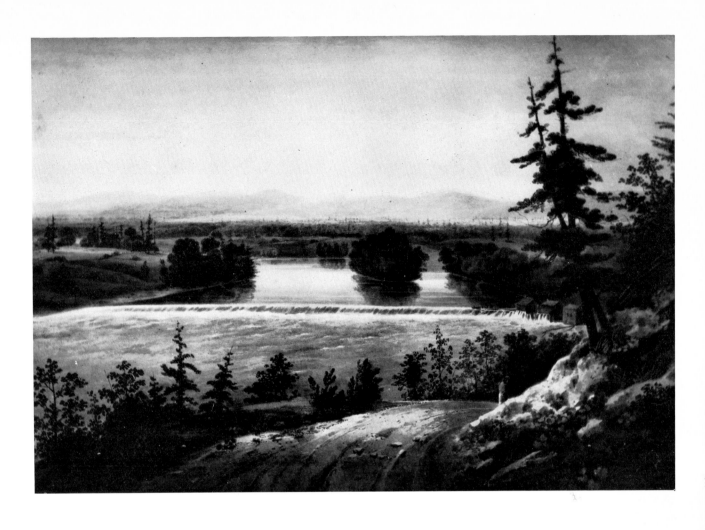

95. William Guy Wall, *Glens Falls*

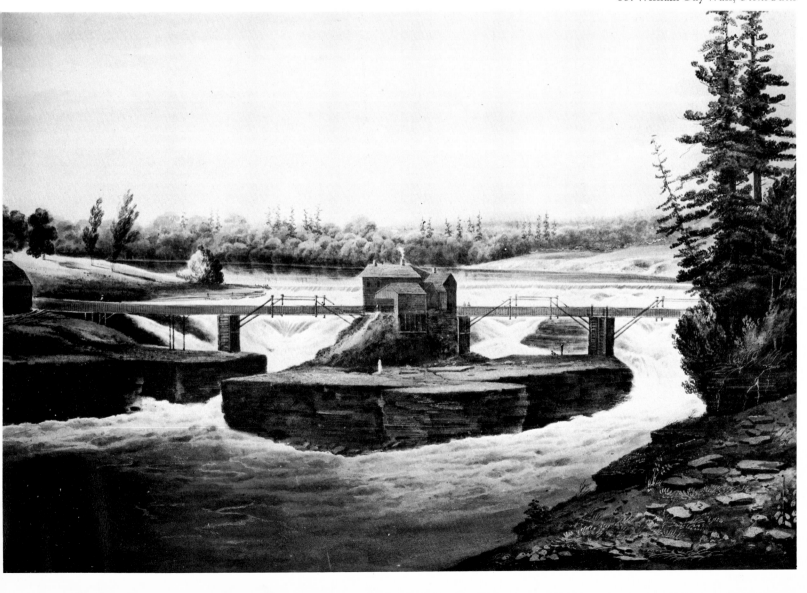

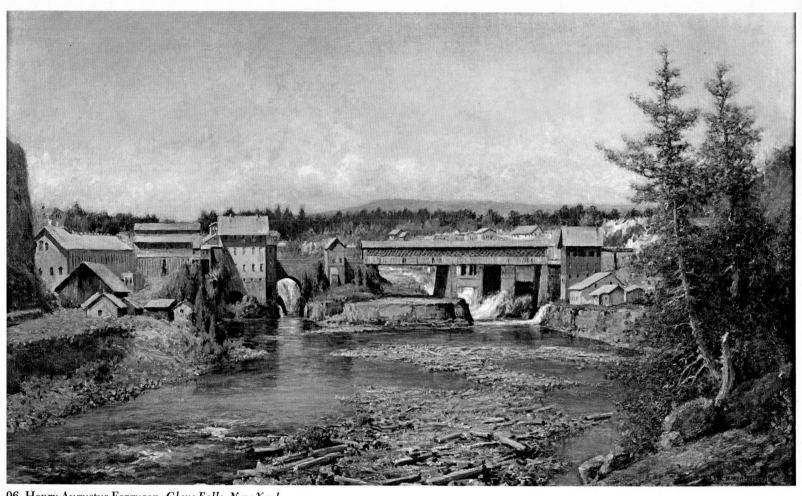

96. Henry Augustus Ferguson, *Glens Falls, New York*

97. Winslow Homer, *The Hudson River—Logging*

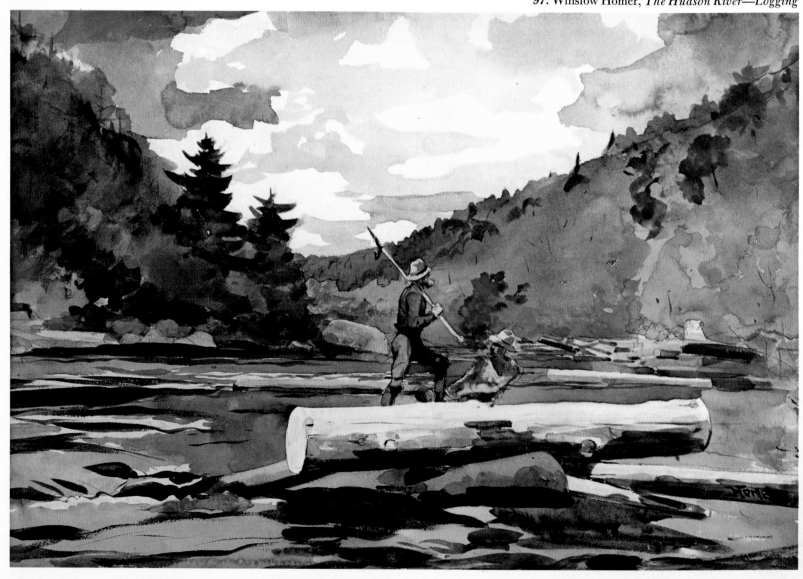

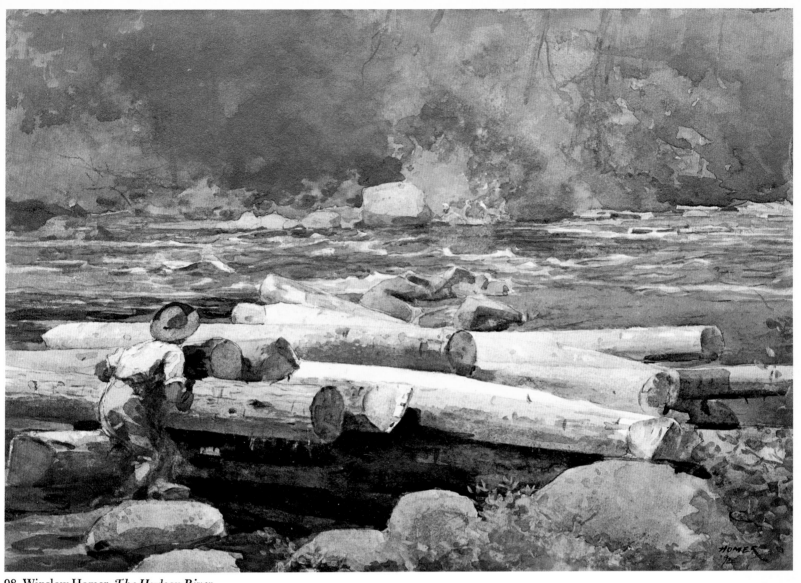

98. Winslow Homer, *The Hudson River*

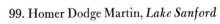

99. Homer Dodge Martin, *Lake Sanford*

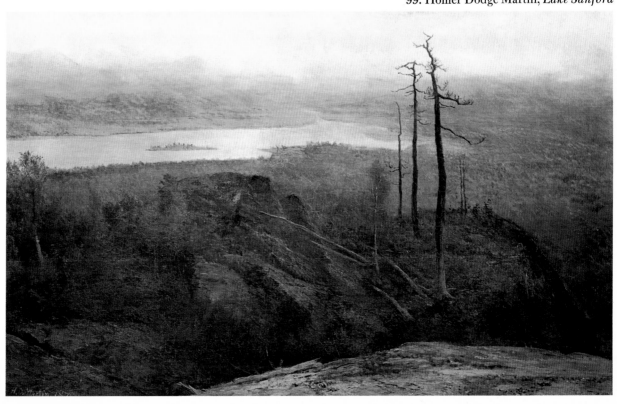

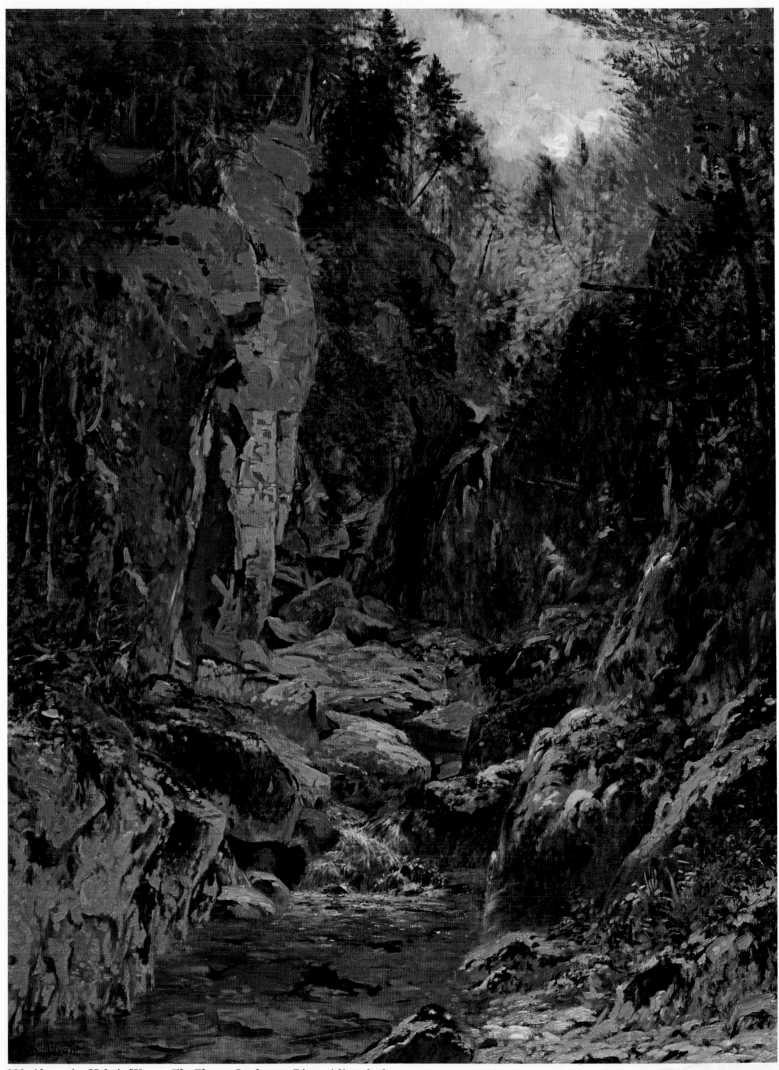

100. Alexander Helwig Wyant, *The Flume, Opalescent River, Adirondacks*

NOTES TO THE PLATES

by John K. Howat and Sandra Feldman

1. Thomas Chambers (1808-after 1866)
Staten Island and the Narrows

Oil on canvas, 22 x 33¼ inches. Brooklyn, New York: The Brooklyn Museum Collection.

Bold color and brushwork, combined with the use of simple outline and two-dimensional forms, distinguish the work of Thomas Chambers. The English-born artist came to New York in 1834, two years after his arrival in America. He moved to Boston in 1843, then to Albany in 1852, and in 1861 returned to New York. The view, which looks southeast toward Lower New York Bay and the Atlantic Ocean through the harbor's main ship channel, was painted from the western shore of New York Bay and was probably inspired by a popular print of the scene. Long Island's almost level shores flank the Narrows at the left, with Staten Island to the right. This island was taken from New Jersey by New York following an agreement signed in 1833, presumably not long before this picture was painted.

2. William Henry Bartlett (1809-1854)
View of the Bay and Harbor of New York from Gowanus Heights, Brooklyn

Watercolor on paper, 7¼ x 11⅜ inches. Inscribed in pencil (lower right): "New York Bay." New York: The Metropolitan Museum of Art, Edward W. C. Arnold Collection of New York Prints, Maps and Pictures.

During the late eighteenth and early nineteenth centuries, English watercolorists developed with great skill the subtle qualities of that medium in landscape painting. The Englishman William Henry Bartlett made four trips to America between 1836 and 1852, producing large numbers of sensitive topographical views in pencil and watercolor. His pictures served as illustrations for N. P. Willis's *American Scenery*, published about 1840, a widely circulated book that provided the basis for compositional study and inspiration to numberless American artists. In this drawing Manhattan extends across the background, lying north of Brooklyn, "a city without public buildings of interest, and without a commerce of its own," according to William Cullen Bryant, "being little more than New York's vast dormitory. . . . Within the precincts of Brooklyn, on what were once called Gowanus Heights, is Greenwood, the handsomest cemetery, probably in the world. It is over four hundred acres in extent, beautiful, undulating . . . varied with several lakes—a rural paradise in its natural attractions."

3. Edward Moran (1829-1901)
New York Harbor

Oil on canvas, 8 x 14 inches. Signed (lower left): "Edw. Moran." New York: Lee B. Anderson Collection.

Although trained as a weaver in his native England, Edward Moran came to America in 1844 with his family and, like his brothers Thomas and Peter, pursued painting as a career. By 1857 he was an established Philadelphia artist. In 1862 the Moran brothers left for England, and Edward enrolled in the Royal Academy. Ten years later he settled in New York where he acquired a studio.

The Statue of Liberty, presented to the United States by France honoring the centennial of the Declaration of Independence in 1876 and erected ten years later, is shown here silhouetted against the expansive bay and sky. The view looks northwest from Brooklyn toward the New Jersey shores. As in most of Moran's paintings, the heightened color and dramatic conceptions of Joseph M. W. Turner are recalled in this glowing celebration of a New York sunset.

4. Sanford Robinson Gifford (1823-1880)
Sunset over New York Bay

Oil on canvas, 23 x 40 inches. Signed and dated (lower right): "S. R. Gifford 1878." Ansonia, Connecticut. Robert Paul Weimann, Jr.

Gifford, a gifted landscapist and handler of paint and an artistic free spirit, was raised in Hudson, New York, and trained from 1845 to 1846 in the art of drawing under John Rubens Smith and at the National Academy of Design in New York City. His painter's instinct convinced him that he must go "to nature as it had been formed by the Creator; that no historical or legendary interest attached to the landscape could help the landscape painter." A two-year trip visiting Europe's most celebrated ateliers, begun in 1855, served to reaffirm his belief in nature while exposing him to the simplicity and suggestiveness possible through the controlled effects of light. Today he is recognized as a leading Luminist, a poet of light and atmosphere. The painting is an example of his mature style, exploiting every subtlety of color, tone, light and dark.

5. William Guy Wall (1792-after 1864)
The Bay of New York and Governor's Island Taken from Brooklyn Heights

Watercolor and white on paper, 20⅝ x 29⅝ inches. New York: The Metropolitan Museum of Art, Edward W. C. Arnold Collection of New York Prints, Maps and Pictures.

The Irish-born William G. Wall arrived in America in 1818, and by 1820 had published a large number of his watercolors in the *Hudson River Portfolio*, engraved by J. R. Smith, I. Hill, and John Hill. This renowned publication, which contributed to the growing awareness of American landscape and which drew particular attention to the Hudson River, established Wall's reputation. This scene of Governor's Island was one of his numerous subjects not published in the *Portfolio*. Governor's Island, at the entrance to the East River, had once been referred to by the Dutch settlers as Noten (Nut) Island "on account of the chestnut, oak, and hickory trees with which had once abounded," and is said to have been the first place the Dutch occupied in the bay. The picture is typical of Wall's work in its expansive feeling and pastel tonality.

6. Anonymous (after Thomas Kelah Wharton, 1814-1862)
New York from Brooklyn Heights

Black and white sandpaper drawing, 18¾ x 27 inches. After 1834. New York: Courtesy of Kennedy Galleries, Inc.

"The panoramic view as you pass the city is extensive and grand ... exhibiting the Jersey shore on the west, with great distinctiveness in the picturesque scene. In this mass of architecture and of life composing the city which seems extending as you are gazing, more than a hundred spires of houses of religious worship arise, 'as so many electrical conductors to convey away the wrath of God for the sins of a people.' ... " Samuel Knapp's description of New York, written in 1835, captures the feeling of this folk drawing, which was made after a smaller line engraving published in the *New-York Mirror* in 1834; the original was painted by Wharton, engraved by A. W. Graham, and is now number 153 in the Eno Collection of New York City Views, The New York Public Library. Wharton moved to New York City two years after his 1830 arrival in America from England with his family. Although employed as an architect, he exhibited landscape paintings at the National Academy of Design and made city views in pencil and lithograph.

7. Charles Herbert Moore (1840-1930)
Morning over New York

Oil on canvas, 11⅞ x 30 inches. 1861. Poughkeepsie, New York: Vassar College Art Gallery.

The taste during the mid-nineteenth century for the impartially objective and highly finished painting was nurtured by the development of photography and the popularity of the art academy at Düsseldorf, Germany. Although Moore was born and trained in New York City, his early works owe much to these trends. The breadth of composition contrasted with the darkly silhouetted New Jersey shores in the foreground descriptively sets forth the character of the scene. According to one tradition, Indians in 1609 named the island where the city of New York now stands *Man-a-hat-ta-nink*, "island of general intoxication," supposedly after tasting Henry Hudson's fire-water. The English conquest in 1664 changed New Amsterdam to New York. Greater New York only came into being by a charter in 1897. By that time Moore had taught the principles of design at Harvard University, had studied in 1876 with Ruskin in Venice, and in 1896 had become the first director of the Fogg Museum at Harvard.

8. Thomas Chambers (1808-after 1866)
Villa on the Hudson near Weehawken

Oil on canvas, 17½ x 24 inches. Cooperstown, New York: New York State Historical Association.

The travel book *Picturesque Tourist*, published in 1858, described Weehawken: "on the Jersey shore, north of Hoboken, and 3 miles from New York, a high wooded cliff, with its bold rocky bluffs partly veiled with trees and partly bare, and a handsome villa on its summit, is one of the finest points in the scene as you move up the river. At the foot of this cliff, and on the margin of the river, a small obelisk of white marble for many years marked the spot where Alexander Hamilton fell in his fatal duel with Aaron Burr, on 12th July, 1804." Chambers' re-creation of the scene is a colorful, decorative, and charming composition based on a Bartlett print published in 1838 in *American Scenery*. Chambers deleted the Bartlett figures and lowered the horizon line, while creating bolder forms through the use of hard outlines and saturated colors. The picture may have been painted in Boston in the late 1840s during Chambers' residence there.

9. Sanford Robinson Gifford (1823-1880)

Sunset on the Hudson

Oil on canvas, 8⅞ x 15⅞ inches. Signed and dated (lower right): "S. R. Gifford '76." Hartford, Connecticut: The Wadsworth Atheneum, Ella Gallup Sumner and Mary Catlin Sumner Collection.

This view of the Palisades, William Cullen Bryant's "brow of rock that overlooks the Hudson's western marge," concentrates on the light of the setting sun rather than on the location. Gifford believed that the impression received by the viewer is governed by the color of the sky, the "key-note" of the picture, and that different impressions of air produce different impressions on the mind. To create this effect, he painted in the horizon and sky first, working from carefully finished oil sketches. His last step was to apply several layers of varnish, which correspond to the natural veil of the atmosphere, reflecting and refracting light, creating a transparent picture surface.

10. Jasper Francis Cropsey (1823-1900)

Shad Fishing on the Hudson

Oil on canvas, 12 x 20 inches. Signed and dated (lower right): "J. F. Cropsey 1874." Private collection.

This nostalgic view looking upstream past the Palisades documents pictorially the activity of shad fishermen, who, according to *Valentine's Manual* of 1924, had in the nineteenth century "spread all along the shores opposite Yonkers," interfering with river navigation. "In those days one could row out to where the fishermen were hauling in their nets, and get all the delicious roe shad he wanted for a quarter. This is only a few years ago, but it is morally certain that shad have virtually disappeared from the sludge-infested waters of the Hudson." Cropsey, who took such care to describe accurately the fishermen, their boats, and the familiar location, lived the late years of his life on the river at Hastings, not far north of this scene. He was born in Staten Island and studied painting while serving an architectural apprenticeship in New York. In 1846 he left for a trip through Europe with his new bride, and occupied Cole's old studio in Rome. He returned to New York in 1849, and during the 1850s his landscape themes fluctuated between the real and the ideal, reflecting the romantic, imaginative landscapes of Cole. A visit to London in 1856 lasted seven successful years, and by the 1860s he was producing panoramic compositions, usually characterized by the highly colored glow found in this attractive picture.

11. Pavel Petrovich Svinin (1787-1839)
The Packet "Mohawk of Albany" Passing the Palisades

Watercolor on paper, 9³⁄₁₆ x 15⁵⁄₁₆ inches. New York: The Metropolitan
Museum of Art, Rogers Fund, 1942.

After the development of the steamboat, the sailing packet was used almost exclu-
sively as a freight carrier. Here it dominates the composition, creating a pleasant
diagonal movement contrasting to the vertical Palisades, "a name given probably
for the ribbed appearance of some parts of the cliff, which seem, like rude basaltic
columns, or huge trunks of old and decayed trees, placed close together in a
perpendicular form for a barricade or defense," as J. S. Buckingham wrote in *America:
Historical, Statistic and Descriptive*, published in 1841. Svinin painted the scene from
life in his usual direct and precise manner. He was born in Russia and educated
at the Academy of Fine Arts of Saint Petersburg. After entering the Foreign Office,
he was sent to America in 1811 as secretary to the Russian Consul General. During
the two years of his stay Svinin traveled along the East Coast and painted watercolors
of the American scene as he found it. He also kept an account of his observations
on American political institutions, steamboats, climate, cities, and outstanding men,
which was published upon his return to Russia under the title *Picturesque Voyage
in North America*.

12. John George Brown (1831-1913)
View of the Palisades

Oil on canvas, 38 x 71⅛ inches. Signed and dated (lower left): "J. G.
Brown / N.Y. 1867." Private collection.

The quiet monumentality in Brown's painting is achieved through a subtle use
of warm rich tones, which serve to tie the composition together, and beautifully
handled details such as the crisply painted steamboat. The picture displays a fine
understanding of coloristic unity. Brown studied painting first in his native England,
then in Scotland. When he came to America he found employment in a Brooklyn
glass factory but by 1860 had established a studio in New York City. Although,
in his own words, Brown placed great emphasis in his pictures on "contemporary
truth," he made his reputation as the "shoe-black Raphael," the somewhat sentimen-
tal portrayer of New York's street urchins. A broadly painted and straightforward
picture such as this is a rare and delightful variation from Brown's accustomed
genre.

13. Frederick Rondel (1826-1892)
The Hudson River, Viewed from Lovat, the Fraser Home

Oil on canvas, 31½ x 47½ inches. Private collection.

The panoramic view was a common type of mid-nineteenth-century American landscape painting. Rondel used a broad and deep perspective with a foreground specificity reminiscent of Durand's, while cloaking the scene in a subtly clear light. He had received formal painting instruction in Paris, his birthplace, from the romantic marine and landscape painters Auguste Jungelet and Theodore Gudin. Beyond his arts, Rondel is memorable for giving Winslow Homer his only art instruction. In 1855, 1857, and 1858 Rondel lived in the greater Boston area; from 1859 to 1860 and in 1868 he lived in New York City. He visited Europe in 1862. The remainder of his life was spent in the New York and New England area. This view looks upstream from Hastings, across the Tappan Zee toward Hook Mountain at Nyack. The Lovat home, which still exists, was built in the popular "Hudson River Bracketed" style, a term based upon the enthusiastic acceptance of the style in the Hudson River area. Hastings, which lies four miles north of Yonkers, New York, was the location, according to Wallace Bruce's 1894 guidebook *The Hudson,* where "a party of Hessians during the Revolutionary struggle were surprised and cut to pieces by troops under Col. Sheldon. It was here also that Lord Cornwallis embarked for Fort Lee after the capture of Fort Washington, and here in later days Garibaldi, the liberator of Italy, frequently came to spend the Sabbath. ... Although there is apparently little to interest in the village, there are many beautiful residences in the immediate neighborhood. ... "

14. Anonymous nineteenth-century American artist
Mill, Philipse Manor and Church, Tarrytown

Oil on canvas, 34 x 28 inches. Irvington, New York: Sleepy Hollow Restorations.

Inspiration for many scenes of Sleepy Hollow at Tarrytown, New York, came from prints published in travel books and from novels. To the self-trained artist, these prints were guides to the creation of formal compositions and the basis for pretty pictures which might contain historical or legendary significance. In this case, the artist has enriched the composition with the addition of the columned portico on the oldest church in New York State (shown in the right background of the picture), built in the Dutch style by "Frederic Philips and Catherine Van Cortland, his wife, in 1699," according to an inscription on a marble tablet in front. The Sleepy Hollow Bridge (shown at the right) crosses the Po-can-te-co stream, the Indian name for a "run between two hills," and Philipse's milldam (at the left) fronts the Philipse Manor. The folk artist has added foliage to complete the painting in a charming and decorative manner. The area was immortalized by Washington Irving in his *Legend of Sleepy Hollow* as the setting for the encounter between the headless horseman of Sleepy Hollow and Ichabod Crane.

15. Harry Fenn (1838-1911)

Palisades, Hudson River

Watercolor on paper, 8¾ x 15¾ inches. New York: Courtesy of Kennedy Galleries, Inc.

Even the acid-tongued Mrs. Trollope thought the lower Hudson offered certain pleasures. "For the first twenty miles, the shore of New Jersey ... offers almost a continued wall of trap rock, which from its perpendicular form, and lineal fissures, is called the Palisades. This wall sometimes rises to the height of a hundred and fifty feet, and sometimes sinks down to twenty. Here and there, a watercourse breaks its uniformity; and everywhere the brightest foliage, in all of the splendour of the climate and the season, fringed and checkered the dark barrier." Trained as a painter and wood engraver in his native England, Harry Fenn came to America in 1857 for a six-year visit, then left for further study in Italy. Upon return to America Fenn pursued a wood engraver's career and illustrated many popular books, Bryant's *Picturesque America* among them. The sensitive handling of figures and landscape, drawn from nature, is rendered in minute detail; yet there is a lyrical, light storytelling quality characteristic of his work that recalls the stylish sketches of his Parisian contemporary Constantin Guys.

16. Francis A. Silva (1835-1886)
The Hudson at Tappan Zee

Oil on canvas, 24 x 42⅛ inches. Signed and dated (lower left): "Francis
A. Silva / '76." Brooklyn, New York: The Brooklyn Museum Collection,
Dick S. Ramsay Fund.

A simple approach to form and a quiet monumentality distinguish Francis A. Silva's
marine paintings. Born in New York City, Silva displayed an early gift for art in
pen drawings exhibited at the American Institute from 1848 to 1850. Opposed in
his wishes to be an artist by his father, Silva tried several trades before serving
an apprenticeship as a sign painter. After the Civil War, in which he was an army
officer, Silva returned to New York City and in 1868 began the career of a professional artist. His luminous technique, entirely self-taught, led to his election to
membership in the American Water Color Society in 1872. The name Tappan derives
from the Indian *Tup-hanne*, "cold stream." The painting looks north toward the
artificial island of Kingsland Point, upon which a lighthouse was located. At this
point the Hudson is more than four miles wide. There is a folk tale associated
with this area: the "Flying Dutchman," Mr. Van Dam, still rows until Judgment
Day across the Tappan Zee between Kakiat and Spuyten Duyvil.

17. Robert Havell, Jr. (1793-1878)
View of the Hudson from Tarrytown Heights

Oil on canvas, 22 x 30 inches. New York: Courtesy of the New-York
Historical Society.

The detailed interpretation of the scene draws upon Havell's experience as an
engraver combined with his direct observation from nature. Born and educated
in Reading, England, Havell continued his family profession of engraving. His sense
of design and skill of translation into aquatint of the Audubon drawings for *Birds
of America*, engraved from 1827 to 1838, contributed to the popularity of these books.
When Havell came to America with his wife and daughter in 1839, he journeyed
up the Hudson to the West Point area, then visited with the Audubons in New

York City. He lived in Brooklyn until 1841, when he bought a house at Sing Sing. The last twenty-one years of his life were spent at nearby Tarrytown. Although the painting was once thought to represent the Havell home at Sing Sing (at the right), modern research marks the location as the heights north of Tarrytown. In his book *The Hudson,* Lossing records: "The natives called this place A-lip-conck, or Place of Elms, that tree having been abundant there in early times, and still flourishes. The Dutch called it Terwen Dorp, or Wheat Town, because that cereal grew luxuriantly. ... As usual, the English retained a part of the Dutch name, and called it Terwe Town, from which is derived the modern pronunciation, Tarrytown." The painting looks upstream past Kingsland Point (in the center) toward Teller's Point, named in memory of an Indian sachem (later renamed Croton Point by Dr. T. R. Underhill, who owned the land with his brother).

18. Anonymous nineteenth-century American artist
Old Mill of Sleepy Hollow

Oil on canvas, 27 x 21 inches. Irvington, New York: Sleepy Hollow Restorations.

The area of Sleepy Hollow, Slaeperigh Hol in Dutch, excited the imaginations of both poet and artist—stimulated, to quote Lossing in *The Hudson,* by "a pretty little lake above an ancient and picturesque dam, near the almost as ancient church. This little lake extends back almost to the bridge in the dark weird glen, and furnishes motive power to a very ancient mill that stands close by Philipse Castle, as the more ancient manor-house of the family was called." According to a pamphlet published recently by Sleepy Hollow Restorations, the gristmill included a wharf and granary, located "in a northern sector of Philipsburg Manor, near where the Pocantico and Hudson Rivers meet. ... [Philipse] called this trading center Upper Mills to distinguish it from his other milling operation in the southern part of the manor which is now the City of Yonkers. The grain from the surrounding Pocantico tract was milled and sent down the Hudson to New York City in sloops."

19. Jasper Francis Cropsey (1823-1900)
Hudson River near Hastings

Watercolor on paper, 6 x 12½ inches. Signed and dated (lower right):
"J. F. Cropsey / 1886." Courtesy of Mrs. John C. Newington.

During the 1860s, Cropsey turned increasingly to watercolor as a medium of expression; he helped found the American Water Color Society in 1866 and exhibited annually thereafter in their shows. This scene taken from Cropsey's home, high above the Hudson, looks across the Tappan Zee, capturing in his best impressionistic manner the lively shipping driven both by steam and sail.

20. Albert Bierstadt (1830-1902)
View on the Hudson

Oil on academy board, 14 x 20 inches. Signed (lower right): "ABierstadt." New York: Courtesy of Kenneth M. Newman, The Old Print Shop, Inc.

In 1866 Albert Bierstadt built an expansive thirty-five-room mansion at Irvington-on-Hudson, where he lived and worked for the next sixteen years. According to Tuckerman in 1867, "It was because of his conviction that the patient and faithful study of nature is the only adequate school of landscape art, that Bierstadt, like Cole and Church, fixed his abode on the banks of the Hudson. His spacious studio ... commands a beautiful and extensive view of the noble river, in the immediate vicinity of the Tappan Zee and the Palisades. ... " This picture, looking west across the Tappan Zee toward a stormy sunset sky, is typical of the artist's grandly conceived pictures. Born in Düsseldorf, Germany, Bierstadt grew up in New Bedford, Massachusetts. He studied painting at Düsseldorf in the early 1850s, traveled in Europe, then returned to this country. In 1859 he joined a military expedition for the first of several trips he made through the American West. The finished and enlarged versions of oil sketches he made en route established Bierstadt as the pre-eminent painter of the Rockies, the Sierra Nevadas, and the California redwoods. Here the artist has applied his romantic vision successfully to the less overwhelming landscape outside his window.

21. Robert Havell, Jr. (1793 -1878)

Key to the View of Haverstraw Bay from Sing Sing

Pastel crayon and ink on paper, 7 x 11¼ inches. New York: Courtesy of Kennedy Galleries, Inc.

As was recorded by the popular nineteenth-century American writer Nathaniel Parker Willis in *American Scenery*, 1840, "Sing Sing is famous for its marble, of which there is an extensive quarry near by; for its State prison, of which the discipline is of the most salutary character; and for its academy, which has a high reputation." By a fluke, Havell purchased a home here in 1841. He had been traveling around the countryside with his family in a homemade, horse-drawn trailer which created quite a stir in the country villages. When they encountered a real estate auction in progress at Sing Sing, his travel-weary wife placed a bid on a house. Only when the auctioneer's aide overtook the trailer did the Havells learn of their purchase. The drawing, which may have been intended as a preliminary guide for a painting of the area, is an interesting document and provides insight into Havell's working method: he has carefully observed the particulars of the location, recorded details in a key, and captured the effect of sunlight on the landscape with a quick and spontaneous line.

22. Sanford Robinson Gifford (1823 -1880)

Hook Mountain, near Nyack, on the Hudson

Oil on canvas, 8⅛ x 19 inches. New Haven, Connecticut: Yale University Art Gallery, gift of Miss Annette I. Young, in memory of Professor D. Cady Eaton and Mr. Inness Young.

Hook Mountain is part of the Ramapo Mountains, referred to as "Hook" or "Point-No-Point" by the old-time mariners. Wallace Bruce described these mountains coming "down to the river in little headlands, the points of which disappear as the steamer nears them." The painting looks south from Haverstraw Bay, past Hook Mountain, toward Nyack. The exaggerated use here of a horizontal format and the perfect handling of local tone, texture, and color are typical of Gifford's mature work. More unusual is the almost brittle clarity and contrast of forms and color which lend the picture such a poignant calm and soundlessness.

23. Samuel Colman (1832-1920)
Looking North from Ossining, New York

Oil on canvas, 15½ x 30 inches. Signed and dated (lower left): "S. Colman '67." Yonkers, New York: Hudson River Museum.

The microscopic view of nature brought into paintings by Asher B. Durand was communicated to his pupil Samuel Colman. Colman's artistic studies were encouraged by his father, a publisher and fine-arts bookseller, who had settled in New York City shortly after his son's birth in Portland, Maine. From 1860 to 1862 Colman traveled and studied in France, Spain, and Morocco, and from 1871 to 1875 visited northern and southern Europe. Colman was elected the first president of the American Water Color Society, organized during the latter part of 1866. Nineteenth-century Ossining was remembered by Lossing, in *The Hudson*, as "a very pleasant village ... [lying] upon a rudely broken slope of hills, that rise about one hundred and eighty feet above the river, and overlook Tappan Bay, or Tappaanse Zee, as the early Dutch settlers called an expansion of the Hudson. ... [The name Sing Sing originates from] Sint-sinck, the title of a powerful clan of the Mohegan or river Indians, who called this spot *Os-sin-ing*, from *ossin*, a stone, and *ing*, a place—stony place. ... The land in this vicinity, first parted with by the Indians, was granted to Frederick Philipse ... in 1685."

24. Pavel Petrovitch Svinin (1787-1839)
Shad Fishermen on the Shore of the Hudson River

Watercolor on paper, 10¹⁄₁₆ x 15½ inches. New York: The Metropolitan Museum of Art, Rogers Fund, 1942.

A genre quality reflects Svinin's interest in all facets of American life which he observed during his two-year stay here. He painted more than fifty watercolors capturing the American scene; this one looks upstream from Crugers toward Verplanck's Point, an area steeped with historical significance. Lossing wrote, "The Indians called this place *Me-a-nagh*. They sold it to Stephen Van Cortlandt, in the year 1683. ... The purchase was confirmed by patent from the English government. On this point Colonel Livingston held command at the time of Arnold's treason, in 1780; and here were the head-quarters of George Washington for some time in 1782. It was off this point that Henry Hudson first anchored the *Half-Moon* after leaving Yonkers. The highland Indians flocked to the vessel in great numbers. One of them was killed in an affray, and this circumstance planted the seed of hatred of the white man in the bosom of the Indians in that region."

25. Jasper Francis Cropsey (1823-1900)
Autumn on the Hudson River

Oil on canvas, 60 x 108 inches. Inscribed, signed, and dated (lower center): "The Hudson River / J. F. Cropsey / London 1860." Washington, D.C.; National Gallery of Art, gift of the Avalon Foundation, 1963.

Cropsey celebrated in this grandiose composition the overwhelming spectacle of an American autumn, which was so hard for the English viewer to comprehend. One of the largest paintings ever attempted by Cropsey, it took over a year to complete and received such an enthusiastic reception in London that the artist and his wife were presented to Queen Victoria in 1861. In order to satisfy the incredulous English of the accuracy of his color, Cropsey showed real autumn leaves from the Hudson Valley to settle any argument. The picture, showing the Highlands in the distance, is a tour de force of careful planning, detailed observation, and appreciation of the most impressive aspects of local light and color.

26. Asher Brown Durand (1796-1886)
River Scene

Oil on canvas, 24 x 34⅛ inches. Signed and dated (lower left): "A. B. Durand 1854." New York: The Metropolitan Museum of Art, bequest of Mary Starr Van Winkle, 1970.

Born in New Jersey and apprenticed as an engraver, Durand achieved prominence in that field and as a portraitist. Then at thirty-eight he began a career as a landscape painter. He spent 1840–1841 traveling and studying the art and scenery of Europe, then resumed residence in New York City upon his return home. The formal composition of this picture and the introduction of cattle as subject matter harks back strongly to Dutch and English landscape traditions, despite Durand's stated rejection of European models in his work. Durand, in his usual manner, combines closely rendered foreground details, such as rock and shrubbery, with tantalizingly distant vistas along woodland paths and into the hazy distance. The view is toward the southern entrance to the Highlands from Peekskill Bay. "It is said," wrote Wallace Bruce, "that the stream and the town took their names from a worthy Dutch skipper, Jans Peek, who imagined he had found the head waters of the Hudson, and ran aground, on the east side. ... It was called by the Indians the unpoetic name of Sackboes."

27. John Frederick Kensett (1816-1872)
Lakes and Mountains

Oil on canvas, 27½ x 44½ inches. Initialed and dated (lower left):
"J.F.K. '65" Baltimore: The Baltimore Museum of Art, gift of Mrs.
Paul H. Miller.

Born in Connecticut, Kensett was trained as an engraver first by his father, an immigrant English engraver and printer, then by an uncle. After working in New Haven, Albany, and New York as a bank-note engraver, Kensett sailed in 1840 for London in the company of engravers-turned-artists Asher B. Durand and John Casilear, and the painter Thomas Rossiter. Kensett saw at first hand the art collections of Europe and received training at the Paris academies—an education considered requisite to the success of the nineteenth-century artist. By 1845 he had assumed a full-time painting career. Kensett returned to America toward the end of 1847 and established a studio in New York City, taking subsequently numerous summer trips around upstate New York and New England. He revisited Europe in 1856 and 1861, possibly in 1865, and in 1867, and later he accompanied two colleagues, Sanford Gifford and Worthington Whittredge, to Colorado and the Rockies. An entry in the unpublished diary of W. H. Willis, written May 22, 1834, describes a trip on the Hudson at the entrance to the Highlands (the area shown in the painting): "The passage of the Highlands ... strikes the imagination with peculiar force, especially of him who views for the first time the bold scenery through which the noble Hudson winds its way to the ocean. Their mountain peaks rising abruptly from the water, the deep shadows cast upon the tranquil stream ... and the silence broken only by the swift prow plunging through the foam, and the occasional whistle of the whip-poor-will, heard as you near the shore—all contribute to heighten the interest of this romantic voyage."

28. William Guy Wall (1792-after 1864)
View near Fort Montgomery

Watercolor on paper, 14 x 21 inches. New York: Courtesy of the New-York Historical Society.

Fort Montgomery, named for Gen. Richard Montgomery, who was killed during an unsuccessful attack on Quebec in December 1775, is situated on the western shore of the Hudson diagonally opposite Anthony's Nose. During the War for Independence a massive chain on timber floats was stretched across the river at these two points to obstruct passage of British ships up the river. The chains were destroyed when the British captured the fort during the autumn of 1777. Wall's painting is the original watercolor for plate 18 of the *Hudson River Portfolio*. The composition looks upstream toward Sugar Loaf Mountain on the eastern bank. The inclusion in the foreground of the carefully rendered lumber raft and figures add scale to the painting and a reference to contemporary commercial life on the river.

29. Homer Dodge Martin (1836-1897)
On the Hudson (near Peekskill)

Oil on canvas, 24 x 34 inches. Signed and dated (lower right): "H. D. Martin 1881." New York: Collection of Mr. and Mrs. I. D. Orr.

A personal view of nature sustained by a congenital eye weakness sets forth the character of Homer D. Martin's paintings. He was born and raised in Albany, New York, where he showed a predilection for drawing while still a child. His formal education ended when he reached thirteen years of age, and the only art tutelage he received consisted of two weeks' study under James Hart in Albany. In 1863 he moved to New York City. While on a trip through Europe in 1876, Martin struck up a friendship with James Abbott McNeill Whistler, which he renewed on a second trip abroad in 1881. Martin occasionally painted in Whistler's studio. *On the Hudson* reveals an affinity with Whistler in the reflective, rather than literal, transcription of nature. Martin moved away from the dark tonalities of this picture toward a lighter impressionist touch after he returned to America in 1886. During his last years Martin relied on an inward vision to paint due to his almost total blindness.

30. William Henry Bartlett (1806-1854)

Entrance to the Highlands near Anthony's Nose, Hudson River

Pencil and watercolor on paper, 16 x 22 inches. Inscribed (across top):
"Entrance to the Highlands Near Anthony's Nose"; descriptive notations over sheet. Utica, New York: Munson-Williams-Proctor Institute.

Landscape art in America was based, in part, on travel books illustrated with prints.
As a leading English topographical artist, Bartlett traveled throughout the Western
world, painting carefully in watercolor scenes which caught his eye. In 1850 he
wrote for *Sharpe's London Magazine* that the study of topography offers the advantage
"that it makes every country, also every market-town ... an object of interest,
affords a plea for excellent excursions by rail or road, and induces a healthy habit
of taking periodical journeys for change of air and scene." Since the drawing was
intended to be reproduced as an aquatint for Willis's *American Scenery*, Bartlett added
descriptive notations across the sheet to aid accurate translation of the scene to
the other medium. There are several different stories attached to the origins of
the name "Anthony's Nose," but one amusing version tells of a mate under
the command of a ship's captain named Anthony Hogan who noticed a similarity
in size and shape between the mountain and the captain's nose. "What?" said
the captain. "Does that look like my nose? Call it then, if you please, Anthony's
Nose."

31. A. Van Zandt

The Hudson River North, from West Point

Wash heightened with white, on paper, 19½ x 69 inches. Signed (lower
left): "A. Van Zandt." Yonkers, New York: Hudson River Museum,
purchase William Collins Memorial Fund, 1968.

"The dark pile of old Cro' Nest, guarding the northern side of West Point, rises
fourteen hundred and eighteen feet, one of the noblest mountains of the Highlands.
Beyond it, the Storm King and Mount Taurus are the northern portals of the pass,

with Pollopell's Island, rocky and tree-clad, lying in the river between, and farther on the distant hazy shores enclosing Newburg Bay. These buttresses of the northern entrance solidly rise as protectors of the pass into the valley:

> 'Mountains that like giants stand
> To sentinel enchanted land.' "

Joel Cook in volume 2 of *America, Picturesque and Descriptive*, published in 1900, identifies the scene painted by A. Van Zandt. Although no information has been found on this artist, the painting reveals a spontaneous and adroit handling of the watercolor medium, painted directly from nature. The monochromatic palette achieves a photographic effect, while an aerial perspective is created through the subtle lightening and graying of tone in the background forms, suggesting an artist who has received some formal art instruction.

32. John Frederick Kensett (1816-1872)
View near Cozzens Hotel from West Point

Oil on canvas, 20 x 34 inches. Initialed and dated (lower center): "J.F.K. '63." New York: Courtesy of the New-York Historical Society.

This painting was referred to as *Hudson River, from Fort Putnam* by Henry Tuckerman, who described it and other Kensett views as "memorable illustrations of the scope and character of our natural landscape. ... Kensett does not merely imitate, or emphasize, or reflect nature—he interprets her—which we take to be the legitimate holy task of the scenic limner. ... The calm sweetness of Kensett's best efforts, the conscientiousness with which he preserves local diversities—the evenness of manner, the patience in detail, the harmonious tone—all are traceable to the artist's feeling and innate disposition, as well as to his skill. " An almost impressionistic urge is seen in the suffused atmospheric light which is subtly reflected in the waters of the Hudson.

33. David Johnson (1827-1908)
West Point from Fort Putnam

Oil on canvas, 42½ x 64¼ inches. Signed and dated (lower right): "David Johnson / 1867." Private collection.

An intense realism executed with a firmly drawn hand characterizes the early style of David Johnson. Although he took frequent sketching trips into New England, New Jersey, and upstate New York, Johnson made New York City home base throughout his lifetime. His professional training consisted of a few lessons with the landscape artist Jasper F. Cropsey in 1852. The historic picturesqueness associated with Fort Putnam appealed, during the nineteenth century, to America's poets and landscape artists. The poet and author William Cullen Bryant, one of the leading supporters of the Hudson River School, wrote in 1830 in *The American Landscape:* "Fort Putnam was formerly the principal fortress ... erected during the war of Independence, for the defence of the passes of the Hudson and the Highlands, at West Point. ... [Located] on the western bank of the Hudson, where the river, deviating from the usual majestic directness of its course, bends suddenly around that bold and lofty promontory, [the site] was selected ... from the natural strength of its position. ... The preservation of this post was the cardinal point in the plan of more than one eventful campaign, and its surrender to the enemy was the great object of Arnold's treason. It was called at that time, and with justice, the Gibraltar of North of America. ... Immediately beneath you, you perceive the plain of West Point, surrounded by the buildings of the national Military Academy, and gay with the tents of the encamped cadets. ... "

·34. Pierre Charles L'Enfant (1754-1825)
West Point

Watercolor and ink on paper, 10%₁₆ x 56¾ inches. Washington, D.C.: Library of Congress.

L'Enfant, later distinguished as the designer of the street plans for the City of Washington, D.C., came to America from Paris as a volunteer soldier for United States independence when he was twenty-three years old. Two years after his arrival on our shores he was wounded in an advance on Savannah, Georgia, became a prisoner in Charleston, and was finally exchanged in January 1782. The drawing, which depicts the encampment of the Revolutionary army in the Highlands, was probably executed from life after this exchange. West Point is located in the center, middle ground. At its right sits Constitution Island, which Ben Frazier noted "shows the original fortification of the entire area. Fort Constitution was built in 1775 because it could fire straight down the river [flowing to the left in the picture] and this is where the chain was stretched from 1778 until the end of the war. The reasons for this are the two right angle turns, one around West Point, the other around Constitution Island, which were very difficult for a sailing ship to negotiate. It is also very deep and narrow, with strong currents; and the winds due to the mountains are apt to be gusty. The Americans chose (this) easiest spot to hang onto the mountain range so the British could not split the colonies into two pieces ... and so communications with New England and the South could be maintained. ... "

35. Anonymous nineteenth-century American artist
Hudson River Scene

Keg top, oil on wood, 15¾ inches (circular). Williamsburg, Virginia: Abby Aldrich Rockefeller Folk Art Collection.

The folk artist–craftsman working about 1830 has schematically suggested the bends in the river, possibly looking north from the Highlands, West Point area. The scene, decoration for the top of a keg, repeats the curves of the mountains and the clustered foliage in a highly imaginative manner. Observations made by the visiting Scandinavian writer, Fredrika Bremer, on October 7, 1849, catch the spirit of the painting: "The river was full of life. ... On the shores glistened white country-houses and small farms. I observed a great variety in the style of building ... the prevailing color being white. Many private houses, however, were of a soft gray or a sepia tint."

36. Thomas Chambers (1808-after 1866)
View from West Point

Oil on canvas, 18 x 24 inches. Cooperstown, New York: New York State Historical Association.

Although Chambers relied upon William H. Bartlett's engraving of the scene, as published in Willis's *American Scenery*, he is somewhat more fanciful and emphatic in his use of color and repetition of shapes. Willis's text accompanying the Bartlett illustration boasted that "of the river scenery of America, the Hudson, at West Point, is doubtless the boldest and most beautiful. This powerful river writhes through the highlands in abrupt curves, reminding one, when the tide runs strongly down, of Laocoön in the enlacing folds of the serpent. The different spurs of mountain ranges which meet here, abut upon the river in bold precipices from five to fifteen hundred feet from the water's edge. . . . Back from the bluff of West Point extends a natural platform. . . . This is the site of the Military Academy, and a splendid natural parade. . . . forward, toward the river, on the western edge, stands a spacious hotel, from the verandahs of which the traveller gets a view through the highlands, that he remembers till he dies." Willis's words and Bartlett's view north past Anthony's Nose and Storm King are probably the most memorable of countless similar reactions to the superb location.

37. Samuel Lancaster Gerry (1813-1891)
West Point, Hudson River

Oil on canvas, 23½ x 28¼ inches. Private collection.

"On the extreme edge of the summit, overlooking the river, stands a marble shaft, pointing like a bright finger to glory, the tomb of the soldier and patriot Kosciusko." Nathaniel P. Willis's description of the monument to the Lithuanian-born and Polish-educated Thaddeus Kosciusko (1746–1817) was published in *American Scenery*, illustrated by W. H. Bartlett and engraved by R. Young for the publisher George Virtue, London, in 1837. The young Kosciusko supervised the building of the defenses at West Point two years after his appointment, in 1776, by General Washington as engineer in the Revolutionary Army with the rank of colonel. In 1794 he served as generalissimo of the Polish army; and in 1797–1798 he revisited America. Twelve years after his death the monument "was erected by the cadets of West Point," noted a nineteenth-century *Guide to the Hudson River,* "as a tribute of respect for his many private virtues and acknowledged worth." The Gerry painting of 1858 was based on the Bartlett composition. Gerry spent most of his life in Boston, his birthplace, although he toured Europe for three years before establishing a studio at home in 1840. Eighteen years later he was made President of the Boston Art Club. The painting shows an interest in complete finish and attention to detail and reveals a stronger color sense than the Bartlett composition.

38. John Frederick Kensett (1816-1872)
View of Storm King from Fort Putnam

Oil on canvas, 32 x 48 inches. Initialed and dated (lower right): "JF.K. 57." New York: The Metropolitan Museum of Art, gift of Mr. H. D. Babcock in memory of S. D. Babcock, 1907.

Kensett's poetry was based upon carefully delineated forms and subtle handling of color. He executed detailed studies directly from nature, usually during his summer trips, then selected and combined them into large paintings during the winters. The view north toward Storm King from Fort Putnam (the ruins of which are shown in the extreme right foreground opposite Mount Taurus) was likely the result of studies made during an 1853 summer's trip touring West Point and upstate New York. According to the architect Thomas Kelah Wharton (see plate 6) in an unpublished diary written between 1830 and 1834, "The Highlands are conspicuous more for their simple grandeur of their grouping and their majesty of outline than from their height, the highest not exceeding 1600 or 1700 feet—ragged peaks, and barren rocky pyramids. ... Stupendous masses of rock shooting upward far above us into the blue heavens, and clothed with the richest foliage—ridge after ridge and one steep precipice after another."

39. Anonymous nineteenth-century American artist
View of West Point from above Washington Valley

Oil on canvas, ca. 14½ x 20 inches (oval). Boston: Courtesy of the Museum of Fine Arts, M. and M. Karolik Collection.

In this view of West Point from above Washington Valley the artist has achieved subtle luminist colorations in the cloudy sky which is reflected in the sheetlike water. Figures riding in the sailboats add scale to the painting while lending a genre interest, although the boats are naïvely shown floating upon, rather than in, the water. Roe's Hotel (shown in the center of the painting) was the West Point Hotel which Ben Frazier comments was "built in 1829 on the Parade ground, and demolished around the 1930s. There were all kinds of famous initials which the cadets' fiancées had scratched with their diamond rings into the window panes of the hotel; however, as far as I know, nobody has bothered to save any of it." The M. and M. Karolik Catalogue, published by the Boston Museum of Fine Arts in 1949, very tentatively suggests an attribution to either David Johnson or R. G. L. Leonori.

40. John Ferguson Weir (1841-1926)
View of the Highlands from West Point

Oil on canvas, 19 x 33 inches. Signed and dated (lower right): "J. F. Weir / 1862." New York: Courtesy of the New-York Historical Society.

The son of the West Point drawing master Robert Weir, John Ferguson Weir studied painting in his father's studio after completing his early education with the military instructors at West Point. At the age of twenty he established a studio in New York City, and in 1868, six years after completing this picture, he embarked on the grand tour of the European art capitals. The following year Weir was elected Director of the Yale School of Fine Arts in New Haven. He wrote the official report and acted as a Judge on the Fine Arts for the 1876 Centennial Exposition held in Philadelphia. The Highlands drew superlatives from the English visitor Mrs. Frances Trollope in the late 1820s: "The beauty of this scenery can only be conceived when it is seen. One might fancy that these capricious masses, with all their countless varieties of light and shade, were thrown together to shew how passing lovely rocks, and woods, and water could be. Sometimes a lofty peak shoots suddenly up into the heavens, shewing in bold relief against the sky; and then a deep ravine sinks in solemn shadow, and draws the imagination into its leafy recesses. For several miles the river appears to form a succession of lakes; you are often enclosed on all sides by rocks rising directly from the very edge of the stream, and then you turn a point, the river widens, and again woods, lawns, and villages are reflected on its bosom."

41. David Johnson (1827-1908)
Off Constitution Island

Oil on canvas, 15 x 26 inches. Signed and dated (verso): "David Johnson 1872." New York: Photo courtesy Chapellier Galleries.

According to Lossing, "between Cold Spring and West Point lies a huge rocky island, now connected to the main by a reedy marsh ... called by the Dutch navigators Martelaer's Island, and the reach in the river between it and the Storm King, Martelaer's Rack, or Martyr's Reach [signifying] contending and struggling, as vessels coming up the river with a fair wind would frequently find themselves, immediately after passing the point of the island into this reach, struggling with the wind right ahead. The Americans fortified this island very early in the old war for independence. The chief military work was called Fort Constitution (an American reminder that they were fighting for their rights under the British Constitution), and the island has ever since been known as Constitution Island." Johnson has adopted a close-up point of view of the island, maintaining a carefully detailed realism and luminosity which gently envelops the scene.

42. David Johnson (1827-1908)
Foundry at Cold Spring

Oil on canvas, 19¼ x 27¼ inches. Private collection.

Lossing notes that the West Point Foundry, located on the eastern bank of the Hudson at the southern end of Cold Spring, "was established in 1817, by an association organized for the chief purpose of manufacturing heavy iron ordnance, under a contract with the government. . . . The works then consisted of a moulding house; a gun factory; three cupolas and three air furnaces; two boring mills; three blacksmiths' shops; a trip-hammer weighing eight tons for heavy wrought iron-work; a turning shop; a boiler shop; and several other buildings used for various purposes. . . . The establishment is conducted by Robert P. Parrott, Esq., formerly a captain of Ordnance in the United States Army, and the inventor of the celebrated 'Parrott gun', so extensively used . . . during the late Civil War. These, with appropriate projectiles, were manufactured in great numbers at the West Point Foundry, during the war, from 1861 to 1865." Additions made on the little Catholic church, shown at the right of the foundry dock, date the painting after 1867.

43. Régis François Gignoux (1816-1882)
On the Upper Hudson

Oil on canvas, 18 x 34 inches. Signed and dated (lower left): "R. Gignoux / 1862." New York: Courtesy of Sloan & Roman, Inc., Gallery.

Régis Gignoux was trained at academies in Lyons, his birthplace, and Paris. His teacher Paul Delaroche, a renowned French historical painter, impressed by Gignoux's landscape drawings, encouraged him to specialize as a landscapist. Gignoux quickly established himself as a painter of winter landscapes when he came to America in 1840. His versatility and ability as an artist were noted by the art historian Henry T. Tuckerman: "Gignoux has made a study of American scenery under every aspect; he has observed nature in the New World with reference to the modifying influence of the seasons; and in many instances has proved singularly felicitous in his true rendering of atmosphere, sky and vegetation, as they are changed in tone, color, and effect by vernal, summer, autumnal, and wintry agencies. He ... carries into his observation of nature no morbid feeling; but catches her pleasantest language, and delights in reproducing her salient effects." Gignoux lived in Brooklyn but spent summers in the countryside sketching from nature. He spent the last twelve years of his life back in France. This autumnal painting looks at the Highlands just north of West Point.

44. Anonymous nineteenth-century American artist
Untitled *(Storm King)*

Oil on canvas, 18 x 25 inches. Private collection.

Views of Storm King caught the imagination of folk painters as firmly as they had that of professionally trained artists. In this example the artist has simply and directly repeated jagged shapes to create a strong element of design. The scene was undoubtedly copied from printed sources rather than observed directly from nature. "The Storm King," wrote Lossing in *The Hudson*, "seen from the middle of the river abreast its eastern center, is almost semi-circular in form, and gave to the minds of the utilitarian Dutch skippers who navigated the Hudson early, the idea of a huge lump of butter, and they named it Boter Berg, or Butter Hill. It had borne that name (called Klinkerberg previously by Hendrick Hudson on account of its broken and glistening rock) ... when Mr. Willis successfully appealed to the good taste of the public by giving it the more appropriate and poetic title of Storm King."

45. Thomas Prichard Rossiter (1818-1871)
A Pic-Nic on the Hudson

Oil on canvas, 29 x 45 inches. Signed (lower left of center): "T. P. Rossiter." 1863. Cold Spring, New York: Butterfield Memorial Library.

This colorful group portrait of an outing on Constitution Island, in the Hudson south of Cold Spring, is a charming if self-conscious period piece that recalls more jovial Dutch seventeenth-century corporation portraits. The *Pic-Nic* portrays a group of friends and neighbors of the artist, who stands at the far left. The others shown include (from the left): Gen. Truman Seymour (seated), Col. Richard Kemble, Professor Robert Weir (on rock), Miss Louisa Weir, Miss Cora Weir, Lt. Julian James (with cap, standing between unidentified man and woman), unidentified young woman (with hat on back), Gen. Gouverneur Kemble Warren (seated on ground), Mrs. George Pope Morris, George Pope Morris (white beard), Miss Isabel Sloan, Mrs. Frederick P. James (later Mrs. Daniel Butterfield), Capt. Frederick P. James, Jr., Frederick P. James, Mrs. Robert P. Parrott, Gouverneur Kemble (seated, without hat), and Robert P. Parrott, who developed the famous Parrott rifle gun. The picture is a record both of a pleasant moment and of a favorite tourist spot near West Point, where travelers and day trippers resorted in large numbers via steamer during the nineteenth century. The painting is unusual in Rossiter's work for its rich coloring, solid brushwork, and nicely developed landscape interest. Born in Connecticut and trained as a portrait painter, Rossiter opened up studios in New York City in 1839, 1846, and again in 1856. Four years later he moved to a house and studio of his own design at Cold Spring-on-the-Hudson where he spent his remaining years. He was an intimate of such Hudson River School painters as Kensett and Casilear.

46. Anonymous nineteenth-century American artist
Outing on the Hudson

Oil on cardboard, 19 x 24 inches. Williamsburg, Virginia: Abby Aldrich Rockefeller Folk Art Collection.

The folk artist often celebrated nature in a simple and direct way, translating such shapes as mountains into repetitive patterns, and foliage into decorative accents. In this painting the figures loom large with relation to the landscape; there is not the emphasis upon nor the glorification of nature. Indeed, nature serves only as an ornamental backdrop. The artist has employed bright colors and crisp, clean outlines in a highly imaginative way. Perhaps the mountains represented in the background of the painting are the Catskills, viewed from the Hudson's eastern shores. Observations on the area by Joel Cook in *America, Picturesque and Descriptive* fit the character of the scene: "The Hudson stretches a silvery streak across the picture. . . . Its distant diminutive steamboats slowly move. . . . The perpendicular mountain wall brings the valley almost beneath one's feet, the buildings look like children's toy houses, [and] the trees like dwarfed bushes. . . . "

47. William Guy Wall (1792-after 1864)
View near Fishkill

Watercolor on paper, 14 x 21⅛ inches. New York: Courtesy of the New-York Historical Society.

Henry Bailey in his *Local Tales and Historical Sketches* wrote, "The first settlement of the original town of Fishkill dates back as far as 1682. Prior to that [the land] was purchased [from the Wappinger Indians] by Francis Rombout, a distinguished merchant of New York City, and Gulyne Ver Planke for . . . one hun royales, one hun powder . . . white wampum . . . bars of lead . . . black wampum . . . tobacco boxes . . . guns . . . blankets. Rombout's only daughter, Catherine [who was heir to the patent], married . . . Roger Brett, and . . . in the year 1710, located on the patent where the Teller Mansion now stands, and they gave her the title of Madam Brett." This is the original watercolor for plate 17 of the *Hudson River Portfolio*. It looks upstream toward the Catskills in the far distance.

48. Thomas Doughty (1793-1856)
View of Highlands from Newburgh, New York

Oil on canvas, 20½ x 26½ inches. Signed (lower right): "T. Doughty." Private collection.

Most early-nineteenth-century American artists approached landscape as an occasional thing, or as a backdrop for portraits and story illustrations. Doughty, however, pioneered the painting of landscapes for their own sake, and in this sense he may be considered one of the founders of the Hudson River School of landscape artists. He had been an established leather currier in his home town of Philadelphia before turning to painting as a vocation prior to his twenty-seventh birthday. The only art instruction he had received was in India-ink drawing; his experience with oils was entirely self-taught. Doughty's first commissions were for "estate portraits," then for landscapes drawn from nature. He lived in Philadelphia and Boston during the 1820s and 1830s, traveling widely in the northeast and occasionally to England in search of subjects and commissions. New York City became his permanent home in 1840 following a short residence on the Hudson at Newburgh, New York. The scene was possibly painted from this home, looking downstream toward the Highlands. Doughty's peaceful depiction of nature is notable for the diffuse and misty quality of its lighting, which here, as almost always in his work, imparts a delightful mood of calm and idyllic reverie.

49. Robert Havell, Jr. (1793-1878)
West Point from Fort Putnam

Oil on canvas, 28 x 40 inches. New York: Courtesy of Kennedy Galleries, Inc.

Havell always thought of himself as an engraver, although he was proficient in the media of watercolor and oil. His hobby was to go on sketching trips with his family, then later translate his sketches into oils; however, few of these oil paintings were sold during Havell's lifetime. In 1848 he published an engraving of *West Point from Fort Putnam* based on this descriptively panoramic view, with the ruins of Fort Putnam shown above the plain of West Point on a prominent hill six hundred feet high. In a recent interview Mr. Ben Frazier, an expert on the West Point area, identified Roe's Hotel (shown in the painting in the foreground center), Constitution Island (shown on the right half of the middle ground), and Bannerman's Island (center background), called Pollepel, or Drunk's Island by the Dutch. Literally *pollepel* meant wooden spoon: "When people were real drunks they tied a great big wooden spoon onto them—a *pollepel*. The great mystery of how this island got its name, as far as anybody knows, is that in the Dutch days, when they had a real drunk aboard ship, they would put him off onto this island to let him sober up, then picked him up on the return trip."

50. Frederic A. Chapman (1818-1891)

Washington's Headquarters at Newburgh, New York

Oil on canvas, 36 x 60 inches. Signed and dated (lower left): "F. A. Chapman / 1865." New York: Union Club.

Benjamin Lossing described the backdrop of this picture: "The natural scenery around Newburgh has an aspect of mingled grandeur and beauty, peculiar and unrivalled. ... [To the south lie] the group of the Highlands, through which the Hudson flows. These are reflected in a broad and beautiful bay, at all times animated with a variety of water-craft. ... Its broad surface is broken by only a solitary rock island." The Hasbrouck house, which George Washington occupied from August 4, 1782, until August 18, 1783, was situated on the western banks of the Hudson at Newburgh. Artists delighted in drawing and painting this historic dwelling, often using as a model the Bartlett print published in *American Scenery*. Chapman was a Connecticut-born historical, landscape, and portrait painter. In August of 1850 he lived in New York City; then he established himself in Brooklyn until after 1861. He served as the first and only secretary and treasurer of the Brooklyn Art Society from 1859 through January 1861.

51. Edmund C. Coates (active 1837-1857)

Washington's Headquarters at Newburgh

Oil on canvas, 24 x 32¼ inches. Signed and dated (lower center): "E. C. Coates N.Y. / 1867." New York: Courtesy of Kennedy Galleries, Inc.

Coate's view of the house that served as Washington's headquarters looks south toward Storm King Mountain from the northern end of the building. A diary entry dated December 5, 1782, written by a French officer, the Marquis de Chastellux, describes the headquarters as consisting of "a single house, neither vast nor commodious, which is built in the Dutch fashion. The largest room in it (which was the proprietor's parlour for his family, and which General Washington has converted into his dining room) is in truth tolerably spacious, but it has seven doors and only one window. The chimney, or rather the chimney back, is against the wall; so that there is in fact but one vent for the smoke, and the fire is in the room itself.

"I found the company assembled in a small room which served by way of a parlour. At nine supper was served, and when the hour of bed-time came, I found that the chamber to which the General conducted me was the very parlour I speak of, wherein he made them place a camp bed. ... " Little is known about Coates other than that he was active in the New York region from 1837 to 1857 and that he also executed Italian scenes, possibly derived from prints.

52. Samuel Colman (1832-1920)
Storm King on the Hudson

Oil on canvas, 31¾ x 59¼ inches. Signed and dated (lower right): "S. Colman '66." Collection of Fine Arts, Smithsonian Institution.

> ...when the Storm King smites his thunderous gong
> Thy hills reply from many a bellowing wave;
> And when with smiles the sun o'erlooks their brow,
> He sees no stream more beautiful than thou."

Samuel Colman's painting of Storm King could illustrate this enthusiastic poetry of an unknown nineteenth-century poet published in the *Knickerbocker Magazine* and quoted in the *Hudson River Birthday and Anniversary Book*. Lake George, the White Mountains, and the Hudson River provided the basic material for Colman's paintings during the ten years before his 1860 trip to Europe, after which he strove for more exotic subjects. The lucid handling of paint suggests the approach of an artist working in watercolor, a medium Colman preferred during the last twelve years of his life. The pioneer American art historian S. G. W. Benjamin noted in *Our American Artists*, published in 1879: "The style of Mr. Colman, both in oil and watercolors has been very effective; he has painted some very strong effects of light and shade, and his coloring has a brilliance that is so harmonious as to influence one like a strain of music."

53. Anonymous (after William Guy Wall, 1792-after 1864)
View of Highlands Looking South from Newburgh Bay

Watercolor on paper, 13¾ x 22⁷⁄₁₆ inches. New York: Courtesy of the New-York Historical Society.

"The Highlands are here moulded in all manner of heights and hollows; sometimes reaching up abruptly to twelve or fifteen hundred feet, and again stretching away in long gorges and gentle declivities." Susan Warner's description of the Highlands is analogous to the composition; this view is a copy after an unlocated original watercolor by Wall. The subject, however, was not included in the *Hudson River Portfolio* although probably intended for inclusion. The format relates to plate 18, *View near Fort Montgomery,* in the open foreground punctuated by a perspectivally rendered raft and in the background framed by mountains descending toward the river in the center and overlapping another mountain in the very center background. This painting shows a labored and dry handling of textures rather than the fluid and dexterous brushwork found in the trees, rocks, and water painted by Wall.

54. William Guy Wall (1792-after 1864)
View on the Hudson River

Watercolor and mixed media on paper, 14⅞ x 19¾ inches. New York: The Metropolitan Museum of Art, The Edward W. C. Arnold Collection of New York Prints, Maps and Pictures.

In this example, three-dimensional forms emerge from Wall's sensitivity to light and shadows, heightened by the free use of washes and the beautifully rendered details. The greater breadth and luminosity suggest a date later than the watercolors painted for the *Hudson River Portfolio.* Possibly it was executed while Wall was living in Newburgh, New York, during his second visit to America from Dublin around 1856 to 1862. This may have been among the paintings noted by the Newburgh *Daily News* for April 14, 1857: "Mr. Wall has had some of his finest pictures on exhibition at his rooms here." Discouraged by advancing age and growing competition, Wall returned to Dublin in 1862, having filled a vital early role in the development of American landscape painting.

55. Clinton W. Clapp (1831-1915)
Marlborough from New Hamburg

Oil on canvas, 12 x 15 inches. Private collection.

Among the many self-trained amateur or "folk" painters who worked in the Hudson Valley was Clinton Clapp. He was born and raised in the Town of Wappinger; in 1845 he left to study mechanical engineering at New York University and the City Mechanical Institute. When he returned in 1852, he became president of a bicycle-wheel manufacturing company and the local historian for Poughkeepsie papers. He also contributed a chapter on the Town of Wappinger to Hasbrouck's *History of Dutchess County.* The creation of colored-chalk pictures for Sunday-school classes encouraged him to try a permanent medium, and between 1883 and 1887 he executed all his oil paintings. Clapp sailed his steam-powered yacht down Wappinger's Creek to its mouth, where the Hudson fronts New Hamburg. From this point he was afforded a fine view of Marlborough, the center of the local raspberry industry, which supplied New York daily via steamboat with berries during the season.

56. James McDougal Hart (1828-1901)
Picnic on the Hudson

Oil on canvas, 33⅝ x 56 inches (oval). Signed and dated (lower left): "James M. Hart / 1854." Brooklyn, New York: The Brooklyn Museum.

James Hart arrived in America from Scotland in 1831 with his family, which included an older brother William, also a painter. He quickly went beyond the sign-painting and carriage-making apprenticeships in Albany and Troy and in 1851 went to Düsseldorf, Germany, for formal artistic training. After reviewing some paintings sent home by Hart from Germany, an 1852 issue of the Albany *Evening Journal* reported that "while they are characterized by all that accuracy of drawing for which his pictures have ever been distinguished, still [they] show a wonderful increase of his ability to see and portray the poetry of nature." He returned to Albany in 1852 and stayed there until 1856, when he moved to New York City. The *Picnic* may have been painted near Spring Brook, about four miles south of Poughkeepsie, looking downriver toward Newburgh. "Here," records Lossing in *The Hudson*, "during the old war for independence, lived Theophilus Anthony, a blacksmith, farmer, miller, and staunch Whig who ... assisted in making a great chain ... that was stretched across the Hudson in the Highlands at Fort Montgomery, to prevent British ships of war ascending the river and carrying invading troops into the heart of the country." Hart has defined each species of tree and leaf, revealing a love for details drawn from nature. The figures add scale and poetic mood to the gently colored composition.

57. Thomas Doughty (1793-1856)
Autumn on the Hudson 1850

Oil on canvas, 34⅜ x 48½ inches. Washington, D.C.: Corcoran Gallery of Art.

In 1867 Tuckerman, the first important historian of the Hudson River School, wrote that Doughty " ... was one of the earliest American artists to make evident the charm of what is called the 'silvery tone,' and to reproduce with genuine emphasis and grace autumnal effects." His pictures often hark back to compositions by Claude Lorrain, whose works Doughty was exposed to in Europe and through prints circulated in America. Silvery tones here permeate the surely painted atmosphere. The brilliance of the warm autumnal colors prefigures the lively and often explosively colored paintings by Jasper F. Cropsey during the last three decades of the century. Doughty's ambition, expressed to a friend, was "to appeal to the eye and heart through the medium of canvas and color, by presenting to his fellow countrymen those beautiful scenes with which our country abounds." Surely this view looking downstream, possibly from the New Paltz area opposite Poughkeepsie, achieves Doughty's objectives.

58. Jim M. Evans (active *ca.* 1850-1870)
Poughkeepsie, New York

Oil on canvas, 29 x 43 inches. Signed (lower left): "J. M. Evans."
Cooperstown, New York: New York State Historical Association.

The popular tradition of city portraiture evolved from topographic landscapes of the type common in England and America in the eighteenth century, and continued in the nineteenth century as both a folk and academic art form. Jim Evans was a Poughkeepsie resident and was probably self-trained. In 1870 he painted this literal description of the town from nearby Lewisburgh. The courthouse (shown at the center background) is located between Main and Church streets, which run westerly to the river. The city lies upon an elevated plain; to the northeast rises College Hill, crowned by a Greek-style building housing the Poughkeepsie Military Academy. Call (Kaul) Rock, the high bluff that fronts the river at the foot of Church Street, offers superlative views up and down the river.

59. Jasper Francis Cropsey (1823-1900)
Upper Hudson

Oil on canvas, 20 x 34½ inches. Signed and dated (lower right): "J. F. Cropsey / 1871." Courtesy of Mrs. John Newington.

While the tradition of the faithful recording of nature continued in the 1870s and 1880s, Cropsey had begun to modify his faithful realism, adding a remarkable pervasive luminous glow. The horizontal composition is relieved by a group of trees at the left, a favorite device in Cropsey's later paintings, while the tranquil Hudson mirrors the setting sun in the center. Since the railroad ran along the eastern shores in 1871 and had cut off the bays with fill, the painting may represent the western side opposite Hyde Park, near the village of Esopus, where the Hudson River's "Long Reach" comes to an abrupt end—as Joel Cook notes in *America, Picturesque and Descriptive*—"in the bent and narrow pass, where the cliffs compress the channel and form the crooked strait known as Crom Elbow [*Krom Elleboge*, or Crooked Elbow], the Dutch and English words having the same meaning. Above, the western shore for a long distance is lined with apple orchards and vineyards, while the eastern bank for over thirty miles is a succession of villas interspersed with hamlets."

60. William Stanley Haseltine (1835-1900)
Near Hyde Park, Hudson River

Pencil and wash drawing on paper, 14⅝ x 21⅝ inches. Inscribed and dated (lower right): "Near Hyde Park—Hudson River / July 3ᵈ 1860." Boston: Courtesy of the Museum of Fine Arts, M. and M. Karolik Collection.

" ... here the misty summit of the distant Kaatskill begins to form the outline of the landscape; it is hardly possible to imagine anything more beautiful than this place." Mrs. Trollope's enthusiasm for Hyde Park was apparently shared by Haseltine, who caught the view from above the plain of Hyde Park looking northwest past Esopus Island toward the Catskills. Haseltine was well schooled in the art of drawing, studying first with Paul Weber in Philadelphia, then at Harvard University, and in 1855 in Düsseldorf, Germany. In 1858 he returned to New York, where he remained for several years. The last forty years of his life were spent at his palazzo in Rome, with intermittent trips to America. His conscientious observation of nature creates a crisp, true rendering of the scene, with the outline drawn first, then details of color and texture added.

61. Johann Hermann Carmiencke (1810-1867)
Hyde Park, New York

Oil on wood, 12 x 16 inches. Signed and inscribed (lower right of center): "JH Carmiencke / Hyde Park / N.Y." New York: Courtesy of Kennedy Galleries, Inc.

About four miles north of Poughkeepsie, along the eastern shore of the Hudson River, is Hyde Park, named in honor of Sir Edward Hyde, the governor of the province of New York from 1702 to 1708, by his private secretary Peter Faulconier. Time has kindly obscured the fact that Hyde was almost universally detested by his subjects. During the nineteenth century Hyde Park was noted for its unique sturgeon caviar and ice harvesting and storing industries, although in 1870 a visitor noted: "Hyde Park has one feature not often to be found in this country, namely good roads and plenty of shade. For a distance of ten miles there is a road, lined with tall maples, now, just turning crimson, which afford ample shade even from the noonday sun, and makes travel a delight instead of a bore." The German-born Carmiencke served as a painter to the Danish royal court at Copenhagen from 1846 to 1851, then left for New York, where he spent the last sixteen years of his life. His thorough academic training is evident in the dark, coherent palette and the preciseness of touch. The painting, which looks upriver, captures the changing character of the western shores, the cultivated fields on gently sloping banks, the craggy, precipitous bluffs, and the Catskills beyond.

62. George Inness (1825-1894)
Landscape

Oil on canvas, 11½ x 17½ inches. Signed and dated (lower right):
"G. Inness 1868." Private collection.

George Inness was born near Newburgh, New York, and raised in Newark, New Jersey. His interest in art led him away from his father's grocery business to study drawing under John Jesse Barker, a Newark artist and drawing master. While serving an apprenticeship to map engravers in New York City in 1841, Inness began painting. In 1846 he studied briefly with Régis Gignoux in Brooklyn. Inness made frequent study and painting trips to Europe, the first in 1847. As a result of these trips, he was strongly influenced by the French Barbizon landscapists, who had developed a broad *plein-air* style of realistic painting. Inness became a foremost exponent of their work in America and moved away from the minute techniques advocated by Durand and his followers. Inness established a studio in New York City in 1852, from which he moved with his family to Medfield, Massachusetts, outside Boston, in 1859. In 1864 they moved to New Jersey; three years later they moved to Brooklyn. By 1878 they had settled in Montclair, New Jersey. The scene of the painting is near Kingston, New York, on the Hudson's western shores. Lossing wrote, "The village of Kingston [is] ... situated upon a broad plain on the banks of Esopus Creek, with a fine range of the southern Katzbergs in the rear."

63. George Inness (1825-1894)
Landscape, Hudson Valley

Oil on canvas, 30 x 45 inches. Signed and dated (lower left): "G. Inness 1870." Cincinnati, Ohio: Cincinnati Art Museum.

The landscape depicts the Kingston area silhouetted against the Rhinebeck area to the east. "Rhinebeck is two miles from Rhinecliff Landing," Wallace Bruce notes in the 1873 edition of *The Hudson River by Daylight*, "and is one of the finest towns in Dutchess County. It was named, as some say, by combining two words—Beekman and Rhine. Others say that the word *beek* means cliff, and the town was so named from the resemblance of the cliffs to those of the Rhine." Inness often employed a student to lay out colors on the larger canvases, based upon his sketches. The subjects would then be outlined over the stained canvas in charcoal. The principal shadows were laid in thinly and transparently in black. Finally, Inness painted transparent glazes over opaque colors, achieving, as here, a rich surface and glowing tones that were the envy of many imitators.

64. Andrew W. Warren (active 1854-1861, died 1873)
Red Hook Point on the Hudson, opposite Kingston, New York

Oil on canvas, 15 x 27⅛ inches. Signed and dated (lower right): "A. Warren / 1860." New York: Courtesy of Schweitzer Gallery.

Warren was born on a cattle farm at Coventry, New York. Interested in art, he took lessons from the history, genre, and portrait painter Tompkins Harrison Matteson in Sherburne, New York. "Taking a fancy to marine subjects," according to Tuckerman in *American Artist Life*, Warren "shipped as cabin-boy on a vessel bound to South America, that he might see the sea in all its bearings." From 1858 to 1860 he lived in New York City and made frequent trips to Mount Desert Island, Maine. This horizontal waterscape refers in its arrangement back to English and Dutch models, but the colorful luminist shimmer of sky and water are an obvious attempt to emulate Turner. The village of Kingston, at the mouth of Rondout Creek, was one of the earliest Dutch settlements in this part of New York, dating back to 1614. The settlers originally called it Esopus, which means "the river," but the Indian name for the area had been At-kan-karten, "smooth land."

65.   Asher Brown Durand (1796-1886)
Hudson River Looking towards the Catskills

Oil on canvas, 46 x 62 inches. Signed (lower left, on stone): "A. B. Durand / 1847." Cooperstown, New York: New York State Historical Association.

Durand's fidelity to nature was based on a "poetical sympathy," to quote Tuckerman, and an engraver's consciousness of detail. In 1855 he wrote: "I refer you to Nature early, that you may receive your first impressions of beauty and sublimity, unmingled with the superstitions of Art . . . that you may learn to paint with intelligence and sincerity. . . . " His landscapes evoke a reverence for nature in their tranquil and harmonious aspect. The scene looks from the Rhinecliff area, on the eastern shores, toward the Catskills. The pastoral landscape established Durand's fame as an artist. Durand's careful delineations of spacial planes and the pervasive mellow light recall the works of Claude Lorrain and Dutch seventeenth-century landscapes, which Durand saw and copied when he toured the art salons and museums of Europe.

66.   Thomas Doughty (1793-1856)
Scene in the Catskills

Oil on canvas, 35½ x 28½ inches. Garrison-on-Hudson, New York: Collection of Boscobel.

Doughty has carefully organized the elements of water, trees, and mountains to make a well balanced composition. His style during the 1820s was marked by sharply delineated forms and even brushstrokes. The artist has softened the forms of nature and has clothed them in an alluring atmospheric haze. As the *Knickerbocker Magazine* from 1833 commented, Doughty "infuses into his pictures all that is quiet and lovely, romantic and beautiful in Nature." The location depicted has not been specifically identified.

67. Archibald Robertson (1765-1835)
Clermont, the Seat of Mrs. Livingston

Pen and ink drawing on paper, 9 x 11½ inches. Dated (lower right):
"14 September 1796." New York: Courtesy of the New-York Historical
Society.

On the eastern shore of the Hudson across from Saugerties is Clermont, the mansion
rebuilt by the widow of Robert R. Livingston (1718-1775) after British troops burnt
down the original house. Her son, Chancellor Robert R. Livingston, the associate
of Robert Fulton in his steamboat experiments, was born here. "The setting of
the house," wrote Helen Reynolds, " . . . is one of natural beauty. Placed upon
a bluff that literally overlooks the waters of the Hudson, with the full range of
the Catskills spread out on the opposite side of the river; with lawn and garden
near at hand; and, beyond, woods which screen the place completely from the
outer world." A drawing style based upon the formal demands of academic art,
as seen in the perspectival rendering of the house and the compositional enframe-
ment of the tree, characterizes the work of Archibald Robertson. He was trained
in his native Scotland and under Sir Joshua Reynolds and Benjamin West at the
Royal Academy, London. At the invitation of Dr. Samuel Bard and Chancellor
Livingston he came to New York in 1791. A letter of introduction to General George
Washington led to a friendship that resulted in Robertson painting, from life,
miniature portraits of both George and Martha Washington. Robertson was the
operator of a New York City drawing and art school, among the first in America,
and later he was associated with the American Academy of the Fine Arts, New
York's first official art organization.

68. William Guy Wall (1792-after 1864)
Esopus Creek, Saugerties, New York

Watercolor on paper, 8¾ x 12¼ inches. New York: Courtesy of the New-
York Historical Society.

The name Saugerties is a corruption of Zaeger's Kill, the Dutch for "sawyer's creek."
It refers to an early sawmill built here by one Peter Pietersen. Lossing wrote that
Saugerties lies "near the mouth of Esopus Creek, which comes flowing from the
south through a beautiful valley, and enters the Hudson here. Iron, papers, and
white-lead are manufactured there extensively. . . . A once picturesque fall or rapid,

around which a portion of the village is clustered, has been partially destroyed by a dam and unsightly bridge above it, yet some features of grandeur and beauty remain." Wall's version, which was not published in the *Hudson River Portfolio*, is an accurate and simply constructed reinterpretation of the scene.

69. James Bard (1815-1897)
Steamer "America"

Oil on canvas, 33 x 54 inches. Inscribed and dated (lower right): "Picture Drawn and Painted by James Bard 688 Washington St NY 1852." Albany, New York: Collection of the Albany Institute of History and Art.

At mid-century the steamboat was the most important and certainly the most impressive means of Hudson River travel. The marine historian-*cum*-painter James Bard recorded almost every steamer operating in or around New York, Long Island Sound, and the Hudson River. Born in New York City, James and his twin brother John were self-trained artists who mechanically attended to the minutest details with "absolute truthfulness of every part of a steamboat," according to their eulogist Samuel W. Stanton. The *America* was a side-wheel towboat, 212 feet long, navigating the Hudson from 1852 to 1896. In this typical Bard composition it is shown from the broadside, steaming ahead at full speed; the stippled water at the bow seemingly produces a bubbling effect ahead and astern. The background, which may be the Catskills, is incidental to the scene, serving rather to silhouette the steamer. The few figures, dressed in high silk hats and long black frock coats, stand awkwardly. Bard measured and reduced each part to an arbitrary scale selected for the particular steamer. The approved drawing was then transferred to canvas in his studio. As a means of advertising, his address was included with the signature on the front.

70. Jasper Francis Cropsey (1823-1900)
View of Catskills across Hudson

Oil on canvas, 12 x 20 inches. Signed and dated (lower right): "J. F. Cropsey 1877." Courtesy of Mrs. John C. Newington.

In *America, Picturesque and Descriptive*, Joel Cook relates an Indian tradition associated with the Catskills of the sort that appealed to Cole, Cropsey, and many other painters of the school: "Among these mountains was held the treasury of storms and sunshine for the Hudson, presided over by the spirit of an old Indian squaw who dwelt within the range. She kept the day and night imprisoned, letting out one at a time, and made new moons every month and hung them up in the sky, for they first appeared among these mountains, and then she cut up the old moons into stars. The great Manitou also employed her to manufacture thunder and clouds for the valley. Sometimes she wove the clouds out of cobwebs, gossamers and morning dew, and sent them off, flake by flake, floating in the air, to give light summer showers. ... " Although one of his English scenes was recognized for "Beauty" at the Centennial Exhibition of 1876 in Philadelphia, Cropsey's prominence began to fade at that time. In comparison with the personal vision of Homer Dodge Martin, the analytical realism of Thomas Eakins, and the broad handling of Winslow Homer, Cropsey's continuation of a detailed, romantic manner seemed out of date. Successes such as this picture suggest that critical fashion can be mistaken.

71. Thomas Cole (1801-1848)
Catskill Mountain House

Oil on canvas. Private collection.

Thomas Cole, "father" of the Hudson River School, was born in the north of England and was apprenticed at the age of fourteen to an engraver of calico designs before emigrating with his family to America in 1818. He lived and visited intermittently in Philadelphia, Ohio, and the West Indies before finding employment as a wood engraver in Philadelphia. He moved to New York City in 1825 and was soon recognized as a professional landscape painter in oils, one of the first such specialists in America. In the late summer of 1825 Cole took his first sketching tour up the Hudson River, and the following year he settled in Catskill. In succeeding years he lived there and at times in New York, and made several extended painting tours in England, France, and Italy. His pictures are characterized by dramatic intensity, romantic blending of light and dark, and a rich use of paint in delineating the details of nature. To Cole the Catskills, "although not broken into abrupt angles like the most picturesque mountains of Italy, have varied, undulating, and exceedingly beautiful outlines—they heave from the valley of the Hudson like the subsiding billows of the ocean after a storm." The Catskill Mountain House, famous in its day as a luxurious scenic retreat, was a constant resort for landscape artists and those absorbed by the dramatic beauties of nature available there. Nathaniel P. Willis, the mid-century poet laureate of the Hudson Valley, exclaimed that its location was "too near heaven."

72. Anonymous (after William Henry Bartlett, 1809-1854)
Catskill Mountain House

Oil on canvas, 16¼ x 22¾ inches. New York: Dr. Roland Van Zandt; photo courtesy of the Rutgers University Press; photographer Geoffrey Clements.

The aquatints published in N. P. Willis's *American Scenery*, adapted from watercolors executed by William H. Bartlett, were probably the most important graphic source for numerous folk artists working in America before the advent of Currier and Ives. This painting is after *The Two Lakes and the Mountain House on the Catskills*, drawn by Bartlett and engraved by J. C. Bentley in 1838, facing page 105 in the first volume of Willis's work. "From the Mountain-House," observed Willis, "the busy and all-glorious Hudson is seen winding half its silver length—towns, villas, and white spires, sparkling on the shores, and snowy sails and gaily-painted steamers, specking its bosom. It is a constant diorama of the most lively beauty. ..." The painting would have been done sometime after the publication of the book in 1840. It appears to have been painted by an artist reasonably well trained in the oil technique who understood the shadings of atmospheric perspective. The composition conforms in almost every area to the Bartlett source, including the rolling cloud formation at the left background, which serves to effect a changing mood of nature. However, the painter has added more foliage to the trees at either side, creating a more decorative composition.

73. Thomas Cole (1801-1848)
Sunny Morning on the Hudson

Oil on panel, 18¾ x 25¼ inches. Signed (lower center): "Cole." Boston: Museum of Fine Arts, M. and M. Karolik Collection.

Cole's creative freedom and individuality are perfectly embodied in this expressive view from the Catskill foothills south toward the Hudson Highlands painted about 1827. Cole, following to some extent the model of Salvatore Rosa's and John Martin's agitated landscapes, incorporates weather-blasted tree trunks, trailing mists, impressive variations of mass, and theatrical lighting to give the scene an overwhelming sense of the presence of nature. Cole's close friend William Cullen Bryant wrote his impressions of this part of the valley at sunset: "The traveller, as he looks from the shore of the river to the broad woody sides of this mighty mountain range, turns his eye from a scene rich with cultivation . . . to one of primeval forest . . . a wide sylvan wilderness. . . . sometimes . . . [the Catskills] will gather a hood of gray vapours about their summits, which, in the last rays of the setting sun, will glow and light up like a crown of glory." This painting, early in Cole's work, is among his finest in its perfect appreciation of light and atmosphere.

74. Frederic Edwin Church (1826-1900)
Winter Landscape from Olana

Oil on paper, 11⅝ x 18⅛ inches. Hudson, New York: Olana.

Frederic Church, a native of Hartford, Connecticut, began studying art at the age of sixteen and worked with several local painters before moving to Catskill in 1844 to study with his idol, Thomas Cole. Church settled in New York in 1847 and set out on a distinguished career that included extensive sketching tours of North and South America, Europe, Egypt, and the Middle East. From Cole Church learned the cursive handling of paint that characterize his beautiful oil sketches such as this one. An English critic wrote perceptively that his landscapes were "great in conception, brilliant in execution, and with a finer perception of the beautiful, a more tender and elevated poetical feeling, than have been displayed in this branch of the art since Turner." This scene looks south and west from Church's estate, Olana, above Hudson, downriver toward the Catskills, and comes as close to perfection as anything done by American artists painting in the field.

75. Frederic Edwin Church (1826-1900)
Autumn View from Olana

Oil on canvas, 22 x 36 inches. Hudson, New York: Olana.

Frederic Church completed construction of his villa, Olana, in the hills above the town of Hudson in the early 1870s. "The site," according to H. W. French in the book *Art and Artists in Connecticut*, "is the result of a careful study of the river-banks, and commands so many views of varied beauty that all the glories of the Hudson may be said to circle it." The view included the Catskill Mountains, which a critic contemporary to this picture called "Nature's great Academy of landscape art. . . . For studies of our Northern skies, of atmosphere, phenomena of rugged mountain forms, of the manifestations of nature in the seasons, and for the accidental lights and shadows which give variety to a landscape, the Catskills are unrivalled. . . . "

76. Frederic Edwin Church (1826-1900)
Oil Sketch

Oil on canvas, 11⅛ x 15¼ inches. Dated (lower right): "June / 70."
New York: Cooper-Hewitt Museum of Decorative Arts and Design,
Smithsonian Institution, New York.

In another lovely and dramatic oil sketch looking south across the Hudson from Olana, Church captures the majestic breadth of the vista, as well as the accurate appearance of natural phenomena. Henry Tuckerman wrote that "Church chooses his subjects wisely; he works them out scientifically, and the consequence is, that there is a *realism* in his pictures. . . . He has combined, as far as possible in one view, the most characteristic forms and colors." Almost as if he held this sketch in his hand, William Cullen Bryant described the scene: "On the western bank of the river you can see a series of ridges covered with trees, rolling away, one after another, eight or ten miles; and beyond the farthest, lifting their wooded sides up into the clouds that have begun to settle on their peaks, are the famous mountains."

77. Frederic Edwin Church (1826-1900)
Oil Sketch: View of Catskills from Olana

Oil on canvas, 9¾ x 14 inches. Private collection.

A literal transcription of nature was promoted during the mid-nineteenth century by, among other things, scientific explorations and treatises—paramount being *On the Origin of Species* by Darwin and *Kosmos* by Baron Alexander von Humboldt. The latter book played an important role in the development of Romantic-realist painting within a grandiose framework and was especially influential to Church's work after 1850. *Kosmos* was published in Europe in 1845, and in New York, in four editions from 1850 to 1859. The essence of von Humboldt's art ideas is expressed in volume 2: "Landscape painting, though not simply an imitative art . . . requires for its development a large number of various and direct impressions, which . . . must be fertilized by the powers of the mind, in order to be given back to the senses of others as a free work of art." Church scientifically explored the changing aspects of sunlight and clouds, directly from nature. This oil sketch is one of hundreds painted from Olana, looking across the Hudson toward the Catskills, and catches that moment when the sunlight fans out behind a cloud.

78. William Louis Sonntag (1822-1900)
Untitled

Oil on canvas, 20 x 30 inches. Signed and dated (lower left): "W. L. Sonntag 1854." New York: Collection of Mr. and Mrs. I. David Orr.

Born near Pittsburgh, Sonntag worked as an artist in Cincinnati before an extended trip to Europe in the mid-1850s. He studied in Florence in 1856. The Florentine school's interest in the thick, tactile quality of paint and the luminous quality of atmospheric light is reflected in this transparently bright view of the Catskills from Columbia County, south of Troy. "The Catskill Mountains rise in all their glory," wrote Joel Cook in volume 2 of *America, Picturesque and Descriptive,* "spreading across the western horizon at a distance of eight to ten miles from the Hudson River. ... When the Dutch colonists came along, they sent expeditions into the mountains, searching for gold and silver, but chiefly found wildcats, causing them to be named the Kaatsbergs, and from this their present title has come to be, in time, the Kaatskills or the Catskills." The wildcats are not included, but Sonntag presents his view in highly romantic terms.

79. Thomas Cole (1801-1848)
Catskill Creek

Oil on canvas, 26 x 36 inches. New York: Courtesy of the New-York Historical Society.

The Romantic movement in England provided the impetus for Cole's style and subject, but it was the picturesque character of nature herself that most influenced him. In an 1835 *Essay on American Scenery* Cole set forth components he considered essential to the painting of landscapes. Mountains, as the "most conspicuous objects," took precedence. Water was listed next, "without which every landscape is defective. ... Like the eye in the human countenance, it is a most expressive feature. ... " The third element was the waterfall, "which in the same object at once presents ... [the] idea, of fixedness and motion. ... [It is] the voice of the landscape, for [it] strikes its own chords, and rocks and mountains re-echo in rich unison." In conclusion, Cole listed the American forest, with its great variety, and the sky: "The soul of all scenery, in it are the fountains of light, and shade, and color. Whatever expression the sky takes, the features of the landscape are affected in unison. ... " This painting of *Catskill Creek* exhibits in varying degrees each of the aforementioned elements, selected for their picturesqueness and grandeur. To Cole, "The Hudson for natural magnificence is unsurpassed. ... The lofty Catskills stand afar—the green hills gently rising from the flood, recede like steps by which we may ascend to a great temple, whose pillars are those everlasting hills, and whose dome is the boundless vault of heaven."

80. Albertus del Orient Browere (1814-1887)

Catskills

Oil on canvas, 34 x 44 inches. Signed and dated (lower left): "A. D. O. Browere / 1849." Brooklyn, New York: The Brooklyn Museum.

Born at Tarrytown, New York, Browere was the eldest son of and assistant to H. I. Browere (1790–1834), a creator of life masks from eminent Americans. Albertus Browere, however, pursued a painting career and in 1832 won a medal for the best original oil painting at the American Institute in New York. A competition first prize of one hundred dollars was awarded Browere in 1841 at New York's National Academy of Design, where he was a student. The quest for gold led him twice to California; first via Cape Horn in 1852 to 1856, next by mule over the Isthmus of Panama in 1858 to 1861. Browere moved to Catskill, New York, after his father died of cholera in 1834; he lived there, with the exception of his trips to California, the remainder of his life. "These Catskill Mountains," records Joel Cook in *America, Picturesque and Descriptive,* "were purchased from the Indians on July 8, 1678, by a company of Dutch and English gentlemen, who took their title at a solemn conclave held at the Stadt Huis in Albany, where the Indian chief Mahak-Neminea attended with six representatives of his tribe." In the careful recording of a summer's day along the Hudson opposite the Catskills, Browere knowingly differentiates species of trees and captures the textures of rocks and water.

81. Jasper Francis Cropsey (1823-1900)

Sunset, Hudson River

Oil on canvas, 12 x 20 inches. Signed and dated (lower left): "J. F. Cropsey / 1874." Courtesy of Mrs. John C. Newington.

The painting illustrates Cropsey's preoccupation with the ever-changing patterns of the sky, a theme which he discussed in the essay "Up Among the Clouds," written for an 1855 issue of *The Crayon*: "Of all the gifts of the Creator—few are more beautiful and less heeded, than the sky. ... Here we have first the canopy of blue; not opaque, hard and flat, as many artists conceive it and picture patrons accept it; but a luminous palpitating air, in which the eye can penetrate infinitely deep, and yet find depth." The Catskill Mountains, viewed from the Hudson River's western shores, are painted in the warm transparent tones which distinguish Cropsey's palette during the 1870s and 1880s.

82. William Guy Wall (1792-after 1864)
Hudson, New York

Watercolor on paper, 14 x 20¾ inches. New York: Courtesy of the New-York Historical Society.

This watercolor is a variant of the original composition for plate 13 of the *Hudson River Portfolio*, published by Wall in 1820, and relates compositionally to the original watercolor for *Fort Edward*, plate 10. The City of Hudson, on the eastern shore of the River, is depicted here in the middle ground with South Bay in the foreground and Albany and Troy in the distant background. Joel Cook in *America, Picturesque and Descriptive* mentions that Hudson is "a picturesque city sloping up Prospect Hill, which rises five hundred feet for a noble background, and it once had more ships and commerce than the city of New York. A colony of thrifty Quakers from New England started the settlement, which had many fishermen and whalers, and a large fleet of ships sailing to Europe and the Indies, fifteen loaded vessels having cleared from its wharves in a single day. But Napoleon's wars swept away its fleet and commerce, and the last ship was sold in 1845, so that its commercial greatness is only a tradition; although it has become a seat of considerable manufactures. ... Both sides of the river here are inhabited by the Dutch, and in fact theirs is the universal language of the Hudson from Kingston up to Albany."

83. Attributed to Albertus del Orient Browere (1814-1887)

Hudson River Landing

Oil on panel, 25⅝ x 45½ inches. Albany, New York: Collection of the Albany Institute of History and Art.

Utilitarian objects such as storekeeper's signs, weather vanes, buggies, and fireboards were often embellished by professional artists as a means of earning a livelihood. The Albany Institute of History and Art has attributed the painting to Browere on the basis of style; also he was known to have relied upon the painting of objects as well as genre and landscape subjects on canvas. This fireboard, used to cover fireplaces during the summers, is decorated with an everyday scene depicting commerce and packet sloops alongside a river landing. The location may be Catskill Landing, which is just above the mouth of Kauterskill Creek where it joins the Hudson.

84. Victor Gifford Audubon (1809-1860)

Landscape along the Hudson

Oil on canvas, 30 x 45½ inches. Signed and dated (lower left): "V. G. A. / 1842." Newark, New Jersey: Collection of the Newark Museum.

This careful delineation of the upper Hudson by Victor G. Audubon, a wildlife, landscape, and miniature painter, looks northerly toward Albany and Troy. Born in Louisville, Kentucky, Audubon learned painting techniques from his father, John James Audubon—America's outstanding painter of wildlife. Victor was engaged first as a clerk in a commercial house. In 1832, however, he left for England to act as secretary and agent on his father's behalf for the publication of *Birds of America*. During his seven-year stay in London Audubon executed some paintings and exhibited his works at the Royal Academy. The year following his return to America he and his bride established themselves in New York City. Audubon continued to work—with his younger brother John, and their father—to "collect, mount, and draw specimens, copy or color drawings," wrote their biographer Donald Peattie in *Audubon's America*, "and handle the affairs of what had now become a family business." After the elder Audubon's death in 1851, Victor and John pursued the recording of wildlife, Victor painting almost half the plates for *Quadrupeds of America.*

85. William Guy Wall (1792-after 1864)

View near Hudson Looking Southwest to Mount Merino and the Catskills

Watercolor on paper, 14 x 21 inches. New York: Courtesy of the New-York Historical Society.

This watercolor by Wall, executed on the spot, is characteristically lovely in its use of subtly gradated washes that recreate the effect of airiness and atmospheric perspective. However, it was not included with the twenty views published in the *Hudson River Portfolio.* Wall's eminence and sizable production as an artist was commented upon by William Dunlap, who in his *History of the Arts of Design,* published in 1834, wrote: "This gentleman has been indefatigable in studying American landscape, and his reputation stands deservedly high." Henry Hudson anchored his ship, the *Half Moon,* close to Mount Merino after encountering sandbars in the river. Mount Merino, a hill just south of Hudson, received its name from a sheep farm established there in the early nineteenth century.

86. William Hart (1823-1894)

Albany, New York, from Bath

Oil on canvas, 35½ x 48¼ inches. Signed and dated (lower right): "Wm Hart 1846." Albany, New York: Collection of the Albany Institute of History and Art.

Hart's career progressed from coach-maker's apprentice in Troy, New York, at age fifteen, to window-shade decorator, portrait painter, and landscape artist. He had accompanied his family from Scotland to Albany in 1831, and though he traveled extensively throughout the United States after 1840, he returned to Albany in 1847. In 1854 he moved to New York City, then to Brooklyn, where he became first president of the Brooklyn Academy of Design and founder and three-term president of the American Water Color Society. His portrait of Albany, handled in a manner descriptive yet poetic, depicts what Bryant described: "The city rises up from the western bank in irregular terraces, the culminating point being crowned with the capitol, embowered amid the foliage of old trees. ... Up and down the river, the city stretches far and wide. ... Above, the hills of the town rise, covered with fine old houses, and towering churches, and massive legislative halls, and huge caravansaries of hotels."

87. James McDougal Hart (1828-1901)
View from Hazelwood, Albany in the Distance

Oil on canvas, 24 x 27¾ inches. Signed (lower right): "J. M. Hart."
New London, Connecticut: Lyman Allyn Museum.

The highly finished, skillfully painted composition demonstrates within the bounds of academic painting conventions what Frances Trollope, in writing of this area from around 1827 to 1830 in *Domestic Manners of the Americans,* describes as "the liquid smoothness of the broad mirror that reflects the scene, and most of all the clear bright air through which you look at it." No record has been found listing a town of Hazelwood; the name may have referred to an estate located near Albany. Hart's painting career began at Albany, where he gained early recognition. The four years following his return from Düsseldorf in 1852 were spent here also. The December 1857 issue of the *Cosmopolitan Art Journal* took notice of a remark made in 1854 by "a connoisseur, writing from Albany, [who] thus refers to him: ' . . . His studies from nature evince industry and application, and his fancy sketches betray the touch of genius. . . . ' "

88. Asher Brown Durand (1796-1886)
View of Troy, New York

Oil on canvas, 24 x 40 inches. Albany, New York: Collection of the Albany Institute of History and Art.

This painting looks south from Mount Olympus, north of Troy, and presents, as the *Picturesque Tourist* celebrated: "an extensive and charming prospect . . . embracing a view of the valley of the Hudson for miles, the city of Albany. . . . a landscape presenting more beauty and a greater variety of scenery can hardly be imagined." From this elevation "the eye rests at once, as on a map spread out before it, on city and village teeming with life and activity—the broad Hudson rolling on in majesty to the ocean, . . . on woodlands and cultivated fields harmoniously blended—and on a western horizon of undulating highlands, which toward the south blend with the famed Catskill Mountains, lifting their giant heads to the clouds." Durand generally painted a place as one actually sees it. He was an early American practitioner of painting out of doors. Tuckerman observed that in Durand's work "the aerial perspective, the gradations of light, the tints of foliage, the slope of the mountains—in a word, the whole scenic expression is harmonious, grand, tender, and true."

89. William Guy Wall (1792-after 1864)
View of Cohoes, New York

Oil on panel, 20 x 29½ inches. Private collection.

This topographical view shows the manufacturing town of Cohoes, located on the western bank of the Hudson north of Albany, where the Mohawk joins the Hudson. "Its name," wrote Wallace Bruce in *The Hudson* (1907), "is of Indian origin and signifies 'the island at the falls,' " and it "has one of the finest water powers in the country." William Cullen Bryant observed: "Very much depends upon the season of the year as regards the impression which the falls make upon the mind of a traveller. In the dry season there is but little water, and hence the upper part of the falls appears like a series of grand rapids. ... The banks on either side are high and shaly, crowned generally with dark pines at the summit, and showing, below, a diagonal stratification, as if they had been upheaved." The painting lacks the sense of spontaneity usual in Wall's watercolors—the oil medium may account for this difference: the picture may have been drawn on the spot, from nature, and finished in the studio. This was normal procedure for artists who chose not to burden themselves in the field with heavy canvases and paraphernalia.

90. John William Casilear (1811-1893)
Upper Hudson River Landscape

Oil on canvas, 22 x 30 inches. Initialed (lower left): "J.W.C." New York: Courtesy of Kennedy Galleries, Inc.

Apprenticed as a bank-note engraver at sixteen years of age, Casilear worked first under Peter Maverick, then under Asher B. Durand. Durand and Thomas Cole taught Casilear the rudiments of landscape art, and what he had learned from them was reinforced by trips through Europe in 1840-1843 and 1857-1858. Although his interest focused on landscape painting, he also continued to work as a master engraver. New York City was Casilear's home throughout his lifetime, but he spent summers in Vermont and upstate New York. This composition, set somewhere upriver of Troy, recalls Durand's familiarity with the works of Claude in the graceful framing trees set into a dark foreground and in the establishment of subtly defined spacial planes. Dutch landscapes are also recalled by the cows at the left, which invoke a pastoral mood, echoing landscapes by Durand. Tuckerman noted that Casilear's "habit of dealing strictly with form gives a curious correctness to the details of his work ... indicative of a sincere feeling for truth, both executive and moral. ... "

91. Anonymous nineteenth-century American artist
View of the Hudson River near Troy

Oil on canvas, 36¼ x 54 inches. Albany, New York: Collection of the Albany Institute of History and Art.

The scene appears to be the upper Hudson River, possibly at Hudson, New York, where a public promenade was laid out along the banks of the river. Lossing in *The Hudson* mentions that "it is adorned with trees and shrubbery, and gravelled walks, and affords charming views up and down the river of the beautiful country westward, and the entire range of the Katzbergs, lying ten or twelve miles distant. In the north-west, the Helderberg range looms up beyond an agricultural district dotted with villages and farmhouses. . . . The country around Hudson is hilly and very picturesque. . . . " The imaginative treatment of bright color, dramatic clouds, and fancifully exaggerated reflections in the water suggests the picture may have been inspired by a print.

92. William Guy Wall (1792-after 1864)
Fort Edward

Watercolor on paper, 14 x 21 inches. New York: Courtesy of the New-York Historical Society.

Wall's original watercolor for plate 10 of the *Hudson River Portfolio* represents the bend of the Hudson River at Fort Edward, where it moves in a broad curve from west to south. Fort Edward, long an English frontier post, was the site where Israel Putnam, one of the American Revolutionary War heroes, first distinguished himself. He fought a fire over a powder shed, at great danger to his own life, until the fire was quenched and the post at Fort Edward saved. The shooting and scalping of Jane McCrea by Indians seeking bounties from the English for prisoners occurred near here. This atrocious murder of an attractive young woman rallied the locals to fight the English and contributed considerably to Gates' defeat of Burgoyne at nearby Saratoga.

93.   William Guy Wall (1792-after 1864)
Baker's Falls

Watercolor on paper, 14 x 21 inches. New York: Courtesy of the New-York Historical Society.

"Baker's Falls are about half-way between Sandy Hill and Fort Edward," recorded Lossing. "The river is about four hundred feet in width, and the entire descent of water, in the course of a mile, is between seventy and eighty feet. As at Glen's Falls, the course of the river is made irregular by huge masses of rocks, and it rushes in foaming cascades to the chasm below." Wall, following common watercolor practice, prepared his composition by drawing slight guide lines in pencil, over which he brushed graduated transparent color washes. The male figures are dressed in overcoats and top hats, characteristic Wall touches, summarily handled. This is the original watercolor for plate 8 of the *Hudson River Portfolio*.

94.   William Guy Wall (1792-after 1864)
View near Sandy Hill

Watercolor on paper, 13½ x 20½ inches. New York: Courtesy of the New-York Historical Society.

The Hudson makes a sweeping curve at the mill town of Hudson Falls, formerly the village of Sandy Hill, and changes its direction from a southerly to an easterly course. This watercolor was the original painting translated into an aquatint for plate 7 of the *Hudson River Portfolio*. Sandy Hill, incorporated in 1810, is on the eastern bank of the Hudson where in a space of half a mile the river falls more than seventy feet, making it a natural mill site.

95. William Guy Wall (1792-after 1864)
Glens Falls

Watercolor on paper, 14 x 20⅞ inches. New York: Courtesy of the New-York Historical Society.

"Perhaps you have heard of Glens-Falls," wrote Eliza S. Bowne to her mother in 1802; "they are said to exceed in *beauty* the Falls of *Niagara*. ... I never imagined anything so picturesque, sublime and beautiful as the scenery around this enchanting place. The rocks on the shores have exactly the appearance of elegant, magnificent ruins, they are entirely of *slate*, and seem piled in regular forms with shrubs and grass growing in between. ... " This watercolor is the original painting for plate 6 of the *Hudson River Portfolio*. Glens Falls provided in part the setting for James Fenimore Cooper's *Last of the Mohicans*. There Cooper described the river at the falls: "Sometimes it leaps, sometimes it tumbles; in one place 'tis white as snow, and in another 'tis green as grass; hereabouts it pitches into deep hollows that rumble and quake the earth; and thereaway it ripples and sings like a brook." Initials and names inscribed in the rock beds here led J. S. Buckingham to exclaim, "I scarcely remember visiting any place at all remarkable in this country, without finding every accessible space of wall or surface covered with names, initials, and dates of visitors ... as if the parties thought it a wonderful achievement to have journeyed so far from home!" Originally the village of Glens Falls had been known by the Indian name Kay-an-do-ros-sa and by the English names "The Corners," "Glenville," and "Pearl Village." In 1788, however, as payment of a debt of honor owed to Col. Johannes Glen of Schenectady by the Quaker leader and landowner Abraham Wing, the name was changed from Wings Falls to Glens Falls.

96. Henry Augustus Ferguson (1843/45-1911)
Glens Falls, New York

Oil on canvas, 15 x 26 inches. Signed and dated (lower right): "Henry A. Ferguson / 1882." Glens Falls, New York: Courtesy of the Crandall Library.

Ferguson was born and raised in Glens Falls but followed his artistic inclinations by moving to Albany to join his brother Hiram, a wood engraver. Shortly afterward he moved to New York, then traveled extensively throughout Mexico, South America (he crossed the Andes six times), Europe, and Africa. He returned to New York, where he maintained a painting and restoration studio until his death. The meticulous attention to detail of the picture reflects Ferguson's training in graphic techniques. His painting anticipates Cook's later observations on Glens Falls in *America, Picturesque and Descriptive*: "Along the north side of the ravine, upon a beautiful plain, is the manufacturing settlement of around 10,000 people. ... Vast numbers of logs coming down the Hudson are gathered in a boom above the town, and sawmills cut them into lumber. Papermills cluster about the falls, and marble-saws work up the black rocks. In the center of the ravine, above the falls, a cavern is hewn where a rocky inlet makes a rude abutment for a bridge pier."

97.   Winslow Homer (1836-1910)
The Hudson River—Logging

Watercolor on paper, 14 x 21 inches. Signed (at right, on log): "Homer."
Washington, D.C.: Collection of the Corcoran Gallery of Art.

Homer was born in Boston and lived his early life in the vicinity. As an apprentice to the lithographer J. H. Bufford from 1854 or 1855 to 1857, he learned the techniques of graphic expression and reportage and became a leading illustrator for *Harper's Weekly*. In 1866-1867 Homer visited France, where he took note of the work of his French contemporaries. Aside from attending a drawing school in Brooklyn around 1860 and some classes at the National Academy of Design night school around 1861, the only training he received in oil painting was from Frederick Rondel, who Barker claims "could hardly have done more than show him how to use brush and pigment." Watercolor became his primary medium of expression during and after trips to England in 1881 and 1882, and the theme of man and the sea began to dominate his compositions. He established a permanent residence on the Maine coast at Prout's Neck in 1883 but spent summers hunting, fishing, drinking, and painting in the Adirondacks. The monumental strength of this composition illustrates the "immense numbers of logs" described by Lossing as "filling the river for two or three miles ... assorted by the owners according to their private marks, and sent down to Glen's Falls, Sandy Hill, or Fort Edward, to be sawed into boards at the former places, or made into rafts at the latter, for a voyage down the river." This picture was done in 1897.

98. Winslow Homer (1836-1910)
The Hudson River

Watercolor on paper, 14 x 20 inches. Signed and dated (lower right):
"Homer / 92." Boston: Boston Museum of Fine Arts.

Before Homer, watercolor painting in America followed the formal and careful precepts established by European and American drawing academies. Homer, however, brought the medium to new heights, employing vividly rich colors in a very free and simplified manner. In his selection and abstraction of nature he departed markedly from Hudson River School precedent. Homer built up his compositions with washes over summary pencil sketches, painted directly from nature. His attempt to re-create nature in a controlled mood produced a simplified rendering, an approach that echoes Walt Whitman's prose: "Give me solitude, give me Nature, give me again O Nature your primal sanities!"

99. Homer Dodge Martin (1836-1897)
Lake Sanford

Oil on canvas, 24½ x 39½ inches. Signed and dated (lower left): "H. D. Martin 1870." New York: The Century Association.

Martin, departing from Durand's Hudson River manner, effected a broader approach. His feeling for mood and general breadth of handling is combined here with an unusual sensitivity to light and shade. Martin's technique was to paint in oil over sketches made in charcoal. "Color to him," wrote his wife, "was an instrument, not an end. He used it as a poet uses words. He made it reflect not so much what is obvious in nature as that duplex image into which eternal nature fused itself with him, who was also part of nature." Martin often spent summers in the Adirondacks, his "favorite sketching ground." According to Lossing, Lake Sanford, located in the Adirondacks about nine and a half miles northeast of the town of Newcomb, in Essex County, New York, "is a beautiful body of water, nine miles long, with several little islands. From the road along its shores ... there is a fine view of the three great mountain peaks ... Tahawus or Mount Marcy, Mount Colden and Mount McIntyre."

100. Alexander Helwig Wyant (1836-1892)
The Flume, Opalescent River, Adirondacks

Oil on canvas, 48 x 36 inches. Washington, D.C.: Smithsonian Institution, National Collection of Fine Arts.

The Flume or fall into the Opalescent River, located between Mount Marcy, the highest point in New York State, and Lake Henderson, was called "one of the most picturesque cascades of the Adirondacks" by Bryant, perhaps America's most noted connoisseur of the picturesque. The ever-useful Lossing described the Opalescent River as "one of the main sources of the Hudson. ... [It] falls into Sanford Lake. The Indians called this cascade She-gwi-en-dawke, or the Hanging Spear. ... It is to the abundance of ... the beautiful labradorite or opalescent feldspar ... that the river is indebted for its beautiful name." Wyant, a traditional figure between the tight realism of the Hudson River School and the American Impressionist movement, began as a harness maker's apprentice and sign painter in his native Ohio. Impressed by George Inness's paintings, he met the artist in the late 1850s and with his help went to Düsseldorf to study in the 1860s. In the late 1860s he returned to America. A stroke in 1873 forced Wyant to use his left hand, which encouraged him in developing a looser technique. The summers from 1874 to 1880 were spent in the Adirondacks, and in 1889 Wyant and his wife moved to Arkville, in the Catskills. Although his detailed earlier style linked him with the Hudson River School, his mature work was strongly influenced by the Barbizon painters and showed a more intimate view of nature, as in this outstanding example.

BIBLIOGRAPHY AND INDEX

SELECTED BIBLIOGRAPHY

General Works—Painting

Nineteenth-Century Sources

Benjamin, S. G. W. *Our American Artists.* Boston, 1879.
    Art in America, a Critical and Historical Sketch. New York, 1880.

Clement, Clara Erskine, and Laurence Hutton. *Artists of the Nineteenth Century and Their Works . . .*, rev. ed. Boston and New York, 1884.

Cummings, Thomas S. *Historic Annals of the National Academy of Design.* Philadelphia, 1865.

Dunlap, William. *History of the Rise and Progress of the Arts of Design in the United States,* 2 vols. New York, 1834. New edition, ed. by Frank W. Bayley and Charles E. Goodspeed, 3 vols. Boston, 1918. Rev. enl. edition, ed. by Alexander Wyckoff, preface by William P. Campbell, 3 vols. New York, 1965.

——*Diary of William Dunlap: The Memoirs of a Dramatist, Theatrical Manager, Painter, Critic, Novelist and Historian,* ed. by Dorothy C. Barck, 3 vols. New York, 1930.

French, H. W. *Art and Artists in Connecticut.* Boston and New York, 1879.

McCoubrey, John W., ed. *American Art 1700–1960, Sources and Documents,* Sources and Documents in the History of Art Series. Englewood Cliffs, New Jersey, 1965.

Sheldon, G. W. *American Painters, with Eighty-Three Examples of Their Work Engraved on Wood.* New York, 1879.

——*Hours with Art and Artists,* New York, 1882.

Tuckerman, Henry T. *Artist-Life: or Sketches of Eminent American Painters.* New York, 1847.

——*Book of the Artists: American Artist Life.* New York, 1867. New edition, ed. by James F. Carr. New York, 1966

Dictionaries

Dictionary of American Biography, ed. by Allen Johnson and Dumas Malone. New York, 1928–1964.

Fielding, Mantle. *Dictionary of American Painters, Sculptors, and Engravers*. Philadelphia, 1926.

Groce, George C., and David H. Wallace. *The New-York Historical Society's Dictionary of Artists in America, 1564–1860*. New Haven and London, 1957.

Collection Catalogs

Metropolitan Museum of Art. *American Paintings: A Catalogue of the Collection of the Metropolitan Museum of Art, I, Painters Born by 1815*, by Albert TenEyck Gardner and Stuart P. Feld. New York, 1965.

Museum of Fine Arts, Boston. *M. and M. Karolik Collection of American Paintings, 1815 to 1865*, introd. by John I. H. Baur. Cambridge, Massachusetts, 1949.

—— *M. and M. Karolik Collection of American Water Colors and Drawings, 1800–1875*. 2 vols. Boston, 1962.

Surveys, Exhibitions, and Recent Studies

Art Institute of Chicago (Feb. 15–Mar. 25, 1945); Whitney Museum of American Art, New York (Apr. 17–May 18, 1945). *The Hudson River School and the Early American Landscape Tradition*, by Frederick A. Sweet. Chicago, 1945.

Barker, Virgil. *American Painting, History and Interpretation*. New York, 1950.

Born, Wolfgang. *American Landscape Painting, an Interpretation*. New Haven, 1948.

Caffin, Charles H. *The Story of American Painting*. New York, 1907.

Callow, James T. *Kindred Spirits, Knickerbocker Writers and American Artists, 1807–1855*. Chapel Hill, North Carolina, 1967.

Clark, Eliot. *History of the National Academy of Design*. New York, 1954.

Detroit Institute of Arts and the Toledo Museum of Art. *Travelers in Arcadia: American Artists in Italy, 1830–1875*, by E. P. Richardson and Otto Wittmann, Jr. Detroit, 1951.

Flexner, James Thomas. *America's Old Masters, First Artists of the New World*. New York, 1939.

American Painting: The Light of Distant Skies, 1760–1835. New York, 1954.

—— *That Wilder Image: The Painting of America's Native School from Thomas Cole to Winslow Homer*. Boston and Toronto, 1962.

Gardner, Albert T. *History of Water Color Painting in America*. New York, 1966.

Garrett, Wendell D., Paul F. Norton, Alan Gowans, and Joseph T. Butler. *The Arts in America: The Nineteenth Century.* New York, 1969.

Harris, Neil. *The Artist in American Society: The Formative Years, 1790–1860.* New York, 1966.

Isham, Samuel. *A History of American Painting.* New York, 1905. Reprinted, with additions by Royal Cortissoz. New York, 1927.

Larkin, Oliver W. *Art and Life in America.* New York, 1949. Rev. ed. New York, 1960.

McLanathan, Richard. *The American Tradition in the Arts.* New York, 1968.

Metropolitan Museum of Art. *19th-Century America: Paintings and Sculpture,* by John K. Howat, John Wilmerding, and Natalie Spassky. New York, 1970.

Miller, Lillian B. *Patrons and Patriotism: The Encouragement of the Fine Arts in the United States, 1790–1860.* Chicago and London, 1966.

New York State University College at Geneseo, Fine Arts Center. *Hudson River School,* exhib. cat. by Agnes Halsey Jones. Geneseo, New York, 1968.

Novak, Barbara. *American Painting of the Nineteenth Century: Realism, Idealism, and the American Experience.* New York, 1969.

Prown, Jules David. *American Painting from Its Beginnings to the Armory Show,* introd. by John Walker. Geneva, 1969.

Richardson, Edgar Preston. *American Romantic Painting.* New York, 1944.

——*Painting in America: The Story of 450 Years.* New York, 1956. Reprinted. New York, 1965

Sears, Clara Endicott. *Highlights Among the Hudson River Artists.* Boston, 1947.

Whitney Museum of American Art, New York (Jan. 19–Feb. 25, 1938). *A Century of American Landscape Painting, 1800–1900,* by Lloyd Goodrich. New York, 1938.

Wilmerding, John. *A History of American Marine Painting.* Boston and Toronto, 1968.

Sources for Individual Artists
References are arranged alphabetically by artist.

ALLSTON, WASHINGTON
Richardson, Edgar Preston. *Washington Allston: A Study of the Romantic Artist in America.* Chicago, 1948.

BARD, JAMES and JOHN

Sniffen, Harold, and Alexander Brown. "James and John Bard, Painters of Steamboat Portraits." *The Mariners' Museum Publication*, no. 18. Newport News, Virginia, 1949

BARTLETT, WILLIAM HENRY

Barteaux, Eleanor. "W. H. Bartlett, of 'Bartlett Prints.'" *The Dalhousie Review*, vol. 24, no. 4 (Jan. 1945).

Cowdrey, Bartlett. "William Henry Bartlett and the American Scene." *New York History*, vol. 22, no. 3 (Oct. 1941).

BIERSTADT, ALBERT

B[ierstadt, Albert]. "Country Correspondence: Rocky Mountains, July 10, 1859." *The Crayon*, vol. 6 (Sept. 1859), p. 287.

Santa Barbara Museum of Art. *A Retrospective Exhibition, Albert Bierstadt 1830–1902*, introd. by Thomas W. Leavitt. (Aug. 5–Sept. 13, 1964.) Santa Barbara, California, 1964.

Hendricks, Gordon. "The First Three Western Journeys of Albert Bierstadt." *The Art Bulletin*, vol. 46, no. 3 (Sept. 1964), pp. 333–365.

BIRCH, THOMAS

Philadelphia Maritime Museum. *Thomas Birch, 1779–1851, Paintings and Drawings*, introd. by William H. Gerdts, (Mar. 16–May 1, 1966). Philadelphia, 1966.

Gerdts, William H. "Thomas Birch: America's First Marine Artist." *Antiques*, vol. 89, no. 4 (Apr. 1966), pp. 528–534.

Wilmerding, John. *A History of American Marine Painting.* Boston and Toronto, 1968.

BROWERE, ALBERTUS D. O.

Conkling, R. P. "Reminiscences on the Life of Albertis del Orient Browere." *Los Angeles County Museum Quarterly*, vol. 8, no. 1 (1950), pp. 2–6.

Smith, Mabel P., with Janet R. MacFarlane. "Unpublished Paintings by Alburtis Del Orient Browere." *Art in America*, vol. 46, no. 3 (Fall 1958), pp. 68–71.

CHAMBERS, THOMAS

Merritt, Howard S. "Thomas Chambers—Artist." *New York History*, vol. 37, no. 2 (Apr. 1956).

CHURCH, FREDERIC EDWIN

Noble, Louis Legrand. *Church's Painting, The Heart of the Andes.* New York, 1859.

Gardner, Albert TenEyck. "Scientific Sources of the Full-Length Landscape: 1850." *The Metropolitan Museum of Art Bulletin*, n.s. vol. 4, no. 2 (Oct. 1945), pp. 59–65.

Huntington, David C. "Landscape and Diaries: The South American Trips of F. E. Church." *The Brooklyn Museum Annual*, vol. 5 (1963–1964), pp. 65-98.

——— *The Landscapes of Frederic Edwin Church: Vision of an American Era*. New York, 1966.

National Collection of Fine Arts, Smithsonian Institution (Feb. 12–Mar. 13, 1966); Albany Institute of History and Art, Albany, New York (Mar. 30–Apr. 30, 1966); M. Knoedler and Co., New York (June 1-30, 1966). *Frederic Edwin Church*, introd. by David C. Huntington. Washington, 1966.

COLE, THOMAS

Noble, Louis Legrand. *The Life and Works of Thomas Cole*. New York, 1853. Ed. by Elliot S. Vesell. Cambridge, Massachusetts, 1964.

The Baltimore Museum of Art. *Annual II. Studies on Thomas Cole, An American Romanticist*. Baltimore, 1967 [1968].

Memorial Art Gallery of the University of Rochester, Rochester, New York (Feb. 14–Mar. 23, 1969); Munson-Williams-Proctor Institute, Utica, New York (Apr. 7–May 4, 1969); Albany Institute of History and Art, Albany, New York (May 9–June 20, 1969); Whitney Museum of American Art, New York (June 30–Sept. 1, 1969). *Thomas Cole*, by Howard S. Merritt. Rochester, 1969.

Bryant, William Cullen. *A Funeral Oration Occasioned by the Death of Thomas Cole, Delivered Before the National Academy of Design, New-York, May 4, 1848*. New York, 1848.

CROPSEY, JASPER FRANCIS

University of Maryland Art Gallery, J. Millard Tawes Fine Arts Center, College Park, Maryland. *Jasper F. Cropsey 1823–1900: A Retrospective View of America's Painter of Autumn. An exhibition of oil paintings and watercolors by the artist along with selected works by Thomas Cole, David Johnson and George Inness*, by Peter Bermingham, preface by George Levitine, foreword by William H. Gerdts. (Feb. 2–Mar. 3, 1968). College Park, 1968.

Cleveland Museum of Art, Cleveland, Ohio (July 8–Aug. 16, 1970); Munson-Williams-Proctor Institute, Utica, New York (Sept. 14–Oct. 25, 1970); National Collection of Fine Arts, Washington, D.C. (Nov. 23, 1970–Jan. 3, 1971). *Jasper F. Cropsey 1823–1900*, by William S. Talbot. Washington, D.C., 1970

DOUGHTY, THOMAS

Doughty, Howard N. Unpublished biographical sketch of Thomas Doughty. Ms. dept., The New-York Historical Society.

——— "Thomas Doughty, Painter of Scenery." *Appalachia*, n.s., vol. 13, no. 103 (June 1947), pp. 307-309.

DURAND, ASHER BROWN

Asher B. Durand papers. The New-York Historical Society and the New York Public Library, Manuscript Division.

Durand, Asher B. "Letters on Landscape Painting." *The Crayon,* vol. 1 (Jan.–June 1855), pp. 1-2, 34-35, 66-67, 97-98, 145-146, 209-211, 273-275, 354-355; vol. 2 (July –Dec. 1855), pp. 16-17.

Durand, John. *The Life and Times of A. B. Durand.* New York, 1894.

GIFFORD, SANFORD ROBINSON

Metropolitan Museum of Art. *A Memorial Catalogue of the Paintings of Sanford Robinson Gifford, N.A., with a Biographical and Critical Essay by Prof. John F. Weir.* New York, 1881.

University Art Museum of the University of Texas, Austin, Texas (Oct. 25-Dec. 13, 1970); Albany Institute of History and Art, Albany, New York (Dec. 28, 1970–Jan. 31, 1971); Hirschl and Adler Galleries, New York (Feb. 8-27, 1971). *Sanford Robinson Gifford (1823–1900),* by Nicolai Cikovsky, Jr. Austin, Texas, 1970.

GUY, FRANCIS

Pleasants, J. Hall. *Four Late Eighteenth Century Anglo-American Landscape Painters.* Worcester, Massachusetts, 1943. Reprinted from *The Proceedings of the American Antiquarian Society* (Oct. 1942).

HASELTINE, WILLIAM STANLEY

Plowden, Helen H. *William Stanley Haseltine, Sea and Landscape Painter (1835–1900).* London, 1947.

HOMER, WINSLOW

Adirondack Museum. *Winslow Homer in the Adirondacks,* introd. by Lloyd Goodrich. Blue Mountain Lake, New York, 1959.

Downes, William Howe. *The Life and Works of Winslow Homer.* Boston and New York, 1911.

Goodrich, Lloyd. *Winslow Homer.* New York, 1944.

—— *Winslow Homer.* The Great American Artists Series. New York, 1959

Gardner, Albert TenEyck. *Winslow Homer, American Artist: His World and His Work.* New York, 1961.

INNESS, GEORGE

Inness, George, Jr. *Life, Art and Letters of George Inness.* New York, 1917.

Ireland, LeRoy. *The Works of George Inness: An Illustrated Catalogue Raisonné.* Austin, Texas, and London, 1965.

University Art Museum of the University of Texas. *The Paintings of George Inness (1844–94)*, preface by LeRoy Ireland, introd. by Nicolai Cikovsky, Jr., notes by Donald B. Goodall. (Dec. 12, 1965–Jan. 30, 1966.) Austin, Texas, n.d.

KENSETT, JOHN FREDERICK

American Federation of Arts. *John Frederick Kensett 1816–1872*, by John K. Howat. New York, 1968.

Century Association. *Eulogies on John F. Kensett. Proceedings at a Meeting of the Century Association held in Memory of John F. Kensett, December, 1872.* New York, 1872.

Cowdrey, Bartlett. "The Return of John F. Kensett, 1816–1872, Painter of Pure Landscape." *The Old Print Shop Portfolio*, vol. 4, no. 6 (Feb. 1945), pp. 121-136.

Johnson, Ellen H. "Kensett Revisited." *The Art Quarterly*, vol. 20, no. 1 (Spring 1957), pp. 71-92.

MARTIN, HOMER DODGE

Martin, Elizabeth Gilbert Davis. *Homer Martin: A Reminiscence.* New York, 1904.

Meyer, Ann Nathan. "Homer Martin: American Landscape Painter." *International Studio*, vol. 35, no. 140 (Oct. 1908), pp. 255-262.

Mather, Frank Jewett, Jr. *Homer Martin, Poet in Landscape.* New York, 1912.

MORSE, SAMUEL FINLEY BREESE

Mabee, Carleton. *The American Leonardo: A Life of Samuel F. B. Morse.* New York, 1943.

National Academy of Design. *Morse Exhibition of Arts and Science . . .* , exhibited at the American Museum of Natural History, New York (Jan. 18–Feb. 28, 1950). New York, 1950.

Larkin, Oliver W. *Samuel F. B. Morse and American Democratic Art.* New York, 1954.

SVININ, PAUL

Yarmolinsky, Avrahm. *Picturesque United States of America, 1811, 1812, 1813: Being a Memoir on Paul Svinin.* New York, 1930.

TRUMBULL, JOHN

Sizer, Theodore. *The Works of Colonel John Trumbull, Artist of the American Revolution,* with the assistance of Caroline Rollins. Rev. ed. New Haven and London, 1967.

VANDERLYN, JOHN

Schoonmaker, Marius. *John Vanderlyn, Artist 1775–1852.* Kingston, New York, 1950.

Mondello, Salvatore. "John Vanderlyn." *The New-York Historical Society Quarterly*, vol. 52, no. 2 (Apr. 1968), pp. 161-183.

WALL, WILLIAM GUY

Shelley, Donald A. "William Guy Wall and His Watercolors for the Historic Hudson River Portfolio." *The New-York Historical Society Quarterly*, vol. 31, no. 1 (Jan. 1947).

WHITTREDGE, THOMAS WORTHINGTON

[Whittredge, Worthington]. "The Autobiography of Worthington Whittredge, 1820–1910," ed. by John I. H. Baur. *Brooklyn Museum Journal* (1942), pp. 7-68.

Munson-Williams-Proctor Institute, Utica, New York (Oct. 12–Nov. 16, 1969); Albany Institute of History and Art, Albany, New York (Dec. 2, 1969–Jan. 18, 1970); Cincinnati Art Museum (Feb. 6–Mar. 8, 1970). *A Retrospective Exhibition of an American Artist*, introd. by Edward H. Dwight. Utica, New York, 1969.

WYANT, ALEXANDER HELWIG

Clark, Eliot. *Alexander Wyant.* New York, 1916.

——— *Sixty Paintings by Alexander H. Wyant.* New York, 1920.

Travel Books, Guides, Gazetteers, and Poetry Relating to the Hudson Valley

Bailey, Henry. *Local Tales and Historical Sketches.* Fishkill, New York, 1874.

Brown, Henry Collins. *The Lordly Hudson.* New York, 1937.

Bruce, Wallace. *The Hudson River by Daylight, New York to Albany.* New York, 1873.

——— *The Hudson.* Boston, 1881.

Bryant, William Cullen, ed. *Picturesque America.* New York, 1874.

Buckingham, J. S. *America, Historical, Statistical and Descriptive.* New York, 1841.

Buckman, David Lear. *Old Steamboat Days on the Hudson River.* New York, 1907.

Colvin, Verplanck. *Topographical Survey of the Adirondack Region of New York to the Year 1879.* Albany, New York, 1880.

Cook, Joel. *America, Picturesque and Descriptive.* Philadelphia, 1900.

Eberlein, Harold D. *The Manors and Historic Homes of the Hudson Valley.* Philadelphia and London, 1924.

Ely, W. W., compiler. *Colton's Map of the New York Wilderness.* New York, 1872.

French, John H. *Gazetteer of the State of New York.* Syracuse, New York, 1860.

Guide to the Hudson River. New York, 1860.

Hoffman, Charles Fenno. *Love's Calendar, Lays of the Hudson, and Other Poems.* New York, 1858.

Irving, Washington. *The Works of Washington Irving.* New York, 1859.

Lossing, Benson J. *The Hudson from the Wilderness to the Sea.* Troy, New York, n.d.

New York State Education Department, Office of State History. *The Hudson Valley and the American Revolution.* Albany, 1968.

Panorama of the Hudson. New York, 1888.

Smith, Mabel Parker. *Greene County, New York: A Short History,* 4th ed. Greene County, 1970.

Trollope, Frances. *Domestic Manners of the Americans,* ed. by D. Smalley. New York, 1949.

Van Zandt, Roland. *The Catskill Mountain House.* New Brunswick, New Jersey, 1966.

Wade, William. *Panorama of the Hudson River, from New York to Albany.* New York, 1846.

Willis, Nathaniel Parker. *American Scenery; or Land, Lake, and River.* London, 1840., ed. *The Legendary, consisting of original pieces, principally illustrative of American history, scenery, and manners.* Boston, 1828.

——— *Outdoors at Idlewild.* New York, 1855.

Wilson, H. *Wilson's Illustrated Guide to the Hudson River.* New York, 1854.

Wise, Daniel. *Summer Days on the Hudson.* New York, 1876.